Retrieving Experience

Retrieving Experience

Subjectivity and Recognition
in Feminist Politics

Sonia Kruks

CORNELL UNIVERSITY PRESS

ITHACA AND LONDON

Copyright © 2001 by Cornell University

First published 2001 by Cornell University Press
First printing, Cornell Paperbacks, 2001

Printed in the United States of America

Library of Congress Cataloging-in-Publication Data
Kruks, Sonia.
  Retrieving experience : subjectivity and recognition in feminist politics / Sonia Kruks.
      p. cm.
  Includes bibliographical references and index.
  ISBN 0-8014-3387-8 (cloth : alk. paper) —
  ISBN 0-8014-8417-0 (pbk. : alk. paper)
  1. Feminist theory. 2. Existential phenomenology.
3. Subjectivity. 4. Postmodernism. I. Title.
  HQ1190 .K78 2001
  305.42'01—dc21   00-010474

Cloth printing   10 9 8 7 6 5 4 3 2 1
Paperback printing   10 9 8 7 6 5 4 3 2 1

For Ben and Gabi—
and in loving memory of Gabe,
who died too soon

It was a desire, a sound; she could drape it in colours, see it in form, hear it in music, but not in words; no, never in words. She sighed, teased by desires so incoherent, so incommunicable.

—Virginia Woolf,
Night and Day

There is no liberation that only knows how to say "I"; there is no coalition movement that speaks for each of us all the way through.

—Adrienne Rich,
"Notes toward a Politics of Location"

Contents

Acknowledgments

No book is solely the work of its author, and numerous people have contributed to the process of writing this one: some through providing comments on the whole or a part of the manuscript, others through discussion and sharing their own work, or by offering encouragement or support when it was needed. I would especially like to thank William McBride and Iris Young for their careful readings of the entire manuscript, and Hazel Barnes for her comments on several of the chapters and her generous encouragement.

Various networks of colleagues and friends have supported and sustained me over the years in which this work has been written. Some of the most important have been overlapping groups of Sartre and Beauvoir scholars. In particular, I thank Ronald Aronson, Linda Bell, Elizabeth Bowman, Michèle Le Doeuff, Thomas Flynn, Lewis Gordon, Monika Langer, Phyllis Sutton Morris (alas, posthumously), Michel Rybalka, and Bob Stone. For helping me to think specifically about Beauvoir, I also thank Debra Bergoffen, Eleanore Holveck, and Margaret Simons.

Several parts of the book were presented along the way at meetings of the American Political Science Association, where political theory colleagues offered valuable comments and insights. They include Romand Coles, Fred Dallmayr, Christine Di Stefano, Hwa Jol Jung, Kirstie McClure, Shane Phelan, Marion Smiley, Joan Tronto, and Linda Zerilli. Discussions with Linda Zerilli were especially important in clarifying my ideas on Beauvoir. Conversations with Hester Eisenstein, Rachel Joffe Falmagne, and Patricia Jagentowicz Mills, as well as their careful readings of different chapters, have also been immensely valuable, not to mention enjoyable. Jane Mansbridge provided much needed encouragement at an early stage of the project.

At Oberlin College I have also enjoyed the support of many colleagues. Special thanks to Wendy Kozol, for the scotch as well as the comments. Thanks also to Harlan Wilson for his thoughtful criticisms, and to Ben Schiff for rescuing me from crisis with the computer system. Other colleagues (and now former colleagues) who read and commented on various chapters include Anna Agathangelou, Leela Fernandes, Wendy Hesford, Chris Howell,

Anuradha Dingwaney Needham, Carol Tufts, and Sandra Zagarell. I thank them all. My two student research assistants at Oberlin, Cecily Beane and Susan Dennehy, also have helped immensely.

Institutional support has been important for this project. Oberlin College granted me a sabbatical and two research grants. The first versions of chapters 4 and 5 were written during two separate periods at the Five College Women's Studies Research Center at Mount Holyoke College: Dickinson House was a wonderfully warm environment in all senses of the word. My thanks to all my co-visitors there, who listened and made suggestions.

Another kind of thanks goes to Alison Shonkwiler, formerly my editor at Cornell University Press, and to Catherine Rice who has seen the project through to the end there. Both have been calm and supportive presences, as I struggled to bring this book to such closure as it now possesses.

Finally, throughout the complex weave of our commuting lives, Ben Wisner has remained a constant support, enabling me to carve out the needed stretches of time to work, listening to my musings, and reading sections as I wrote. Over the years our daughter, Gabi, generously endured my absences, and addressed with gentle irony what she regards as my obsession with Beauvoir. My love and thanks to both.

SONIA KRUKS

Oberlin, Ohio

Abbreviations

ASJ   Jean-Paul Sartre, *Anti-Semite and Jew*, [1946] 1976.

BN   Jean-Paul Sartre, *Being and Nothingness*, [1943] 1956.

BSWM Frantz Fanon, *Black Skin, White Masks*, [1952] 1967.

CDR   Jean-Paul Sartre, *Critique of Dialectical Reason*, [1960] 1976.

GT   Judith Butler, *Gender Trouble*, 1990.

PP   Maurice Merleau-Ponty, *Phenomenology of Perception*, [1945] 1962.

SS   Simone de Beauvoir, *The Second Sex*, [1949] 1989.

Retrieving Experience

Introduction

We have come to believe an oft-told tale. For just as frequent repetition makes an act appear natural, so too repeating a story gives it the appearance of truth. This tale is variously called the transition from modernity to postmodernity, from Enlightenment to post-Enlightenment (or poststructuralist) thought, from humanism to antihumanism. It has had a profound impact on contemporary feminist thought, as well as on many other areas of current intellectual and political life.

The all-too-familiar transition tale runs something like this: since long ago, and increasingly since the Enlightenment, the Western intellectual tradition has been marred by its logocentric drive for rational comprehension of all things natural and human. In this drive, truth has been conceived as unambiguous, grounded in identity or sameness, and cumulative, leading to "metanarratives" of progress; while the knower of truth—the "subject"— has been portrayed as autonomous, stable, and unitary, as a constituting— and self-constituting—consciousness. The Western intellectual project, so conceived, has consisted of the violent imposition of order on things by the knowing subject, hostile to differences, ruthlessly totalitarian in impulse and, in some versions of the story, profoundly masculinist.

Happily, however, a new and radically distinct generation of thinkers has swiftly changed all of this for the better. In the hands of the postmoderns, the Western project has become one of destabilizing or deconstructing knowledge, displacing metanarratives, and decentering the knowing subject. The subject has now been properly "stripped of its creative role" and reduced to "a variable and complex function of discourse" (Foucault 1977b, 138). It is now no more than "a post through which various kinds of messages pass" (Lyotard [1979] 1984, 15). The subject is "determined by the displacement of the signifier . . . regardless of character or sex" (Lacan [1955] 1966, 30) and "is only the signifying process" (Kristeva [1974] 1984, 215). Postmodernism sets out zealously to debunk the totalizing myths of Enlightenment thought and resolutely to expose the dangerous power plays implicit in all truth-claims, particularly those of "humanism."

Although some precursors are acknowledged, this story is usually told as one of dramatic, even heroic, rupture. For although Nietzsche and Heidegger offered earlier intimations, the narrative tells of the travails of a small group of thinkers, distinct in location (France) and time (since the 1960s), who have performed the truly Herculean task of capsizing the entire previous Western tradition. Today, "French Theory" is synonymous with postmodernism in the Anglo-American academy.[1] Both terms refer primarily to the ideas of a particular cluster of thinkers who began publishing in France in the 1960s or 1970s, as well as to more recent work that is inspired by theirs. The names associated with postmodernism/French Theory are, above all, those of Foucault, Derrida, Lyotard, and (although his early work overlaps with that of a previous generation) Lacan, plus, in the "French feminist" version of the tale, such neo-Lacanian thinkers as Irigaray and Kristeva. Although there are also profound disagreements and differences of focus among these thinkers, what they have in common is their iconoclasm toward the prior Western tradition.

"French feminism" has been an important episode in this tale: a blend of deconstruction and psychoanalysis that has subverted the masculine One and its discourse through the celebration of the "essentially" different and diffuse feminine. But, as longtime French feminist Christine Delphy has pointed out, " 'French Feminism' is not feminism in France" (1995, 190). Rather, it is an Anglo-American construct, formed to serve political ends and to fulfill agendas specific to (primarily) academic feminism in the United States. As such, Delphy suggests, the deployment of French Feminism involves a distortion and appropriation for other ends of a feminism that is, in France, a complex and far from unified set of theories and practices. In her account of how what she calls "Made-in-America 'French feminism' " came to be fabricated in the United States, Claire Moses also points out that embracing French feminism was an astute political move for women struggling for professional recognition in the American academy, where the work of male French theorists was already central (1998, 262).

But why, we might ask, was (masculine) French Theory already so central in the American academy? How did this tale come into being? Strangely

---

1. The anglophone academic reception of French Theory began in the United States, where postmodernism began to sweep into literary studies in the late 1970s (Lamont 1987). From there it entered other fields, including philosophy and feminist theory. Postmodernism had a later and somewhat different reception in other anglophone countries. In what follows I will sometimes refer specifically to the U.S. context and at other times to a broader anglophone context, in which case I will use the term Anglo-American.

perhaps, at least in the beginning, it had authors. The French Theorists themselves, at numerous conferences and in diverse essays and published interviews, explained repeatedly to American audiences what they had accom-
plished—and so, with time and much reiteration, it came to pass that the
story acquired the status of indubitable truth. As Foucault so authoritatively
affirmed in 1968, traditional philosophy, preoccupied by weighty questions
about life, death, freedom, and so on, had simply become "obsolete" (Foucault
[1968] 1989, 35). But from there the tale also took on a life of its own. New
versions proliferated, as French Theory/postmodernism rapidly spread
through diverse disciplines and into discourses of politics beyond the
academy.[2]

This is not to say that postmodernism went unchallenged. But it became
so pervasive that intense "for and against" debates centrally structured theory in many fields, including feminist theory. Although somewhat less intense in the last few years, arguments about postmodernism have sharply
divided feminist theorists over the last two decades. The debate, especially
in the late 1980s and early 1990s, was heated, frequently vituperative, and
often overly polarized. It seemed one had to choose: Did one support
Enlightenment or postmodern positions? Humanism or antihumanism? The
Cartesian knowing subject or the death of the subject? Some, such as Jane
Flax, went so far as to claim that feminist theory is *inherently* postmodern.
She argued that feminism, with its deconstruction of what appears "natural" in our society, its focus on "difference," and its subversion of the stable
phallocentric norms of Western thought, "properly belongs in the terrain of
postmodern philosophy" and that "feminist notions of the self, knowledge,
and truth are too contradictory to those of the Enlightenment to be contained

---

2. Attempts to account for the sweeping popularity of French Theory among
American academics and intellectuals have pointed to a range of possible factors. These
include a natural affinity between homespun American pragmatism and postmodernism, the attraction of American intellectuals to the exotic and the esoteric, or just plain
skilled self-marketing by the French Theorists and those who have made their own ca-
reers in promoting them (Lamont 1987; Mathy 1995).

A more embracing explanation might be found in the dwindling of "New Left" radi-
calism by the end of the 1970s. The war in Vietnam was long over, the civil rights and
early women's movements had garnered enough formal advances for their concerns to
be less urgently pressing, the last colonial struggles in Africa had ended, and Reagan came
to power in 1980. Such a quiescent period was fertile for the reception of a new intellectual orientation, one that belied individual agency and cautioned that the impulse of
movements for liberation could also be totalitarian.

In addition, there was also clearly an affinity between the postmodern orientation to
the local and particular and growing attention to diversity and what came to be called
"multiculturalism" on the Left. More recently, "postcolonial" articulations of postmodern thematics have also become influential via the works of Said (1978), Spivak
(1988), and others.

within its categories"(1987, 625). Similarly, Susan Hekman concluded that "Feminism and postmodernism are the only contemporary theories that present a truly radical critique of the Enlightenment legacy of modernism. No other approaches on the contemporary intellectual scene offer a means of displacing and transforming the masculinist epistemology of modernity. This fact alone creates a bond between the two approaches" (1990, 189).

Others emphatically disagreed. They argued that postmodern deconstructions of the "subject" and excessive focus on discursivity risked depoliticizing feminism, threatening to put women's newly found voice and agency into question. Among others, Linda Alcoff (1988), Susan Bordo (1990), and Nancy Hartsock (1990) urged feminists to have little truck with postmodernism, claiming that the problems it presents for feminist practice are overwhelming: its radical constructivism (including a constructivist account of the body) and its discourse-boundedness preclude a grasp of the real, even objective, conditions of women's lives. In addition, they argued, the postmodern refusal to conceive of the self, or subject, as a knowing and volitional agent—a notion that had underpinned prior feminist visions of political action—implied an unacceptable passivity, reducing women to the victims of a "discourse determinism" (Holloway, cited in de Lauretis 1987, 15) As Hartsock put it, "rather then getting rid of subjectivity or notions of the subject, as Foucault does and substituting his notion of the individual as an effect of power relations, we need to engage in the historical, political, and theoretical process of constituting ourselves as subjects as well as objects of history" (1990, 170). But what very few on either "side" questioned was that there was indeed a rupture: to most critics as well as advocates within the feminist debates, it seemed a truism that postmodernism did constitute a radical break in Western thought.

But the postmoderns have taught us to be suspicious of tales of truth and narratives of progress, and their own case is no exception. For although there may well be rupture in intellectual life, there is also continuity. Although postmodernism certainly contains original elements and has a distinctive set of intellectual preoccupations and styles, it is not as radically discontinuous from earlier thought as is often proclaimed. To the contrary, its debt to earlier theory is high. As Habermas has argued, there are important general continuities between Enlightenment and postmodern thought. For the postmodern dedication to radical interrogation and critique itself denotes a persistence of the Enlightenment attitude of critical reflection (Habermas 1991). But there are also more local, specifically French, continuities that have been either forgotten in Anglo-American versions of the tale or else actively suppressed by the French Theorists themselves. It is often forgotten today in Anglo-American feminist theory that it was the earlier French structuralists who initiated the "antihumanist" turn in the late 1950s and early 1960s.

Lévi-Strauss's blistering attack on Sartre and his call to "dissolve man" ([1962] 1968) were typical of the structuralist attack on "the subject" that the postmoderns (or poststructuralists as we might better call them in this context) then reiterated.

There is also an earlier cluster of French thinkers who today are excluded from the highly selective "canon" of French Theory and whose effacement has been deliberate and more complete. I refer here to the French existential thinkers: not only Sartre but others who were associated with him, including of course Simone de Beauvoir and also Maurice Merleau-Ponty.[3] Since these thinkers largely configured philosophical debate in France in the late 1940s and 1950s, when most of the postmodern generation were students, a less grandiose and more parochial story might be one of local inter-generational rebellion. One could tell an equally plausible tale in which the overthrow of the fathers was a key impetus for the postmodern turn in France. Indeed, one commentator has appropriately referred to the treatment, particularly of Sartre, as "parricide":

> Sartre was one of the first French philosophers to think through some of the implications of what has been called the 'divided subject' (or the 'split subject' for Lacanians). . . . Sartre's own discussions became an embarrassment, coming so close in many ways to the points the philosophers of the 1960s and 1970s wished to make, but without the brutal iconoclasm then in favor. The solution was parricide. Only certain aspects of Sartre's thinking were recognized, and he was accused of that very bourgeois humanism and individualism he so profoundly attacked." (Howells 1992, 326)[4]

For, as Fredric Jameson has also suggested, in its militant anti-essentialism and anti-foundationalism, French existentialism already anticipated significant elements of the later theories. Indeed, Jameson also points out that the postmoderns, far from effecting an absolute rupture "have passed their own Sartrean heritage over in what may not necessarily be a guilty, but what is certainly a suspicious, silence" (1995, 11). But why? And does it matter? What's in a tale?

I want to suggest that a great deal hangs by this tale and that it does matter for contemporary feminist thinking where postmodernism (as I shall most commonly call it), although not unchallenged, today continues centrally to

---

3. I also include Frantz Fanon here. Interest in Fanon in the United States has been high in recent years, but the most prominent readings have wholly obliterated the existential import of his work. I address this issue in chapter 3.

4. One might add that Beauvoir was subjected to a parallel "matricide" at the hands of postmodern feminists both in France (notably Kristeva [1979] 1986) and in the United States.

structure discourse and debate. For what is at issue here is a question not just of historical accuracy (though it is also that) but of theoretical difficulties created and valuable insights lost. Here, indeed, is the central premise of this book: in taking the postmodern tale at face value, we have unwisely cut ourselves off from the rich heritage of existential thought. Feminist (and other social) theory would now do well to retrieve and employ it.

In the chapters that follow, I offer a range of projects of retrieval and application. Some are textual re-readings—particularly of Beauvoir, Sartre, and Fanon—that function as interventions in current feminist debates: about the status of the subject, about the relevance of discourse theory for feminism, about gendered and raced identities, and about how far such identities shape experience and knowledge. In others, I move further from the texts to offer my own reflections and more free wheeling applications of existential problematics to pressing issues, particularly those of difference and fragmentation in feminism. Here my questions focus primarily on the possibilities and limits of forms of solidarity that are respectful of differences among women. In a phenomenological vein indebted above all to Merleau-Ponty and Beauvoir, I explore women's embodied experiences. I ask whether they might not offer some means to help build affective bonds among women who are in many ways radically different from each other.

BUT first I need to offer an alternative tale, one that will take us back to the 1940s and to the history of French existential thought. The postwar existentialist generation in France has commonly been characterized as the "generation of the three *H*s"—the generation that discovered and synthesized Hegel, Husserl, and Heidegger (Descombes 1980). While this is an oversimplification, it does broadly serve to characterize the core of what structured philosophical discourse when Foucault, Derrida, Lyotard, and others of the postmodern generation were students and young "Left" intellectuals in Paris in the immediate postwar decade. In the public eye, Sartre held center stage in the late 1940s, and "Left Bank Existentialism" became the rage. But other thinkers, including not only Merleau-Ponty but also figures with less public presence outside the academy, such as Jean Hyppolite (an academic adviser to both Derrida and Foucault), Maurice de Gandillac, Jean Wahl, Emmanuel Levinas, and Gaston Bachelard, were also key. They offered new readings of Hegel or introduced Husserlian phenomenology or Heideggerian *Existenz* philosophy to the next generation.

Historically, existentialism and phenomenology emerged as two distinct strands of European thought. But they shared a critical orientation to rationalism, abstract system building, and other objectifying modes of thought such as positivism. Existentialism may be broadly characterized as "the deliberate and intentional use of the *concrete* as a way of approaching the abstract, the *particular* as a way of approaching the general" (Warnock 1970, 133). It per-haps finds its originary formulations in the mid-nineteenth century, in Kierkegaard's turn to the exploration of concrete, personal experience as a critical response to Hegel's abstract "grand system." Phenomenology finds its locus classicus in Husserl's early-twentieth-century critique of the objec-tification of experience, as produced both by our everyday, or "natural," as-sumptions about the world and by the "scientific attitude." Husserl believed that a sufficiently rigorous method of suspending or "bracketing" our pre-suppositions (*epoché*, leading to the phenomenological "reduction") would enable us to arrive at the pure, "lived," forms of certain kinds of experience, uncontaminated by preconceptions: "a return to the things themselves."

It was arguably Heidegger, in *Being and Time* (1927), who first conjoined these two approaches, using phenomenological method (albeit unfaithfully) to explore, in their immediacy, such fundamental experiences of human existence as time and death. For the "generation of the three *H*s," Hegel's *Phenomenology*, only recently re-discovered,[5] additionally offered a series of new themes for phenomenological investigation. These included, in par-ticular, self-other relations (Hegel's much-cited "master-slave dialectic") and experiences of alienation, or the "unhappy consciousness."

In the hands of the thinkers with whom I am most concerned—Beauvoir, Sartre, Fanon, Merleau-Ponty—existential phenomenology, as we might now call it, became increasingly concerned with social and political phenomena: with disclosing the "lived experience" of being a woman in the hands of Beauvoir, or of being a Jew or a black for Sartre and Fanon respectively, as well as with addressing issues of violence, responsibility, and meaning in the world of politics. Many of these themes were responses to the pressing prob-lems of the immediate postwar period: how to account for Nazism and French complicity with it; how to evaluate the Soviet experiment (in a France where the Communist Party almost uniquely defined "Left" politics) and re-trieve Marxism from deterministic Soviet orthodoxy; how to engage in sup-port of anti-colonial struggles.[6]

For the French existentialists, Husserl's maxim, "a return to the things themselves," functioned more as a heuristic than as a strict method for at-

5. Lectures on the *Phenomenology* given in Paris by the Russian emigré scholar Alexandre Kojève in the mid-1930s were one important source of the new interest in Hegel (Kojève [1947] 1962). Also highly influential were the translations and commen-taries of Jean Hyppolite, notably his *Genesis and Structure of Hegel's Phenomenology of Spirit* ([1946] 1974).

6. Many of these questions were explored at length in articles in *Les Temps Modernes*, the influential monthly periodical that Sartre, Merleau-Ponty, Beauvoir, and others founded at the end of the war. For an intellectual and political history of the jour-nal, see Davies 1987.

taining certain knowledge. For as Merleau-Ponty observed, the process of "bracketing" is always open-ended, and we could never arrive at a definitive, or final, phenomenological reduction. Since no "pure" return to unmediated experience is possible, "the unfinished nature of phenomenology and the inchoative atmosphere which has surrounded it are not to be taken as a sign of failure" ([1945] 1962, xxi). This open-ended attempt to describe our experiences, while as far as possible "bracketing" our prior preconceptions, still remains valuable today. It is a method that feminist theory can usefully draw upon. For it enables us to destabilize commonly held or naturalized attitudes and assumptions that are constitutive of gender relations, and it opens up valuable spaces for new ways of seeing and understanding.

Given this open-endedness, and as Jameson's comment suggests, a major theme of postwar existentialism was the non-foundational and non-essential quality of human existence. It is here, with her insistence on the contingency of sexual difference, that one can instantly see how Beauvoir anticipated much of later "second-wave" feminist theory. Moreover, if human existence is indeterminate, then (contra the "orthodox," Communist Party Marxism of that era, and as the postmoderns would also later argue) history is no necessary guarantor of a telos or of progress. "Metanarratives" are already being put into question in such works as Sartre's "Materialism and Revolution" (1946) and, yet more strongly, Merleau-Ponty's *Humanism and Terror* (1947) and *Adventures of the Dialectic* (1955). Although they retain a more optimistic horizon than their postmodern successors, both thinkers emphatically reject theories of historical necessity. Indeed, Merleau-Ponty's extended reflections on the contingency of events strikingly anticipate the later postmodern focus on discontinuity and rupture.

However, if forced to choose between two bald alternatives, we would have to categorize French existentialism as a philosophy of the subject rather than a philosophy without a subject. But it is here that the postmodern misrepresentations begin. For French existentialism is not a philosophy of the "Enlightenment," disembodied subject, of the Cartesian cogito. Although there is no one, definitive, "existential" account of the subject, what these thinkers share are notions of a subject that is, above all, *situated:* embodied, sentient, ambiguous, unable ever to coincide with itself in Cartesian self-reflexivity, to act as a pure constituting consciousness, or to engage in what Merleau-Ponty pithily called "high-altitude" thinking (*pensée de survol*).[7] Thus even the early Sartre, who (as I shall argue in chapter 1) at least in *Being*

---

7. As Sartre wrote in a memorial essay after his death, Merleau-Ponty "was infuriated by these well-meaning souls who, taking themselves for small airplanes, indulged in 'high-altitude' thinking, and forgot that we are grounded from birth. They pride themselves, he was later to say, on looking the world in the face. Don't they know that it envelops and produces us?"([1961] 1965, 158).

and Nothingness (1943) still defends an improbable notion of absolute human freedom, does not offer a straightforward Enlightenment account of the subject. Instead of the metaphysical philosophy of presence of which he stands accused, Sartre arguably anticipates Derrida in insisting that the subject's "presence to self" is never possible. It is, rather, he says, "a way of not coinciding with oneself, of escaping identity" ([1943] 1956, 77). Meanwhile, it was Merleau-Ponty who perhaps spoke first of "decentering," of "man" [sic] as "ex-centric to himself" (*excentrique à lui-même*) ([1956] 1964, 123), thus anticipating Lacan's assertion of "the self's radical ex-centricity from itself" (*l'excentricité radicale de soi à lui même*) ([1957] 1966, 524).

But all of this is now forgotten. When existentialism is not simply written out of the record, it is caricatured as no more than an Enlightenment/Cartesian philosophy of "constituting" consciousness, now properly displaced by an account of the constituted subject. In attempting to establish their tale of definitive rupture, the French Theorists either expunged the existentialists from the record or else crudely distorted their positions, forcing them to fit the Enlightenment mold.

These moves were not made from ignorance. Derrida, Foucault, and Lyotard (among others) were profoundly immersed in phenomenological and existential modes of thought. Not only did they study the "three Hs" and postwar French phenomenology extensively, but each also published his earliest work on topics related to phenomenology or existentialism. Derrida's first publication was a major interpretive introduction to Husserl's short essay on geometry ([1962] 1978). Although Derrida engaged critically with Husserl's notion of transcendental consciousness and the metaphysics of presence it implied, he wholly ignored Sartre's prior critical reading of Husserl and gave only the most scant attention to Merleau-Ponty's. Indeed, he later stated that his reading of Husserl was "not—especially not—in the versions proposed by Sartre or by Merleau-Ponty which were then dominant, but rather in opposition to them, or without them" (Derrida [1980] 1983, 38).[8] Lyotard's first book was simply entitled *La Phénoménologie* (1954). In it, he engaged quite extensively with the work of Sartre and Merleau-Ponty, as well as Heidegger. Yet, later, in *The Postmodern Condition* ([1979] 1984)—a text that has been highly influential in presenting postmodernism to North American audiences—the suppression of these thinkers has become so total that they are present only as an absence: they have disappeared from the story of the transition to postmodernity without a trace.[9]

8. Recently, however, Derrida has begun to tell an intriguingly different tale. Not only does he acknowledge that Sartre was an important influence on him, but he also puts it so strongly as to describe himself (perhaps with allusion to his *Specters of Marx*) as "haunted" by Sartre (1999, 82–83).

9. The only reference to any of these thinkers is a brief discussion of Heidegger, concerning his unfortunate speech legitimizing Nazism in 1933 (Lyotard [1979] 1984, 37).

As for Foucault, who was the most vehement in affirming the rupture, his first publications, *Maladie mentale et personnalité* (1954) and his extended introduction to Binswanger's "Dream and Existence" (1954), were both concerned with existential psychoanalysis. In the latter work he affirmed that the aim of the analysis of dreams is to be able "to arrive at an understanding of existential structures" (cited in Macey 1993, 68). He also promised a further work of his own that would "attempt to situate existentialist analysis within developments in contemporary thinking about man; by following phenomenology's drift towards anthropology, we will attempt to demonstrate the foundations that have been proposed for concrete thinking about man" (cited in Macey 1993, 67). Not only was that work never written, but Foucault later actively attempted to hide the embarrassing traces of his youthful interests, prohibiting republication of *Maladie mentale et personnalité* and persistently citing *Madness and Civilization* (1961) as his first book (Macey 1993, 64).

How then to explain this deliberate and militant effacement of the earlier generation by the postmoderns? Beyond the psychological, we might point also to the history and social organization of French thought. Since the mid-nineteenth century, French thought has been marked by a series of conflictual oscillations between objectivist and subjectivist positions. Intellectually, the oscillations might be read as a series of continuing struggles with the ghost of Descartes, whose powerful and divisive presence still reverberates down through the generations. But the potential for sharp intergenerational conflict has been exacerbated by the remarkably centralized nature of French academic and intellectual life. A unified national *lycée* syllabus in philosophy, the presence in Paris of those very few elite institutions that train France's leading philosophers and other theoreticians, and the absolute centrality of Paris as the locus of intellectual life make for a hothouse atmosphere, in which competition for the intellectual laurels is intensified and often personalized.

Thus, the battle between positivists and neo-Kantians in the mid-nineteenth century, was replayed at the turn of the century as the heated conflict between Durkheimian advocates of objective "social facts" and Bergsonian exponents of the experience of "inner time." Similarly, as students in the 1930s, the generation of the "three Hs" saw itself as overthrowing the Kantian idealism of their professors (notably Brunschvicg) in favor of a return to the "real," to the world of concrete lived experience. Thus, within a longer time frame, one may read the claims of today's French Theory to effect a radical rupture as just another round of the same game, yet another version of the "death and resurrection of philosophy without a subject" (Bourdieu and Passeron 1967) through which previous generations have also defined and demarcated themselves.

However, the game is not played quite identically each time. The subject put to death in this round is one that was already distinct from the classical Cartesian knowing subject. Existential accounts of the subject, particularly those of Beauvoir and Merleau-Ponty, had already significantly confounded subject/object distinctions. Thus, paradoxically, this particular "death" of the subject has often involved the "resurrection" of such distinctions. For since this subject was cast as pure subjectivity, its overthrow has also led to the privileging of peculiar new forms of objectivism.

What we are dealing with here is a case of the return of the repressed. For the attempt to deny what still persists gives rise to strange displacements, lacunae, and incoherences in French Theory. A certain remainder, certain unacknowledged "existential" postulates, continue to work against the grain of the explicit theory, often undermining it. I am referring here not to the real aporias and incommensurabilities to which, at its best, postmodern theory often points us but rather to difficulties that could be addressed were there less investment in suppressing this remainder. Moreover, such difficulties also surface in those feminist theories that espouse postmodern problematics too uncritically—as I will detail in later chapters. But first, let me explain more generally what I mean.

PERHAPS the most striking—and problematic—displacements in postmodern thought involve the shift of such "interior" attributes of the classical Enlightenment subject as intentionality or volition, as well as agency and freedom, from individuated human selves to discursive practices, language games, the free play of signifiers, and so on. Although there is no longer an overarching telos, Hegel's "cunning of reason" still continues to resound here in the continued attribution of such human qualities to discursive structures and systems. What is valuable and exciting about postmodern theory includes its ability to demonstrate the power of discursive systems. But the fact that this power is so often described through *personification* is a symptom that something is amiss here. When Foucault tells us, for example, that discipline "had to solve a number of problems," and that it "clears up confusion" and "establishes calculated distributions" ([1975] 1977a, 219), or when Lyotard tells us that "the language game . . . positions the person who asks" ([1979] 1984, 16), we cannot but be struck by the fact that conscious volition, agency, and even rationality are here being imputed to structures.[10] We should, I think, be suspicious when doctrines that deny any interior or

10. This is, of course, hardly new even though it was previously harnessed to more teleological ends. Its antecedents are not only Hegel's Mind but also Adam Smith's "unseen hand," Comtian positivism, the "laws of motion of capital," and, more recently, the self-equilibrating systems of functionalist sociology.

initiating qualities to the (individuated human) subject seem unable to proceed except by metaphorically displacing these qualities elsewhere. For discipline cannot literally solve problems, clear up confusion, or calculate; nor can language games literally position people.

In these displaced versions, postmodern freedom displays peculiarly strong Enlightenment attributes: autonomy, self-referentiality, lack of exterior determination. The "free play of signifiers," or the "autonomy" of incommensurate language games, is as absolute as was the freedom of the Enlightenment knowing subject. This one-sided attribution of agency to discursive systems, made at the cost of evacuating all initiative or freedom from the individual subject, reduces the latter to no more than a hapless vehicle or conduit through which agency passes. This reduction is highly problematic. For many kinds of human action, including collective movements of resistance, can take place only if at a certain point individuals make a commitment that could also be refused—that is, if they exercise freedom. There is a gap, a "nothing" as Sartre puts it ([1943] 1956, 34), between motives (which may indeed be accounted for as discursive effects) and acts that here precludes determination.

For example, although shifts in the discursive field certainly enabled the civil rights movement to articulate demands that would not previously have been possible, there still remains that moment when each individual rider actually does—or does not—get off the bus, when each potential demonstrator actually leaves for the demonstration or decides to stay home. For resistance to catch on, something more than the relevant discursive shifts (analogous to what Marxists used to call the correct objective conditions?) is necessary. This, among other reasons, is why metanarratives of history are inadequate: change is mediated through the actions of individual agents who are not passive vehicles. Action is not always predictable because even though shifting discursive fields do significantly constitute selves and their experiences and options, a margin of freedom, a "creative role," however slight, still always remains in the ways individuals assume these and translate them into action.

"Freedom" is not a common word in the postmodern lexicon and is explicitly denied as an attribute of the human subject in various versions of the transition tale. However, a degree of individual freedom usually continues to be assumed as an implicit, or suppressed, postulate in postmodern theory. Unacknowledged, it surreptitiously cuts across the general import of postmodern analysis. Lyotard, for example, talks about "one's mobility" in relation to "language game effects"([1979] 1984, 15). Thus the question is implicitly posed: What might such a "one" be that is (after all) more than a "nodal point" in a signifying system? But this is a question Lyotard ignores. Likewise (and as I discuss more fully in chapter 2), Foucault's account of how disciplinary practices produce the subject presupposes, in spite of his explicit claims to the contrary, an interiority of the subject and an active faculty for compliance or resistance.

Similarly, feminists (and others) who wish to harness postmodern theory to radical ends often reluctantly grant an element of freedom to the subject. But they also do so only at the cost of tacitly abandoning the theoretical frameworks they claim to espouse. For example (as I consider in chapter 5), in her essay on "experience," Joan Scott seeks to deny any original interiority to the subject, arguing instead that "historical processes . . . through discourse position subjects and produce their experiences" (1992, 25). But she still wants to insist that the subject has "agency," because it is positioned among conflicting discursive systems that "enable choices" (34). The problem then becomes how to theorize this subject that has agency and choice, yet which she (presumably?) does not conceive as the classical subject of Enlightenment freedom and reason. But here again, the theoretical work is not undertaken. Thus the status of this subject that is, after all, capable of an active response, an initiating agency, remains a mysterious lacuna.

Here, certain existential accounts of the subject as situated and embodied may serve us well. For they offer us ways to grasp the freedom-in-constraint, the socially imbued interiority, of a subject that is neither constituted through and through nor yet a pure constituting consciousness. In their strenuous efforts to demarcate themselves from the generation of the three Hs, the postmodern French Theorists have cut off access for others, including later postmodern feminists, to that intermediate domain of embodied and situated subjectivity. By insisting that either the subject is constituting and self-constituting or else it is constituted, and by depicting existential accounts of the situated subject as uniquely the former, the postmoderns preclude investigation of the mutual co-constituency of subjectivity and social processes that we find, for example, in Beauvoir's account of women's "lived experience," or Fanon's account of black embodiment.

Another strength of the existential focus on "lived experience," absent from postmodern theory, is its call to focus our attention on the importance of sentient and emotional aspects of human life. Such areas of experience are occluded by reductionist conceptions of the subject, as either a rational knower or a discursive effect. A focus on what we might call a *sentient* subject allows us to rethink a range of questions: about volition, knowing, acting; about relations with others; and about how differently sexed and raced (and aged and enabled) bodies imbue subjectivity differentially. Such a focus enables us to rebut the claims to disembodied autonomy and self-constitution of the rational knowing subject. But it also calls for an account of the subject which acknowledges that it exceeds the boundaries of the discursive. I am not here referring to the unconscious which is, the Lacanians tell us, already discursively structured. Rather I refer to those modalities of experience that, in themselves, elude speech—and yet which we come to "know" through forms of non-intellectual, embodied, cognition. For we often experience what is not only unspoken but even unspeakable.

For example, we often have difficulty "putting into words" experiences of pain, anger, or joy, yet they are no less "real" to us for that. And that our pain or joy might well be "explained" as an effect of our discursive position, or that we may sometimes be able to describe it post hoc, does not mean that the experience was *itself* discursively produced. The postmodern subject, like the classical knowing subject, is pitifully thin. An effect of surface inscription, it lacks sentience, affects, feelings, and emotions. Yet, as I shall argue, these experiential realms often significantly inform our commitments and shape our predispositions. Feminist theories that follow the postmoderns too closely, ignoring these aspects of subjectivity, are also frequently too uni-dimensional.

Another area where postmodern theory can be problematic for feminism is the domain of values. Certainly, postmodernism has often served as a resource for feminism in unmasking the masculinist (and other) interests invested in allegedly universal values. It has also proven useful for women of color and others, who have found in it an ally in exposing privileges, such as that of racial whiteness, within feminism's own "universal" demands for "equality" or for the "emancipation" of "women."[11] But difficult issues remain concerning whether or how postmodern theory can move *beyond* critique and whether it can sustain those ethical, indeed utopian, impulses that are integral to a politics of social transformation such as feminism.

Some have argued that postmodernism offers, as Derrida has claimed of his own work, "an openness towards the other" that is profoundly ethical in import (cited in Kearney 1984, 124). But, given indefinite deconstruction, or a suspension of judgment in the name of undecidability, it is not evident that this impulse can inform concrete social or political practices. Derrida himself recognizes this difficulty when he says, "I try where I can to act politically while recognizing that such action remains incommensurate with my intellectual project of deconstruction" (120). But feminism still presupposes a value-laden, even what one might call a utopian, horizon (even if today it

---

11. Thus bell hooks writes that criticism of postmodernism "should not obscure insights it may offer that open up our understanding of African-American experience. The critique of essentialism encouraged by postmodernist thought is useful for African-Americans concerned with reformulating outdated notions of identity" (1990, 28). More recently, Patricia Hill Collins has argued that postmodernism's "reliance on exclusionary language" often makes it yet another tool to prevent many black women from claiming an authorial voice (1998, 142). However, she also sees it as providing "powerful analytical tools and a much-needed legitimation function" for black women in the academy (154).

no longer endeavors to construct utopias). It affirms a desire, however inchoate, for that which does not yet exist. It presupposes what Seyla Benhabib
has called a "longing for the 'wholly other,' for that which is not yet . . . a
regulative principle of hope" (1995, 30). This hope is not easily conjoined
with the postmodern rejection of anything that might possibly smack of
metanarrative. Thus, an end point of—at least a consistent—postmodernism
has been to put into question not only the category of "women,"[12] but the
very desirabilty of a liberatory project such as feminism.

But I do not think we are yet ready for "postfeminism" (Brooks 1997). For
while feminism has not been innocent of its own totalizing impulses and
power effects, and a critique of feminist metanarratives certainly has its
place, there is also an unwarranted temptation here to abandon the field and
to opt for political quietism. There is an invitation to hide behind "the
scruple of undecidability" (Kearney 1998, 228) rather than risk getting "dirty
hands" in the messy world of politics (even feminist politics), where harm
is often a question of degree and any action has its costs.[13] But the forms of
exclusion, exploitation, and oppression against which feminism as a social
movement has been developing for over two centuries certainly have not disappeared. Nor have "women" ceased to exist, even if exclusion, exploitation,
and oppression have a differential impact on different groups of women, so
that many of us are, along different axes, at once oppressed and the bene-
ficiaries of others' oppression.

To the contrary, new and virulent forms of exploitation are emerging
today, for example in the global sex markets and in the systematic use of rape
against women as a terrorist tactic in war. Meanwhile, the old inequities in
women's access to material, cultural, and political resources have diminished only for a very select few. Feminism does not necessarily act from formal, "universal," principles. Indeed (as I discuss in chapters 5 and 6), more
often it affirms "lived" values: values that are submerged and tacit yet "disclosed" in its practices. But these still inform its ethical horizon, its utopian
impulses. They imply that—however complex and difficult they may be in

12. Deconstruction has tended so remorselessly to destabilize identities as to put into
question categories such as gender, or race, or class that have traditionally served as
referents for radical politics. Thus there has been much discussion of whether, for
example, the "category" of women exists, whether feminism needs "women" as its (collective) subject, or whether a "strategic essentialism" might not be necessary for a feminist project to continue (Kristeva 1981; Riley 1988; Fuss 1989; Butler 1990; Mouffe 1992;
Schor and Weed 1994).
13. As Merleau-Ponty wrote, with regard to living in German-occupied Paris, " one
compromised whether one stayed or left; no one's hands are clean. . . . The moral man
does not want to dirty his hands. It is because he usually has enough time, talent, or
money to stand back from enterprises of which he disapproves" ([1948] 1964, 147). See
also, on this issue, Sartre's classic play *Dirty Hands* ([1948] 1955).

practice to untangle—oppression, injustice, and subordination are still morally unacceptable.

Thus feminism is still necessary today, as a politics committed to a range of practical struggles in which such values as justice, respect, recognition, and freedom are implicit. There can be a peculiar purism to a postmodernism that prefers to avoid "dirty hands" by taking the high ground of critique, disclosing the power effects of utopias, emancipatory narratives, and practical projects, instead of accepting their risks and ambiguity. We need to distinguish better between those grand ideological utopian projects that, in the name of dogmatic claims about the future, have tried violently to force the world to conform to their goals, and those horizons of possibility, or longings for the "wholly other," that can guide more open projects of emancipation. As Kearney has nicely put it, "to forswear all utopias because of the pathological nature of ideological utopianism is to renounce the possibility of a commonly shared horizon of history which never reaches its end but perpetually motivates moral agents to bring it nearer" (1998, 227).

Postmodernism can also invite us to quietism, not only through its anti-utopianism but also insofar as its attribution of primary agency to discursive systems strips individual actors of a "creative role." This last point raises the further vexed issues of authorial agency and responsibility. For if the subject is but an effect of discourse, so too is the "author": an author who is now merely a point or node through which discourse passes, or a post in a communication system where nobody "possesses" the through-put and for which nobody is thus accountable.

"What does it matter who is speaking?" Foucault asks, via Beckett ([1979] 1984, 101)—and we must surely reply that it does matter for feminism. For the author as nodal point is suspiciously like the disembodied and dispassionate Enlightenment knower of old, denying his own implication in and responsibility for the production of knowledge. Yet, against the grain of this ostensibly value-free, objectivist stance, postmodern thinkers (happily) do continue to affirm values that structure their projects. Indeed the very project of writing theory presupposes that "it matters," that it is important to an author to write. Thus, for example, Lyotard's critique of totalizing metanarratives and his defense of "open" language games against the "terrorism" that simply eliminates opponents from the game ([1979] 1984, 65–66) tacitly presuppose freedom as a value. While, as his discussion of homosexuality in various interviews makes clear, Foucault's own concern to describe the functioning of discipline and normalization is hardly disinterested! Although subjects are necessarily the effects of "subjectification" for Foucault, certain subjectifying practices are apparently invidious in ways that others are not. We are not explicitly told why this is so, but is it perhaps because they produce suffering subjects, and suffering ought (in principle?) to be minimized?

Thus, although postmodernism seeks to destabilize values and to question their foundational status, postmodern theory itself is (and surely must be) tacitly value-laden. Recoiling from Sartrean notions of commitment and responsibility (along with any notion of a subject for whom these might be possible), the postmoderns hide their own values behind the text: ostensibly ungendered, unraced, unclassed, they claim to be merely abstract (non-particular) nodes through which discourse passes. Yet Sartre and Beauvoir have shown us that it is possible to develop a critique of foundationalist ethics that is compatible with the presence of explicit authorial values. Both insisted on the value-laden, or value "disclosing," quality of all human action while also condemning, as "bad faith" and a refusal of responsibility, claims that there exist ready-made, indubitable, and universal principles. Similarly, Merleau-Ponty warned against the dangers of a liberalism in love with "the empyrean of principles" and given to "abstract judgements." Such an abstract, principled, liberalism serves but as a rationalization for violence, he cautioned long ago ([1947] 1969, xxix).

The troubling ethical stance of postmodern theory, combined with other difficulties I have discussed—including those that stem from the displacement of the "creative role" from the subject to discursive systems, and the erasure of those emotional and affective aspects of subjectivity that are not easily amenable to discursive articulation—should certainly make feminists pause before embracing postmodern theory whole-heartedly. This is a body of theory that can be tremendously powerful when used selectively, but when it is adopted wholesale or too uncritically, as in much postmodern feminist theory, the difficulties I have flagged continue to surface. Often this is because the transition tale has now been so widely accepted that many feminists, who turn to postmodern theory for the real strengths it can offer, are no longer aware that possibilities exist other than those of the "Enlightenment versus postmodernism" binary with which they are constantly presented.

However, in other instances, feminist philosophers who are familiar with the full history of Postwar French philosophy still continue to follow postmodern theories over faithfully. Thus, for example, in *Gender Trouble* (1990), Judith Butler protests rather too much that her account of the subject is in no way to be confused with an existential one. There can be no interiority of the subject, she insists. For styles of enactment "produce the coherent gendered subjects who pose as their originators" (140). Yet (as I shall argue in chapter 2) Butler's account of gender as a performance enacted "under duress" still implicitly acknowledges a capacity for resistance on the part of the subject and thus presupposes a degree of interiority and agency.

Likewise, in a recent essay entitled "Postmodern Subjectivity," Tina Chanter effects the—all too predictable and total—collapse of phenomenology into Cartesianism. "Universalist pretensions pervade even the most radical phenomenological analyses," she writes, "and it is here that perhaps post-modernism might be said to offer something new. By providing ways in which difference, multiplicity, and fragmentation might be not only thought but mobilized, postmodernism distances itself from the assumed rationality, unity, coherence, and mastery of the Cartesian subject" (1998, 263). But the rationality, unity, coherence, and mastery of the "Cartesian subject" are hardly the distinguishing characteristics of Beauvoir's woman, Fanon's black, or Sartre's Jew! It is not obvious that there is "something new" here. Indeed, in a later passage, where Chanter further distinguishes postmodernism from rationalism (as if there were no other possible positions but these), she argues in the name of postmodernism a position that is remarkably *akin* to that of the French existentialists!

Rejecting the false alternatives of "freedom or determinism," Chanter calls for a "nuanced, contoured revision that is not content to reduce the subject to one of two extremes." She adds that "individuals may be at the mercy of social and biological forces . . . but we are not completely passive or without resources in the face of such culturally and historically specific determinants" (264–65). I agree with Chanter. But, contrary to the oft-told transition tale she repeats here, it is in existential phenomenology rather than postmodernism that we find such a series of "nuanced and contoured" theoretical revisions. It is in the work of the earlier thinkers that we find developed conceptions of a subject that is neither reduced to pure freedom nor is the passive plaything of social and discursive forces. Thus, in the chapters that follow, it is to existential phenomenology that I turn as a resource for feminism.

To "essay" is to attempt. The chapters that follow may properly be considered essays: that is, they are attempts to think through what selected aspects of existential phenomenology might mean theoretically for feminism, and how feminists might use insights from existential phenomenology for their own ends. They constitute a series of thematically linked endeavors rather than one seamless argument. They also address and draw on the work of a group of thinkers who, although working in a similar vein, still often disagreed among themselves. I have not tried to smooth out those disagreements but rather to draw from their diverse works here and there as I have found useful. For this reason too, this book cannot offer one unified argument. But although the essays each start out from a particular endeavor, they cluster around three distinct foci. Thus I have divided the book into three parts, within each of which the essays are more tightly linked together.

Part 1 is entitled "Simone de Beauvoir in 'Her' World and 'Ours.'" It contains elements of my earliest work on existentialism and feminism and also some of the most recent. Reading Beauvoir was how I first came to think about existential phenomenology and feminism, and I continue to think with and through her richly suggestive work. If there is one theorist whose work has enduringly informed my own, and whose import for feminism continues to reverberate, it is Beauvoir. I already began to argue more than a decade ago (Kruks 1987) that Beauvoir's account of subjectivity is significantly different from, and an advance on, Sartre's. I also began to argue that it shares striking affinities with Merleau-Ponty's account of embodied subjectivity or the "body-subject" (Kruks 1990b, 1991). The early Sartre (of *Being and Nothingness*) certainly does not deserve the postmodern opprobrium he has received. But, as he himself later admitted,[14] he does still over-emphasize the autonomy of the subject. Beauvoir, by contrast, with her greater attention to "the power of circumstance" and embodiment, offers an account of a socially imbued, hence gendered, subjectivity, one that is not necessarily always capable of the freedom that the early Sartre attributes to it.

However, when I developed this reading, I had yet to work through the implications of Beauvoir's account of subjectivity for the postmodernism debates within feminism. I began to do so in an article that was published in *Signs* (Kruks 1992). Chapter 1, "Freedoms that Matter: Situation and Subjectivity in the Work of Beauvoir, Sartre, and Merleau-Ponty" draws on, reworks, and adds to these earlier materials. It now makes the case for Beauvoir's philosophical originality with respect to not only Sartre but also Merleau-Ponty. I show in detail how Beauvoir offers us an account of the subject that sheds what remained problematic in Sartre's early work, and how her account enables us to think about gender as both socially produced and yet actively and individually assumed. In her ambiguous claim that one "becomes" a woman, Beauvoir offers us a notion of constrained or *situated* freedom. Hers is an account that allows for more individual agency than postmodernism (at least explicitly) acknowledges, yet which does not reduce subjectivity to pure interiority or a self-constituting consciousness.

Chapter 2, "Panopticism and Shame: Foucault, Beauvoir, and Feminism," is recently written and stands as a sequel to the first chapter. In it, I engage more directly in the feminist postmodernism debates by reading Foucault and Judith Butler through Beauvoir. Here I flesh out the arguments, made in this introduction, about the difficulties that arise when the subject is stripped of any creative role or any active interiority. In particular, I argue that Foucault's account of panopticism is incoherent and incomplete and that Beauvoir's analysis of the "interior" experience of shame offers a needed complement. Likewise, I argue, Butler's account of gender performance de-

14. In 1969 Sartre looked back critically at his early claims about the subject and stated that "in *L'Etre et le néant*, what you would call 'subjectivity' is not what it would be for me now, the small margin in an operation whereby an interiorization re-exteriorizes itself in an act" ([1969] 1974, 35).

mands recognition of an element of interiority that she seeks to deny but that Beauvoir illuminates.

Sartre has had a bad press from feminists. Indeed, I have been told by more than one colleague that he is such an outrageous sexist that it is really inexcusable to use his work at all![15] Many feminist theorists who will, for example, happily take Freud seriously—in spite of his claims that women are inimical to civilization, incapable of moral development, and so on—shudder at the thought of engaging with Sartre. While I resist the idea of a feminist Index, it was still with some surprise that I found myself turning so extensively to Sartre's works in the essays that compose part 2, "Recognition, Knowledge, and Identity." However, my focus is on later works, *Anti-Semite and Jew* (1946) and the first volume of *Critique of Dialectical Reason* (1960), rather than on *Being and Nothingness*. For already by 1946 Sartre's increasing attention to social relations was bringing about profound shifts in his philosophy. By the time of the *Critique,* his primary focus was on the socially constrained nature of all human action, however individuated and autonomous it might initially appear.

Written in the mid-1990s, the essays in this section represent a shift in my focus from questions raised by postmodernism to (connected) issues of identity politics within feminism. This shift arose with my increasing involvement in the Women's Studies Program at Oberlin College, where questions of identity and difference often were—and continue to be—highly contentious. Given my whiteness and heterosexuality, it became important for me to explore what such categories mean and to ask how far identity matters. Identity politics converges with postmodern feminism in its (rightful) distrust of "universalizing" discourses that can occlude oppression, and it shares the latter's concomitant celebration of multiplicity, fluidity, instability. But observing identity politics in action, both at Oberlin and beyond, I began to meditate also on some of the difficulties it poses for feminist (and other) poli-

---

15. In an infamous passage in *Being and Nothingness,* Sartre equates the "feminine" not only with "nature" but also with an active threat to "man." The feminine threatens treacherously to suck man into its viscous, or slimy, embrace and to destroy "his" freedom. Feminist scholars, beginning with Collins and Pierce's now classic essay (1973), adduce this and other passages as evidence of Sartre's incorrigible sexism.

Recently, however, some feminist scholars have begun to take Sartre more seriously, arguing either that the sexism is contingent rather than central to his philosophic project (Barnes 1990, 1999; Burstow 1992), or else that feminists can selectively appropriate Sartrean insights and analyses in spite of his sexism. Many of the essays in the recent volume *Feminist Interpretations of Jean-Paul Sartre* (Murphy 1999) take this latter approach. In her introduction, Murphy suggests that in scrutinizing his work for sexism, feminists have been unfair to Sartre: he has been held to higher standards than other male philosophers because of his association with Beauvoir (8).

tics. In addition, I began to ask myself questions about its intellectual roots— which, quite unexpectedly, led me back to existential phenomenology!

Thus the first essay in part 2, "The Politics of Recognition: Sartre, Fanon, and Identity Politics," offers an exploration of modern identity politics through a reading of two closely linked historical texts: Sartre's *Anti-Semite and Jew* (1946) and Fanon's *Black Skin, White Masks* (1952). Fanon's text draws directly and extensively on Sartre's in exploring experiences of otherness and is profoundly informed by existential phenomenology. Since Fanon has recently been resurrected as a major figure within the canon of "Critical Race Theory" in ways that totally erase his existential orientation, this essay is partly a project of retrieval, an effort to set the record straight. However, it is also more than that.

For these two classic phenomenologies of oppression, two studies of the "lived experience" of being ineradicably "the other," throw considerable light on dynamics that still endure in identity politics. Through my reading of Sartre and Fanon I argue, against "post-identity" theorists, for the continuing importance of identity politics as a form of self-affirmation and as a demand for the recognition of differences. But I also examine what can be problematic about identity politics: in particular, the tendency to assert differences so strongly that elements of commonality, which might become the basis for solidarity, come to be denied. I also explore how, by privileging the experiential, cultural, and symbolic aspects of identity, identity politics can function to exclude from consideration equally important issues of material redistribution.

The second essay in part 2 moves onto the terrain of epistemology. In "Identity Politics and Dialectical Reason: Beyond an Epistemology of Provenance," my goal is to explore how what Donna Haraway has called "situated knowledges" can avoid slipping into relativistic claims that knowledge is exclusive to particular groups and is simply a function of its provenance. How, I ask, can knowledge be both partial and perspectival and yet also objective, in the sense of shareable and publicly communicable? Although Haraway rightly calls for such "objective" situated knowledges, she does not show us how they might actually be produced.

Here, I selectively use Sartre's later work, the *Critique of Dialectical Reason*, to sketch some answers. In this work, Sartre's initial focus is on *practices:* on what we do in the world, rather than on experience. He sets out to demonstrate the ways in which apparently discrete practices are de facto connected: through their inherence in common social fields and through various and complex material mediations. Demonstrating that knowledge of these connections is possible, Sartre shows us how our own situated, practical, knowledges can also open out into a comprehension of the practices of others, even when our experiences are significantly different. He thus points a way toward those objective and shareable forms of knowledge that a broadly based feminist movement needs. Although such knowledges still emerge from reflection on our specific social locations, they are able to take us beyond the confines of an epistemology of provenance.

The third and final part of the book, "Experience and the Phenomenology of Difference," contains more recent material. It continues to pursue questions about differences among women but in another vein. Here I ask whether there are ways that we can both give differences their full due and also develop forms of solidarity among women. In searching for possible sites where a solidarity respectful of differences might be developed, I argue that we need to move beyond the postmodern fascination with the discursive and to consider more immediate experiences of feminine embodiment. Here my work is informed by Merleau-Ponty's phenomenology of embodied subjectivity, as well as Beauvoir's.

In chapter 5, "Going Beyond Discourse: Feminism, Phenomenology, and 'Women's Experience,'" I begin by setting out more fully than I have done previously the inadequacy of postmodern reductions of subjectivity to the discursive. Taking the much-cited works of Richard Rorty and Joan Scott as illustrative, I show that such attempts undermine themselves and become inconsistent. They also preclude sufficient attention to the domain of affectivity. This lack of attention is problematic, I argue. For a focus on affective aspects of embodied subjectivity, particularly on suffering, may direct our attention to certain areas of experience where it is possible to be open to others whose social identities and interests are different from our own.

The final chapter, "Phenomenology and Difference: On the Possibility of Feminist 'World-Travelling,' " further develops the line of exploration begun in chapter 5. Taking Maria Lugones's notion of "playful world-travelling" as a guiding thread, I further examine situations in which we might be open to others, whose worlds and experiences are not our own. Again, I focus on women's bodies as an important site for such openings, arguing that certain generalities of feminine embodiment may enable us to feel connections with the suffering of other women in ways that are neither objectifying nor appropriative. Such connections could potentially become the bases for forms of respectful solidarity among otherwise different women. However, this possibility is never guaranteed, and I conclude that a willed *choice* of openness to others is also necessary for feminism.

Taken as a whole, these essays offer a set of interventions in feminist theoretical debates and also bear on more concrete political questions about differences among women and the possibility of solidarity. As situated knowers, we commonly tend to be myopic: to see the world only as it is around us now. But if the postmoderns have taught us one thing, it is that the present does not contain its future as any linear projection. Thus, feminism's present condition is no necessary indicator of its future. Moreover, given the fragility of the advances made by women, the relatively few who benefit from them, and the backlash already under way, we might reasonably anticipate that there will be a broad resurgence of feminism within a not too distant future. These essays are thus written in the conviction that feminism is not "over" and that ways will emerge to move creatively, yet without re-erasing differences, beyond feminism's present state of fragmentation. They stand as a small contribution to such a renaissance.

PART 1

Simone de Beauvoir in "Her" World and "Ours"

1 Freedoms That Matter: Subjectivity and Situation in the Work of Beauvoir, Sartre, and Merleau-Ponty

As we move into the new century, the world Simone de Beauvoir inhabited grows ever more distant from ours. Yet I begin my engagement with contemporary feminism through a return to Beauvoir. For as Merleau-Ponty, her one-time friend and collaborator, remarked, there are certain works that endure as classics. "No one," he observed, "takes them literally, and yet new facts are never absolutely outside their competence but draw forth from them new echoes and reveal in them new facets" ([1960] 1964, 11). For feminist theory, *The Second Sex* remains such a work.

The Second Sex ([1949] 1989; cited hereafter as SS) is a vast and unruly work. Within its many hundreds of pages is packed more information (some of it of dubious accuracy) than one could ever absorb; there are long, breathless digressions and multiple, sometimes contradictory, claims. A work of many voices, of suggestive threads and fragments, it has indeed been read in remarkably different ways over the decades. The echoes it sends forth and the new facets it reveals continue to amaze: once read as the Bible of "equality feminism," it has, for example, more recently been read as con-

My initial ideas about Beauvoir's philosophical originality were published as "Simone de Beauvoir and the Limits to Freedom," *Social Text* 17 (fall 1987): 111–22. Later elaborations, on which I also draw here, appeared in *Situation and Human Existence* (London: Routledge, 1990); "Simone de Beauvoir: Teaching Sartre about Freedom," in *Sartre Alive*, ed. Ronald Aronson and Adrien van den Hoven (Detroit: Wayne State University Press, 1991), 285–300; and "Gender and Subjectivity: Simone de Beauvoir and Contemporary Feminism," *Signs: Journal of Women in Culture and Society* 18, no. 1 (1992): 89–110.

sonant with the work of Irigaray (Bergoffen 1997; Schutte 1997), or Kristeva (Zerilli 1992), or as anticipating Foucauldian accounts of the production of gender (Butler 1987).

This chapter returns to Beauvoir and reads her in the context of "her" world, particularly in relation to the thought of two of her key interlocutors: Sartre and Merleau-Ponty. In the chapter that follows I engage with her in "our" world, that of Anglo-American feminism more than half a century later. The two worlds and the two readings are not, of course, wholly discrete. Even when I read Beauvoir in her world, I am not disinterested. I am not involved here in a quest for authorial intent. Rather, I seek to explore a set of conversations that are often partial or implicit among Beauvoir, Sartre, and Merleau-Ponty in order to shed light on issues that still endure for feminism and other would-be liberatory movements in what have been called our "postliberatory times" (Butler 1997, 18). These issues concern how to theorize the "subject": How are we to think about consciousness and the body, about the gendering of the subject, about agency and its limits, about responsibility? And, perhaps most crucially, are there ways that we can still fruitfully reflect on the issue of freedom?

"Freedom" is a word that feminist theorists tend to steer away from today. Freedom, liberation, a world without oppression: all of these ideals now seem too grandiose and too dangerously universalistic to be considered. Resistance? Perhaps, so long as it is local. Counter-discourse? Maybe, so long as it remains on the margins. But freedom? Surely not! Too much violence, too much silencing of others, has taken place in its name. This last point is, of course, historically accurate. Indeed, today the term "freedom" has been hijacked by conservatives, by "libertarian" militia-men and callous slashers of the social safety net, who continue to justify forms of structural violence in its name. But that is no reason to abandon freedom as a value. We have grown overly timid, too determinedly myopic. In returning to a conversation between Beauvoir and her contemporaries that is ultimately about freedom, I want to restore certain theoretical vistas that have today become foreclosed within feminism.

In what follows I chart the course of Beauvoir's thinking as it develops, at once in conjunction with and against the early ideas of Sartre and Merleau-Ponty. Although Beauvoir draws significant insights from both thinkers, I argue that her accounts of the subject and of freedom move beyond theirs in ways that remain of pivotal significance today. Above all, what I draw from her work is an account of the *situated* subject and its partial freedom. This is an account that anticipates later feminist concerns with positionality and location, yet which avoids reducing the subject to a subject-position or to merely an effect of its positionality. I thus reread Beauvoir to address the vexed issue of personal agency across the grain of much recent, especially postmodern, feminist theory.

BEAUVOIR later said that she had begun work on *The Second Sex* in 1946 because she wanted to understand herself: "wanting to talk about myself, I became aware that to do so I should first have to describe the condition of woman in general" (Beauvoir 1964, 185). Yet the reader cannot but be struck by how aloof Beauvoir seems to stand most of the time: it is other women she is discussing and not, it appears, herself. Nor, anywhere in her multiple volumes of autobiography, does she ever admit that she personally experienced her femininity as a handicap, or even that she recognized it as a source of inner conflict in herself. A reading of her posthumously published *Letters to Sartre* (1992) suggests, however, that there was more of an autobiographical edge to *The Second Sex* than she admitted. Moreover, a close scrutiny of her autobiography suggests that characteristically feminine patterns of otherness and subordination, such as Beauvoir described in *The Second Sex*, were often present in her relations with Sartre.

This becomes a matter of importance if one attempts to examine Beauvoir's philosophical relationship to Sartre and to evaluate her own contributions to philosophy. For she always insisted that she lacked originality and was merely Sartre's disciple in matters philosophical. "[On] the philosophical level," she insisted, "I adhered completely to *Being and Nothingness* and later to *Critique of Dialectical Reason*" (Sicard 1979, 325), and she claimed that Sartre's *Being and Nothingness* (published six years previously, in 1943) was the *only* important influence on *The Second Sex* (Simons 1986, 204).[1] Beauvoir certainly tried to work within Sartre's philosophical framework, to remain the docile handmaiden, but (fortunately) she did not wholly succeed. There is a tension that runs through *The Second Sex*, as well as some of her other essays, between her formal adherence to early Sartrean categories and those ideas of her own that are profoundly incompatible with Sartreanism. It is this tension that perhaps accounts for many of the paradoxes and inconsistencies one can find within her work.

For a long time scholars and commentators took Beauvoir at her word and read *The Second Sex* as simply applying Sartre's analyses of "human" existence to women. Many accused her of being male-identified, hostile to women, and, like Sartre, disgusted by the female body (see, among others, Ascher 1981;

---

1. Similarly, Beauvoir told another interviewer: "in philosophical terms, he was creative and I am not. . . . I always recognized his superiority in that area. So where Sartre's philosophy is concerned, it is fair to say that I took my cue from him because I also embraced existentialism myself" (Schwarzer 1984, 109).

Whitmarsh 1981; Siegfried 1985; Okely 1986; Evans 1987). But starting in the 1980s some feminist scholars, myself included, began systematically to challenge the view of Beauvoir as the faithful disciple who merely applied Sartre's concepts in her own work (Le Doeuff 1980, 1991; Simons 1981; Kruks 1987; Singer 1990). Indeed, one more recent reading has gone so far in reversing the earlier view as to suggest that Beauvoir had previously developed all the key ideas of *Being and Nothingness* in her first novel, *She Came to Stay*, and that Sartre effectively "stole" them from her (Fullbrook and Fullbrook 1994). I think this last claim is problematic, as it depends on an overly simple conception of the ownership of ideas. It also assumes a tighter convergence between Beauvoir's and Sartre's ideas than I believe exists. But the claim that Beauvoir's ideas were not philosophically derivative of Sartre's has by now been established definitively (Le Doeuff 1991; Moi 1994; Lundgren-Gothlin 1996; Bergoffen 1997). Moreover, Margaret Simons's recent study of Beauvoir's unpublished diary of 1927 reveals that many of her ideas were already well in formation two years before she had even met Sartre (1999, 185–243). Indeed, a case can plausibly be made that, at certain points in his development, it was Beauvoir who led Sartre intellectually.

This is particularly probable with regard to Sartre's efforts (for a decade beginning in the late 1940s) to develop a social philosophy that could conjoin his still overly individualistic existential phenomenology with a humanistic Marxism. One of the paradoxes of Sartre's work in the immediate postwar period was that he still defended his account of subjectivity as autonomous, elaborated in *Being and Nothingness*, while also trying (in the context of the developing cold war and the beginnings of anticolonial resistance in the French empire) to argue the case for a humanistic socialism and solidarity with colonized peoples.[2] Struggling with the tension between his individualistic ontology and his growing awareness of the collective nature of emancipatory projects, Sartre gradually modified the notion of freedom he had elaborated in *Being and Nothingness*. This shift is initially evidenced, for example, in his abandoned *Notebooks for an Ethics* (1992; written in 1947–48) and reaches a certain resolution in the first volume of the *Critique of Dialectical Reason* ([1960] 1976). Over time he developed a more nuanced position, in which freedom admits of degree and is socially mediated. This account was strikingly akin to the account that Beauvoir had already developed by the late 1940s and which, according to Simons, she was already beginning to elaborate as early as 1927 (1999, 185–243).

2. *Les Temps Modernes,* the independent left-wing journal founded by Sartre, Beauvoir, Merleau-Ponty, and others in 1945, was the first periodical to take a stand against continued French colonialism in Vietnam and elsewhere. In the context of the intensifying cold war in the late 1940s, the journal took a position of "critical support" for the Soviet Union, arguing that although a return to the prewar capitalist status quo was unacceptable, the Soviet Union could not be fully supported either.

❧

IN *Being and Nothingness* Sartre still claims that subjectivity (or, in the Hegelian terminology he uses, "being-for-itself") is autonomous and, because it is unconditioned, free. "Man" is an absolute subject.[3] Although, *pace* his postmodern critics, Sartre's subject remains far from a Cartesian *res cogitans*, since it always exists "in situation" and encounters the givenness or "facticity" of a world of things that it does not constitute, still it does freely choose how to assume the meaning of its own situation. Moreover, relations among human beings, which Sartre characterizes as the fundamentally conflictual relations of self and other, can never destroy this autonomous aspect of the subject. Thus, for Sartre, relations of unequal power have no bearing on the autonomy of the subject. "The slave in chains is as free as his master," Sartre tells us ([1943] 1956, 550; cited hereafter as BN), because each is equally free to choose the meaning he gives to his own situation. Material or political inequality between master and slave is simply irrelevant to their relation as two freedoms, as two absolute subjects.

In this delineation of the subject, Sartre contributes to what many feminists have suggested is a distinctly masculine conception of selfhood, to what Nancy Hartsock has characterized as the "walled city" view of the self. Such a self is not only radically separate from others but also always potentially hostile to them. Hartsock observes that Hegel's account of the emergence of self-consciousness in the "master-slave dialectic," the struggle in which each consciousness "seeks the death of the other"—an account that Sartre appropriates as the relation of self and other in *Being and Nothingness*—expresses a common masculine experience. As she remarks, "the construction of a self in opposition to another who threatens one's very being reverberates throughout the construction of both class society and the masculinist world view and results in a deep-going and hierarchical dualism" (Hartsock 1985, 241).[4]

Although Sartre stressed Beauvoir's importance to him as a critical reader of his work (Sicard 1979, 326), he never acknowledged that she played a significant role in the transformation his thought underwent between *Being*

3. It is not only Sartre who uses such gender-laden language. Beauvoir also repeatedly uses "man" to refer to all human beings, and she usually lapses into masculine forms for any discussion that does not positively require her to use feminine ones. In the interests of historical accuracy, I keep such masculinist language where I cite or paraphrase Sartre and Beauvoir.

4. Hartsock is careful to point out that she is elaborating an "ideal type" here. This point needs to be emphasized since it is important to avoid essentializing or dehistoricizing conceptions of "abstract masculinity" or the "walled city subject." Few individuals correspond exactly to ideal types, and the Western philosophic tradition itself is far more untidy than some feminist readings of it might suggest. There is, for example, an ethical socialist tradition, exemplified in the work of William Morris, that cuts across the abstract/relational dichotomy. Or for a blistering attack on the autonomous or abstract self, but one that functions as an unapologetic *defense* of patriarchalism, one need look no further than Edmund Burke.

and Nothingness (1943) and the *Critique of Dialectical Reason* (1960). Rather, it was to Merleau-Ponty that he attributed the role of mentor and intellectual guide. It was Merleau-Ponty's collection of essays *Humanism and Terror* (1947) that obliged him, he said, to move beyond his earlier individualism, and that taught him about such supra-individual aspects of human existence as history and politics (Sartre [1961] 1965, 174–76). But Beauvoir had grasped the implications of Merleau-Ponty's work earlier than Sartre, and better.[5] It was she, and not Sartre, who in 1945 wrote an extensive review of Merleau-Ponty's *Phenomenology of Perception* for *Les Temps Modernes*. In the review she discussed the profoundly social import of Merleau-Ponty's thought and highlighted his divergences from Sartre. Merleau-Ponty, she pointed out, rejected Sartre's notion of an "absolute freedom" or pure subjectivity. By contrast, he elaborated a notion of an embodied or "incarnate" subject, of a subject that is also, because embodied, historically situated. To be embodied is to exist in ways that always outstrip individual consciousness. For embodiment effects a conjunction of subject and world that precludes the autonomy of the Sartrean absolute subject:

> While Sartre, in *Being and Nothingness*, emphasizes above all the opposition of the for-itself and in-itself, the nihilating power of consciousness in the face of being and its absolute freedom, Merleau-Ponty on the contrary applies himself to describing the concrete character of the subject who is never, according to him, a pure for-itself. . . . [For Merleau-Ponty] history is incarnated in a body which possesses a certain generality, a relation to the world anterior to myself; and this is why the body is opaque to reflection, and why my consciousness discovers itself to be "engorged with the sensible." [Consciousness] is not a pure for-itself, or, to use Hegel's phrase which Sartre has taken up, a "hole in being"; but rather "a hollow, a fold, which has been made and which can be un-made." (Beauvoir 1945, 366–67)

In this passage Beauvoir perceptively puts her finger on the main divergences between the two philosophies. One is a theory of pure consciousness, of an absolute freedom that stands over and against the material world. The other is

5. Margaret Simons reports, on the basis of Beauvoir's unpublished diary, that Beauvoir and Merleau-Ponty engaged in frequent discussions with each other when philosophy students in the late 1920s. At this time Merleau-Ponty was still a practicing Catholic, and Simons suggests that Beauvoir began to develop her own philosophy of the "lived" and of embodiment in opposition to his "metaphysical absolutes" (1999, 202–5). Whether, as Simons also suggests (205), Beauvoir might also have influenced Merleau-Ponty's intellectual development toward a philosophy of the body-subject remains a moot point. There is no evidence in Simons's account that Beauvoir succeeded in swaying Merleau-Ponty to her views. Moreover, his fully fledged philosophy did not emerge until many years later, after his discovery in 1939 of the late Husserl's philosophy of the "life-world."

a theory of a consciousness that is but a "fold" in being, of a consciousness that, because embodied, is not discontinuous with the generality of the material world but rather "engorged with the sensible." What is striking, however, is that Beauvoir also refrains from making any judgment between these two theories. Although not prepared to criticize Sartre in matters philosophical, apparently she was also unwilling to defend him. For in *The Second Sex* Beauvoir develops an account of the subject that is strikingly close to Merleau-Ponty's: an account in which the subject is "never a pure for-itself" but rather an embodied consciousness, a socially situated and conditioned freedom. "I am my body," writes Merleau-Ponty, and Beauvoir cites his notion of embodied consciousness, or the "body-subject," for her own ends.[6]

Merleau-Ponty's notion of the embodied subject in the *Phenomenology of Perception* ([1945] 1962; cited hereafter as PP) implies a radical reconceptualization of both consciousness and the body. Consciousness is seen to be always situated and perspectival, its evaluations of the world anchored in and delimited by the sensory and physical capacities of the body. We experience the world always through the framework of our bodily relations with it (PP 303). Thus, for example, my bodily capacities define how I see the size of things: "Whether or not I have decided to climb them, these mountains appear high to me because they exceed the grasp of my body" (PP 440). Concomitantly, the body can no longer be conceived as an object distinct from consciousness. Rather it is *itself* the site of forms of sentient knowing, arising from perception, touch, and other sensory experiences. The "lived body" of phenomenology (as opposed to the objective body of science) is not the passive recipient of information but itself actively organizes our knowledge of the world in accordance with its own orientation, capacities, and projects. "Consciousness is in the first place not a matter of 'I think that' but of 'I can' " (PP 137).

Moreover, Merleau-Ponty points out, the presence of other people does not *necessarily* constitute a threat to such an embodied consciousness: on the contrary, the commonalities of embodiment point beyond the solipsistic tendencies of Sartrean subjects each of whom objectifies the other. Although we can—and often do—engage in such forms of objectification, Merleau-Ponty argues this is not our primary relation to others.[7] Rather, the "ano-

---

6. She also alters it, a point I discuss more fully later. "Woman, like man *is* her body," Beauvoir writes, with explicit reference to Merleau-Ponty. Yet instantly adds, "but her body is something other than herself" (SS 29).

7. Although many commentators have read Merleau-Ponty as offering a theory of guaranteed, pre-given intersubjectivity and human harmony, the human potential for conflict, objectification, and violence is also a central pre-occupation of his work. Indeed, he may best be read as presenting human existence as a dialectic of communication and conflict, in which, although the former is always possible, it is never assured. I explore this dialectic more fully in Kruks 1990b.

nymity" of human bodies, the pre-personal set of characteristics they commonly share, offers the possibility of an immediate apprehension of the other as *like* myself: "in so far as I have sensory functions, a visual, auditory and tactile field, I am already in communication with others taken as similar psycho-physical subjects" (PP 353).

For example, I have no reason to assume that another person's perception of a landscape that we are both looking at is radically different from my own. Rather, I think of the other person as "someone who has a living experience of the same world as mine, as well as the same history, and with whom I am in communication through that world and that history" (PP 405).[8] Given such a notion of embodied subjectivity, Sartre's account of freedom must also be reformulated. For such a body-subject is situated not only spatially and temporally but also socially. It requires the support of others. For "there is no freedom without a field" (PP 439), and others can either support my field of action or undermine it. Such an embodied freedom is thus always vulnerable to the domination of others: it is this key insight that Beauvoir and Merleau-Ponty share.

In fact Beauvoir's initial disagreement with Sartre over the notion of freedom predates the writing of both *Being and Nothingness* and Merleau-Ponty's *Phenomenology of Perception*. In *The Prime of Life*, published in 1960, she describes a series of conversations she had with Sartre in the spring of 1940. In these conversations Sartre sketched out for her the main lines of the argument of what was to become *Being and Nothingness*. Their discussions, Beauvoir recalled in 1960, centered above all on the problem of "the relation of situation to freedom." In a rare public admission of philosophical disagreement with Sartre, she writes:

---

8. Sullivan (1997) argues that Merleau-Ponty's account of forms of intersubjectivity that are pre-personally grounded in embodiment functions to obscure differences (such as those of gender) among individuals. Rather, she claims, Merleau-Ponty justifies a solipsistic and ultimately imperialistic projection of one's own perceptions onto different others. Such an imperialistic self-projection is of course a risk, and Merleau-Ponty is able to offer no firm guarantees against it. Moreover, Sullivan is right to point out that Merleau-Ponty himself has a tendency to assume that "the" embodied subject is male and probably rather like himself. See on this last point also Butler 1989 and Weiss 1999.

This having been said, Merleau-Ponty's claim that human beings share certain basic orientations to the world by virtue of their common bodily form and capacities (because, for example, they are bipedal, generally walk at around the same speed, cannot lift as much as elephants can, etc.) is not one that *necessarily* effaces differences. On the contrary, it offers us ways to think about our commonalities that may enable us to bridge our differences without denying them. For although we each embody the pre-personal, we are also always particular; each aspect implies the other. For more positive feminist evaluations of Merleau-Ponty than Sullivan's, see Bigwood 1991 and Diprose 1998.

I maintained that, from the point of view of freedom, as Sartre defined it—not as a stoical resignation but as an active transcendence of the given—not every situation is equal: what transcendence is possible for a woman locked up in a harem? Even such a cloistered existence could be lived in several different ways, Sartre said. I clung to my opinion for a long time and then made only a token submission. Basically [she comments in 1960] I was right. But to have been able to defend my position, I would have had to abandon the terrain of individualist, thus idealist, morality, where we stood. (Beauvoir [1960] 1962, 34)

The naive orientalism of Beauvoir's comment notwithstanding, her general point matters: there are situations in which freedom, as Sartre conceives it, ceases to be possible. Although she would never challenge head-on Sartre's conception of freedom, or the notion of the impermeable "walled city" subject that it implied, from this time on she was quietly to subvert them. This becomes clearer in two essays on ethics she wrote prior to *The Second Sex: Pyrrhus et Cinéas* (1944) and *The Ethics of Ambiguity* ([1947] 1967). In *Pyrrhus et Cinéas*, written while *Being and Nothingness* was in press, Beauvoir still begins from the Sartrean autonomous subject but ends by putting in question the theory of fundamentally conflictual social relations that Sartre developed from it. Although freedoms are separate, Beauvoir argues that, paradoxically, they are also intrinsically interdependent. If I try to imagine a world in which I am the only person, the image is horrifying. For everything I do would be pointless if there were not other subjects to valorize it: "A man [sic] alone in the world would be paralyzed by the self-evident vanity of all his goals; he could not bear to live" (1944, 64).

Moreover, Beauvoir argues that for others to valorize one's project it is not enough that they are free merely in Sartre's sense; it is not sufficient for them to be subjects each of whom, like the master and the slave, constitutes the meaning of his or her own discrete situation. Freedom for Beauvoir, far more than for Sartre at this time, involves a *practical* subjectivity: the ability of each of us to act in the world so that we can take up each other's projects and give them a future meaning. And for this to be possible, we also require for each other an equal social field for action:

The other's freedom can do nothing for me unless my own goals can serve as his point of departure; it is by using the tool which I have invented that the other prolongs its existence; the scholar can only talk with men who have arrived at the same level of knowledge as himself. . . . I must therefore endeavor to create for all men situations which will enable them to accompany and surpass my transcendence. I need their freedom to be available to make use of me, to preserve me in surpassing me. I require for men health, knowledge, well being, leisure, so that their freedom does not consume itself in fighting sickness, ignorance, misery. (1944, 114–15)

Already then in 1944, Beauvoir was aware of the interdependence of subjectivities and, in ways that Sartre was not, of the permeability and hence vulnerability of the subject.[9] Indeed, she arguably took the first step here toward adequately linking Sartre's individualistic existentialism with their shared commitment to the egalitarian and solidaristic values of socialism. In *The Ethics of Ambiguity,* Beauvoir went a step further. There she suggested that oppression can permeate subjectivity to the point where consciousness itself becomes no more than a product of the oppressive situation. The freedom that Sartre had associated with subjectivity can, in a situation of extreme oppression, be wholly suppressed even though it cannot be definitively eliminated. In such a situation the oppressed become incapable of a project of resistance, indeed incapable of the reflective distance necessary to be aware that they are oppressed. Then, "living is only not dying, and human existence is indistinguishable from an absurd vegetation" ([1947] 1967, 82–83). Freedom is no longer, as for Sartre, a capacity to choose how to live even the most constrained of situations. Rather it is reduced to no more than a suppressed potentiality. It is made "immanent," unrealizable. Yet, for all this, freedom is neither a "fiction" nor an "imaginary" for Beauvoir. For should oppression start to weaken, freedom can always re-erupt.

It was only in *The Second Sex* (begun in 1946 and completed and published in 1949), however, that Beauvoir attempted systematically—and at length—to analyze oppression. The attempt proved to be impossible within the confines of Sartreanism. Beauvoir begins *The Second Sex* on what appears to be firmly Sartrean ground. "What is a woman?" she asks, and she answers initially that woman is defined as that which is not man—as other: "She is determined and differentiated with reference to man and not he with reference to her; she is the inessential as opposed to the essential. He is the subject, he is the Absolute; she is the Other" (SS xxii).[10]

9. As Simons suggests, on the basis of her reading of Beauvoir's early diaries, Beauvoir's radically different views on self-other relations were formed well before she met Sartre. Beauvoir's problem, she suggests, was never solipsism but rather the loss of one's self in the other. "The existence of the Other is in doubt for Sartre; Beauvoir doubts the existence of the self" (1999, 232).

10. Page references are to the 1989 Vintage edition, but I have frequently amended the translation. The book, published in French in 1949, was translated into English in 1952 by H. M. Parshley, an American professor of biology. Parshley lacked philosophical training and firmly insisted in his preface that the book "is, after all on woman, not on philosophy" (SS xxxviii). He thus set out to make Beauvoir more accessible by rendering her technical philosophical terms into more "commonsense" English whenever

Some feminist critics have used this and similar passages to accuse Beauvoir of taking on board the Sartrean (and Hegelian) notion of the self-construction of subjectivity through conflict.[11] However, Beauvoir profoundly shifts the meaning of this notion of otherness. For Sartre, at least in *Being and Nothingness*, my "being-for-others" is always *self*-referential: that is, it is the awareness of *myself* in relation to another. As Michèle Le Doeuff nicely observes, Sartre's philosophy is "fundamentally shaped by a kind of Robinson Crusoe complex even when he deals with being-for-others" (1995, 63). Thus, in Sartre's account being-for-others must arise conflictually. For it is only when the other attempts to destroy my freedom that I experience myself, as it were, from without and thus as in relation (albeit antagonistic relation) with the other. But since my freedom is indestructible, the other can never finally touch it. Instead, the other attempts to nihilate the visible *exterior* of my freedom: my "being-in-situation." It is when he or she *looks* at me that the other steals my "being-in-situation" from me and incorporates it, object-like, within his or her own situation. But although the other objectifies what we might call the exteriority of my freedom, I still remain free: that is, I remain free to choose my own action in response to the other's transcendence; and I always retain the possibility of turning the tables on the other. Conversely, if I objectify the other's "being-in-situation," I too will fail to reach his or her freedom. The other will thus remain for me always a potential threat; as Sartre dramatically puts it, the other is for me an "explosive instrument" (BN 297).

In this account, Sartre assumes the freedoms in conflict to be not only autonomous but also *equal*. For in relations of looking per se there is no reason to assume that human beings are anything but equal. Thus, when he describes the torture victim turning the tables on his torturer by *looking* at him (BN 405ff.), Sartre is asserting that two equal freedoms confront each other in this encounter, irrespective of the fact that the torturer has the power of physical domination over his victim. Given Sartre's notion of the indestructible freedom of the for-itself, the question of material or political inequality between torturer and victim (or master and slave) is simply irrelevant to their relation as two freedoms. In the same vein, Sartre is able to write—in 1943!—that the Jew remains free in the face of the anti-Semite because he can choose his own attitude toward his persecutor (BN 529).

It is this assumption, that relations of otherness are conflictual relations between two *equal* freedoms, that Beauvoir quietly subverts. Her challenge,

---

possible. The effect was seriously to obscure the philosophical framework and import of the book. Significant cuts were also made in the English version. For a fuller discussion of the Parshley translation, see Deirdre Bair's introduction to the Vintage edition (1989) and also Simons 1983.

11. See, in particular, Hartsock 1985, 286–92, but also O'Brien 1981, 69–72, and Lloyd 1984, 93–102.

as we will see, implies an account of human freedom that is much closer to Merleau-Ponty's than to Sartre's. It implies that there are gradations of freedom, that the boundary between a free and a determined or coerced action may be ambiguous, and that social situations may modify freedom *itself* and not merely its exteriority. As Merleau-Ponty put it, "the rationalist's [i.e., Sartre's] dilemma: either the free act is possible or it is not—either the event originates in me or is imposed on me from outside, does not apply to our relations with the world and our past" (PP 442). Rather, there can be a continuum of different situations in which more or less freedom is possible.

To return to *The Second Sex*: having begun from the Sartrean notion that woman is the other of man, Beauvoir now proceeds to qualify or nuance that notion in several ways. First, she argues that we can distinguish two significantly different kinds of relations of otherness: those between social equals and those that are structured by social inequality. Second, unlike Sartre, she argues that where the relation is one of equality, otherness can be "relativized" by a kind of "reciprocity": in a movement of mutual respect, each can recognize that the other whom he or she objectifies is also an equal freedom. Third, for Beauvoir, such "reciprocity" is not primarily a relationship of the look. Far more than for Sartre, it is expressed and mediated through social institutions and actions.

Finally, Beauvoir goes on to consider what happens in those situations when relations of otherness are also those of social *inequality*. In such circumstances, she argues, "reciprocity" is to a greater or lesser extent abolished. Relations of subjection that are mediated through oppressive social institutions take its place. When one of the two parties in a conflict is privileged through having some material or physical advantage, then "this one prevails over the other and undertakes to keep it in subjection" (SS 61). In relations of subjection, Beauvoir argues that freedom itself undergoes modification. Thus for Beauvoir, the slave is not always as free as his master, for the restrictions that operate on his situation may come to operate internally on his freedom, so as to suppress his very capacity to project any course of action. In reply to her question of 1940, "What transcendence is possible for a woman locked up in a harem?" Beauvoir's answer is now, "sometimes none." It is not, then, woman's otherness per se but her subjection, the *non*-reciprocal objectification of woman by man (which exists in many places other than harems, including North American middle-class suburbs), that needs to be explained.

Woman is not only the other; she is the unequal, the subordinate, other. Why?[12] Beauvoir begins by rejecting the most pervasive explanation: bio-

12. Heinämaa (1997) rightly argues that Beauvoir's project in *The Second Sex* is not one of causal explanation: Beauvoir does not seek to offer a sociological or ideological

logical inferiority. In a move that is foundational for contemporary feminism, she insists that there is no such thing as biological "destiny": the biological facts of sex do not determine what we today call gender.[13] As she writes in the introduction, "not every female human being is necessarily a woman: one must take part in that mysterious and threatened reality known as femininity" (SS xix). Or, as her much cited statement at the beginning of volume 2 goes: "one is not born a woman: one becomes one" (SS 267). Beauvoir, like both Merleau-Ponty and Sartre, here embraces a profound anti-naturalism and anti-essentialism. We can never describe any human condition as simply given in nature, and thus as absolutely necessary. What is often called the "eternal feminine"—gender in today's terminology—is not therefore natural, not an outcome of biological form or function. Moreover, and most important, since it is humanly created it is transmutable.

Beauvoir goes on to point out that though the "eternal feminine" is humanly constituted, not all humans participate equally in its constitution. Although women may frequently be complicit in the perpetuation of their situation, "man" is the one who defines "woman" as other and creates for her a situation of inferiorized otherness. Moreover, as Beauvoir's use of collective nouns suggests, this situation is not constituted by the relations of particular women with particular men. For subtending such direct, personal relations, women also encounter as fundamental to their situation a set of social institutions.[14] These institutions can, however, function *analogously* to natural forces in perpetuating inequality. If all that took place between an

---

account of how "sexual difference" emerges; nor does she offer a voluntarist account of gender as something chosen. Rather, Heinämaa argues, Beauvoir's project is phenomenological: "to study sexual difference as mental and bodily—but always as signifying—phenomena" (22).

Heinämaa is correct to draw our attention back to the centrality of phenomenology in *The Second Sex*, yet it is not unequivocally a work of phenomenology. For although Beauvoir offers no "cause" for women's subordination, she does still raise "why" questions that exceed phenomenological description. Phenomenological description and social explanation are not such mutually exclusive projects as Heinämaa seems to suggest. On the contrary, they imply each other here insofar as Beauvoir maintains that sources of women's subordination are to be found in lived values, disclosed in action.

13. Beauvoir does not herself use the word *gender*, although her insistence on distinguishing "the feminine" or "woman" from the (biological) "female" certainly implies this more recent usage of the term. It should be noted, however, that in many cases the French word *genre* does not translate into the English term "gender." Indeed we often use it untranslated to designate distinctions in style that are not necessarily bound to those of masculinity or femininity, as when we talk of a literary genre or genres in painting.

14. These institutions will also be variable in their impact on women of different social classes or cultural identities. For example, while property laws in France still disadvantaged all women vis-à-vis men in the 1940s, this played out differently for women of various social classes. Some were disadvantaged by a lack of control over their own wages, others by lack of control over inherited wealth or land.

individual man and woman was a Sartrean (or Hegelian) struggle of consciousness between two human beings, one of whom happened to be male and one female, then we could not anticipate in advance which of them would objectify the other. But if, for example, we examine the relations of a "husband" and a "wife," then it is very different. For the social institution of marriage in all its aspects—legal, economic, sexual, cultural, and so on—has formed in advance for the protagonists their own relation of inequality. As Beauvoir points out in a strikingly un-Sartrean passage, "it is not as single individuals that human beings define themselves in the first place; men and women have never stood opposed to each other in single combat; the couple is an original *Mitsein*; and as such it always appears as a stable or transitory element of a larger collectivity" (SS 35).[15]

But although Beauvoir insists that biology is not a "destiny," the social constructions placed on the female body are absolutely central in constituting woman as not only the other but as the inferior other. For if "I am my body," how my body is defined will significantly shape my very existence: "woman's body is one of the essential elements of the situation she holds in the world," Beauvoir writes (SS 37). There is a certain stability to the relationships between sexuality and other social and economic dimensions to life in a given society, and she cites Merleau-Ponty's remark that "the body is generality" as part of the explanation for the ubiquity of woman's oppression (SS 46).

To say the body is generality is not, of course, to say that it constitutes a defining, immutable essence: "obviously when I use the words *woman* or *feminine* I do not refer to any archetype, to any immutable essence; one must understand the phrase 'in the present state of education and customs' after most of my statements," she writes (SS xxxvi; introduction to vol. 2). Yet, as Merleau-Ponty insists, generality is a real phenomenon: around our own individual intentions and projects we discover, as he puts it, "a zone of generalized existence and of projects already formed, significances which trail between ourselves and things" (PP 450). As embodied subjects, we exist *as* such a zone, and for a woman the constructions placed on her body, the "eternal feminine," carry real weight. This becomes particularly clear in Beauvoir's discussion of "the independent woman." For the independent woman is one who cannot avoid living divided against herself as she discovers that her sex continues to define her socially in ways that are not compatible with her free personhood: "She refuses to confine herself to her role as a female, because she does not want to mutilate herself; but it would also be a mutilation to disavow her sex" (SS 682).

15. The term *Mitsein* is used by Heidegger to denote a "being-with" others that he regards as a fundamental, ontological given of human existence. Compare Beauvoir here with Sartre: "The essence of relations between consciousness is not the *Mitsein*; it is conflict" (BN 429).

For Beauvoir, as for Merleau-Ponty, it is the incarnate quality of consciousness, the fact that "I am my body," that accounts for its inherence in a world that is prior to itself, a world that is, for women, *already* structured by certain generalities as one of subordination and immanence. Expanding on the idea that "the body is generality," Beauvoir writes in a most un-Sartrean manner:

> Across the separation of existents, existence is all one: it reveals itself in similar bodies; thus there will be constants in the relation between the ontological and the sexual. At a given epoch, the technologies, the economic and social structure of a collectivity, will reveal to all its members an identical world. There will also be a relation of sexuality to social forms: similar individuals, located in similar conditions, will grasp similar significations from what is given. This similarity does not ground a rigorous universality, but it does enable us to rediscover general types within individual histories. (SS 46–47)

In this important passage Beauvoir carefully navigates (as Merleau-Ponty also does) between universals and particulars. Particular lives *are* unique: there are "individual histories." Yet lives lived within a given epoch and within a certain collectivity will also be in many ways similar.[16] There are "constants," she tells us, that offer certain kinds of structure, "general types," a degree of uniformity to individual experiences. Individuals who are similarly situated will have roughly similar experiences—and they thus will be able to communicate and share them. Here also lies the role of symbolic signification: "Symbolism . . . has been elaborated, just like language, by the human reality which is at once *Mitsein* and separation" (SS 47). Moreover, sexuality is part of this domain that is at once general and particular: there are "constants in the relation between the ontological and the sexual" that have a profound bearing on the collectivity "woman."[17] Thus to "become a woman" is at once to participate in a given gender identity and to engage in a unique existential project.

16. Merleau-Ponty also makes this point, using the example of class consciousness: "What makes me a proletarian is not the economic system or society considered as systems of impersonal forces, but these institutions as I carry them within me and experience them . . . [it is] my way of being in the world within this institutional framework" (PP 443). Similarly, one might "carry" institutions that reproduce ethnic, or racial, or religious differences as integral to one's way of being in the world.

17. Beauvoir's conception of women as a "collectivity" (*collectivité*) here arguably anticipates Sartre's later development of the idea of the "collective" (*collectif*) in *Critique of Dialectical Reason*. For Sartre, a collective is an ensemble of individuals who are aggregated through their location in one and the same field of exterior exigencies. This field imposes on them similar demands but does not produce shared internal and intentional bonds.

Given his radical individualism, the early Sartre cannot account adequately for the existence of "collectivities" or "general types" (such as being "a woman") that are integral to individual lived histories. For Sartre, each of us construes the meaning of both past and present only from the perspective of our own project. But, intriguingly, Sartre here anticipates later feminist critiques of the "view from nowhere," or the "God's-eye view," which characterizes much of Western epistemology (Harding 1986; Haraway 1991; J.R. Martin 1996). He insists that "there is no absolute viewpoint which one can adopt so as to compare different situations; each person realizes only one situation—*his own* (BN 550). Because each situation is uniquely brought into being by an individual free project, we cannot, for Sartre, conceive of a general situation.

Sartre's position has the advantage of avoiding those grand universalizations (the object also of later, postmodern critiques) that obscure differences. But it also prevents us from acknowledging the similar effects that social institutions and general structures can have on different lives. The problem is not Sartre's alone, however. For a reformulation of Sartre's position (along with its attendant dilemmas) has emerged in present-day identity politics. Although in identity politics the subject is now collective (that is, an identity group of some kind and no longer an individual), claims similar to Sartre's are often made about the perspectival quality of knowing, about the impossibility of knowing about the world except from one's own subject-position, and thus about the impossibility—to which has been added the political danger—of generalization.[18]

But Beauvoir, long before Sartre, pointed us beyond such problems. In the passage cited above, although eschewing an "absolute viewpoint," or a disembodied view from nowhere, Beauvoir still argues that there is a generality, a weight, to woman's situation that delimits her possibilities and which she is not free to refuse, or even to define in her own way. Addressing the claim of an American feminist[19] that we are all, both men and women, just human beings, Beauvoir's response is characteristically ambiguous. Yes, she says, "each concrete human being is always uniquely situated." But also, no:

18. In chapter 4 I refer to this position as an "epistemology of provenance," since it claims that what can be known is always a function of who the knower is, of who produces the knowledge. I argue that because identity politics insists on the radical incommensurability of the experience and knowledge of different groups, it poses a problem for any feminism that aspires to become a movement of solidarity among different kinds of women. I also explore some possible ways beyond this impasse, which Sartre later suggested in the *Critique of Dialectical Reason.*

19. The author Beauvoir refers to is Dorothy Parker (1893–1967), popular essayist, social satirist, and author of numerous short stories and poems, many of which well capture the predicaments of "liberated" white American middle-class women of the 1920s and 1930s.

"to reject such notions as the eternal feminine, the black soul, the Jewish character, is not to deny that Jews, Negroes, women exist today. Such a negation does not represent a liberation for those concerned, but an inauthentic flight" (SS xx). One is not, in short, free to choose not to be a woman, a black, or a Jew, if that is how the social world generally designates one's embodied existence.[20] Moreover, insofar as "I am my body," such designations do not, as Sartre had claimed, affect merely my exteriority, my being-for-others. Rather, they may affect my very capacity to conceive of the world as other than it is: my freedom. Contrary to Sartre, Beauvoir suggests that my capacity to define a project, or even to define the meaning of my situation for myself, may be suppressed. Although a woman's situation is humanly created, she may frequently experience it as what Beauvoir calls a "destiny": an exterior conditioning in the face of which freedom ceases to be possible.

Furthermore, for Beauvoir, enduring in such a condition is not necessarily a matter of "bad faith" on a woman's part. For if choice has ceased to be possible, then bad faith as the self-deceiving "flight" from freedom toward an always illusory condition of irresponsible "thinghood" simply does not arise. "Each subject," she writes,

> concretely affirms himself as a transcendence through his projects; he can only realize his freedom through his continual transcendence toward other freedoms; there is no other justification for present existence than its expansion toward an indefinitely open future. Each time that transcendence falls back into immanence there is a degradation of existence into the "in-itself," of freedom into facticity; this fall is a moral fault if the subject agrees to it; it takes the form of a frustration and an oppression if it is inflicted upon him. (SS xxxiv–xxxv)

Woman is locked in immanence by the situation man inflicts upon her— and she is not necessarily responsible. A consistent Sartrean position would make woman responsible for herself, no matter how constrained her situation. But for Beauvoir, although there are certainly many women who in "bad faith" comply with their oppressors and actively participate in their own objectification, this is not always the case. For some there is no moral

---

20. Being a woman, a black, or a Jew are not, of course, mutually exclusive social attributes, although Beauvoir sometimes tends to write as if she assumes they are. Elizabeth Spelman has criticized her for anticipating the later errors of "second wave" feminism in the United States by "making the default position of feminist inquiry an examination of white middle-class women" (1988, 76). Spelman's critique is formally valid, but there is something anachronistic in holding Beauvoir to account for problems that have arisen within the politics of a movement of another time and place. For in the 1940s France was still remarkably racially homogeneous by modern U.S. standards. If Beauvoir is to be faulted for exclusions in her portrayal of women's "lived experience" in volume 2, it is for insufficient attention to class differences among women.

fault because there simply is no possibility of choice. In the notion that freedom can "fall back into the 'in-itself,' " that the for-itself can be turned, through the action of other (that is, masculine) freedoms, into its very opposite, Beauvoir has radically departed from Sartre. According to Sartre's usage of the terms, the "degradation of existence into the 'in-itself' " would have to mean that oppressed woman has actually ceased to be human—which is not at all what Beauvoir means. For Sartre, there is no middle ground. Either the for-itself, the uncaused upsurge of freedom, exists *whatever* the facticities of its situation, or else it does not exist. In the latter case, one is dealing with the realm of inert being. Insofar as Beauvoir's account of woman's situation as one of immanence involves the claim that freedom, the for-itself, can be pervaded and modified by the in-itself, it implies another ontology than Sartre's. Beauvoir is describing human existence as a synthesis of freedom and constraint, of consciousness and materiality that is an impossibility within the framework of Sartre's philosophy. It is, however, explicable within Merleau-Ponty's framework.

BEAUVOIR must have realized there were profound affinities between her ideas and those of her old friend Merleau-Ponty, even if her relationship with Sartre made her unwilling to highlight them. Indeed, she explicitly quotes or refers to Merleau-Ponty at key points in the development of the philosophical framework of *The Second Sex*. We have already seen that she cites his notions that "I am my body" and "the body is generality" in trying to establish the generality of woman's situation of oppression. Like Merleau-Ponty, she insists that the "lived" body literally is one's situation insofar as it is defining of one's possibilities (SS 34).

As Beauvoir observed in 1945, in her review of the *Phenomenology of Perception*, Merleau-Ponty develops an account of embodied consciousness, not of a consciousness that is Sartre's "pure for-itself." It is through our common sentience, through the anonymous or pre-personal body, that Merleau-Ponty argues we can avoid solipsism and the inevitably conflictual social relations that Sartre describes. For our common inherence in sentience grants us, however fragile it may be, the possibility of an "interworld," of an immediate "intersubjectivity." For such an embodied and intersubjective consciousness, freedom "is not distinct from my insertion in the world" (PP 360), but rather "thrusts roots into the world" (PP 456). It thus admits of degree, and we will be more free or less free depending on how far our situation enables us to engage in free actions. By free actions, Merleau-Ponty means those actions that open onto and shape a future. From this perspective, it is clear that situations—particularly social situations—may qualitatively transform and even suppress freedom.

Merleau-Ponty agrees with Sartre's claim that we are not causally determined. But he does not go on to conclude with Sartre that freedom is therefore absolute. It is not the case that either we are free or we are determined, Merleau-Ponty insists, for probability is a real phenomenon and statistical thought is not irrelevant to the question of freedom. Most commonly our freedom "gears" itself to our situation, and it is then improbable (though not formally impossible) that we should overturn an on-going situation in an instant of choice. Arguing that "the probable," though not determining, strongly predisposes us to act in certain ways, Merleau-Ponty suggests that one's past shapes heavily what one is likely to do. The past, "though not a fate, is . . . the atmosphere of my present" (PP 442). Thus, if women, or other oppressed groups, have "geared" their freedom to an oppressive situation— one that effectively denies them the possibility of action that opens onto the future—then resistance, while not precluded, is improbable. Merleau-Ponty therefore has no difficulty in recognizing that freedom may be effectively suppressed. Anticipating Beauvoir's notion of freedom made immanent, he talks of "a freedom devoid of any project" (PP 444). Since freedom involves *action* that is open, we can find ourselves in situations where it is not possible.

Moreover, Merleau-Ponty and Beauvoir both recognized—long before Sartre—that individuals cannot overcome oppression on their own and that oppressive situations must be changed collectively. This insight, already present in *Pyrrhus et Cinéas*, is fleshed out by Beauvoir in the discussion of the "independent woman" at the end of *The Second Sex*. Here, although Beauvoir applauds those who struggle in their individual lives against their oppression, she also points out that such a struggle is doomed to a substantial degree of failure. For the independent woman's existence is shaped not only by her own project but also by the practices, institutions, and values of the world into which she is born. Oppression is socially instituted, and to overcome it requires a social as well as an individual transformation.[21]

21. Beauvoir's discussion here centers on the struggle of middle- and upper-class women for independence. Their struggle crucially requires them to reject their economic dependence on men. Economic dependence breeds the conditions for passivity and for "bad faith" claims of moral irresponsibility, and is thus inimical to freedom in all its degrees. But beyond economic independence, Beauvoir also insists on the need for women to engage in meaningful activity in a profession or a creative pursuit, and it is when she enters such a sphere of activity that the would-be liberated woman discovers she cannot shed her oppressive designation as a woman.

Beauvoir observes that for working-class women employment does not suffice for liberation, for factory work offers them economic independence only as members of an oppressed class and does not free them of "house-keeping burdens" (SS 680). Although she does not dwell at length on the point, it is interesting to note that Beauvoir suggests that peasant women (still a very significant proportion of French women in the 1940s) are the class of women who have escaped most fully from "the traditional feminine world" (SS 680).

Similarly, for Merleau-Ponty, an oppressive situation cannot be lived as a freely chosen individual project; nor can it be overcome by individual initiative alone. Freedom comes into being in slow, tortuous movements born of "the concatenation of less and more remote ends" (PP 445). It cannot emerge until the point is reached where individuals cease to experience themselves as the isolated victims of an anonymous oppressive "fate" and experience oppression as collective (PP 444ff.). Such a transition from immanence can take place only because "my" situation is not, strictly speaking, "mine" but is part of a more general situation that transcends my immediate experiences. Writing in France in the 1940s, Beauvoir could not imagine women's experiences coalescing to a point that could give rise to a collective liberatory movement.[22] Unlike workers or American blacks, she noted, women "do not say 'We' . . . they live dispersed among the males, attached through residence, housework, economic condition, and social standing to certain men—fathers or husbands—more firmly than they are to other women. If they belong to the bourgeoisie, they feel solidarity with men of that class, not with proletarian women; if they are white, their allegiance is to white men, not to Negro women" (SS xxv). How a "we" did later develop in second-wave feminism—and how it has since dissipated again, along some of the fault lines Beauvoir identified—is another story and beyond the confines of this discussion; yet the possibility that this fragile "we" could emerge was anticipated in the account of freedom that both Beauvoir and Merleau-Ponty offered.

ALTHOUGH Beauvoir draws from Merleau-Ponty's notions of freedom and embodiment, she is by no means a mere disciple here either. According to Merleau-Ponty, my body orients me to the world; it is the locus of my sentient knowledge of the world, and it is also projective: that is, it is an instrumentality through which I bring my intentions, my projects, to bear on the world. In *The Second Sex* Beauvoir cites from the *Phenomenology of Perception:* "I am my body . . . [and] my body is like a life model, or like a preliminary sketch, for my total being." But her own formulation is strikingly different: "Woman, like man, *is* her body; but her body is something other than herself" (SS 29). Implicit here is a critique that later feminists have also made of Merleau-Ponty: the body in his account is literally his—

22. One should note, however, that it would have called for truly remarkable powers of imagination to envision a significant women's movement in postwar France. France, in the 1940s, was still a primarily agrarian, Catholic country, in which women had only just obtained the vote and still lacked equal property rights. The early defeat and occupation of France by the Germans meant that the war did not have the effect of pushing women out of their traditional domestic roles and into the workforce there, as it did in the United States and Britain.

it is masculine. For Merleau-Ponty a man normally "is" his body: a simultaneous cohesion of flesh, subjectivity, and situation that is able to form a
project and act on the world.[23] But a woman lacks such cohesion: she is her
body, yet it is not she. What are we to make of this paradox? How can one
be that which is other than oneself? And what kind of freedom is possible
for such an alienated being?

If our body is, as Beauvoir says, "the instrument of our grasp upon the
world, the outline (*esquisse*) of our projects" (SS 34), then it also delineates
our range of possibilities. To "become" a woman is to find oneself in a world
in which possibilities close down rather than open up, in which the field of
free action narrows even, in extreme cases, to the point of disappearing.
Although Beauvoir does not dismiss biological differences between the sexes
as irrelevant to this process, it is the social values placed on such differences
that carry the most weight: "it is clear that if the biological condition of
woman does constitute a handicap, it is because of the viewpoint in which
she is caught" (SS 333). Woman's situation is one in which her body comes
to define her as the other, even as it remains the locus of her grasp upon the
world, integral to her subjectivity and her projects. Unlike a boy, for whom
there is no "fundamental opposition" between his concern with how he appears to others and his desire to realize himself in his specific projects, a
woman always lives in conflict.[24] For her, "there is from the beginning a conflict between her autonomous existence and her 'being-other' (*être-autre*);
she is taught that to please she must *try to please*, she must *make herself*
object; she must therefore *renounce* her autonomy . . . thus a vicious circle
forms; for the less she exerts her freedom in order to understand, grasp, and
disclose the world, the less resources will she find within herself, the less
will she dare to affirm herself as subject" (SS 280; emphases added).

In this passage, the paradox of an active choice of passivity—a choice not
explored by Merleau-Ponty—emerges. To make oneself an object, to renounce
one's autonomy, is to participate in one's own alienation. But can one say that

23. This is not, of course, the case for all men. As Merleau-Ponty himself acknowledges (notably in his discussion of the case of Schneider in part 1, chapter 3 of the
Phenomenology), some men lack the full use of their senses and organs. Perhaps more
important, many men are—like women—also alienated from their own bodies through
being defined as the other. However, this is not an issue that Merleau-Ponty addresses
at any length: Merleau-Ponty's embodied subject is not merely male but assumed also
to be unmarked, for example, by "racial" differences.

24. Beauvoir's boy in this comparison is, of course, French, white, and probably middle class. As Fanon pointed out not long after Beauvoir wrote, those few black men who
came to France also experienced a profound rupture between how they appeared to others
and their projects for self-realization ([1952] 1967, esp. chap.5). But even though Beauvoir
over-generalizes her account of men's experience here, her point about the ubiquity of
the tensions women experience still stands.

such participation is "freely" chosen if one's field of possibilities is so fore-closed that no other "choices" are possible? One must consider a continuum of situations here, since freedom admits of degree. Some (Beauvoir's liberated women) refuse to renounce autonomy but then live the debilitating tension between their own subjectivity and their "feminine" situation. At the other end of the continuum, some (but probably very few) live in immanence, in a situation that simply allows no space for the formulation of a project. But be-tween these poles lies a wide range of other possibilities. These include forms of complicity, for example masochistic or narcissistic styles of taking up one's otherness, resentment, passive resistance, and so on. But in none of these can a woman escape her definition as the other, or fail to take it up and live it in one way or another. Beauvoir suggests that at the transition to "womanhood" a young girl discovers with profound shock the non-coincidence of her sub-jectivity and her being-for-others: "It is a strange experience for an individual who feels himself to be a subject, autonomous, transcendent, an absolute, to discover inferiority as one's already given essence: it is a strange experience for whoever affirms himself as the One to be revealed to himself as otherness. This is what happens to the young girl when, doing her apprenticeship in the world, she grasps herself as being a woman there" (SS 297).

Schooled from early childhood in "the delights of passivity" (SS 298), a young girl most often comes to accept her role as other, even to revel in it. She actively participates in the process of "becoming a woman," and in-creasingly, as she acquires "normal" feminine heterosexual eroticism, she comes to experience herself as doubled, as an object for others. Erotic tran-scendence involves making herself man's "prey." As prey, "she becomes an object; and she grasps herself as object. It is with surprise that she discovers this new aspect of her being: she seems to have made herself double. Instead of exactly coinciding with herself she begins to exist *outside*" (SS 337).

For most, an element of freedom still remains in becoming a woman, even in making oneself prey. Few women are wholly mired in immanence. Rather than immanence Beauvoir uses the term "destiny" to describe this free-yet-coerced taking up of what cannot be avoided as one's own style of existence. She writes: "in thus *accepting* her passive role, the girl also *agrees to sub-mit* unresistingly to a destiny that is going to be imposed on her from with-out . . . she is twelve years old and already her story is written in the heav-ens. She will discover it day after day without ever making it" (SS 298; emphases added). Beauvoir also titles the first section of *The Second Sex*, which examines biology, psychoanalysis, and class analysis as explanations for women's inferiority, "Destiny." There she argues that none of these is a destiny in the sense of possessing natural causality or inevitable determina-tion. Rather, it is through custom, "this second nature," that the "facts" of biology come to play such a dominant role in woman's situation (SS 36).

Merleau-Ponty too would say that biology acquires its significance only in culture. Indeed, Beauvoir approvingly quotes Merleau-Ponty's claim that "man is not a natural species: he is a historical idea" (SS 34). But what Beauvoir adds to Merleau-Ponty's analysis is a phenomenological description of feminine embodiment which suggests that the contingent particularities of bodies (being female in this instance, but one could add others, such as being of a particular "racial" phenotype) differentially affect our lived experience far more profoundly than he realized. Although Merleau-Ponty is, as I have argued, well aware that objectifying and alienating relations are not only possible but often central to social existence, his account of the lived experience of "the" body—the body that perceives, moves, touches, and acts in the world—is not that of a body that is pervasively cast as the other.

Beauvoir's work may thus be read as a much-needed supplement to Merleau-Ponty's. Although the "I cans" of embodied subjectivity are, as Merleau-Ponty argues, general or anonymous, they are also far more permeated with the effects of alienating social identities than he considers. For example, although walking, the human gait, is a pre-personal or anonymous characteristic of our embodied existence and delimits a specifically human way of traversing terrain that is not that of a snail, a beetle, a hen, or a wolf, our *style* of walking is not so anonymous. For walking is not just the human species' way of traversing space; it is also a way of being in the world. Gender, and many other social relations, are present and presented in the way we walk: through the length of our stride, the firmness of our step, the undulation of our pelvis, the set of our back and head, and so on. Although such characteristics may be shaped in part by anatomical differences (such as sex-specific differences in the average width of the pelvis), they are predominantly expressions of cultural norms.

IN 1960, the year Sartre published *Critique of Dialectical Reason*, Beauvoir, it will be recalled, looked back on their debate of 1940 and commented: "to have been able to defend my position, I would have had to abandon the terrain of individualist, thus idealist, morality where we stood." By 1949, in *The Second Sex*, she had abandoned that terrain. The embodied subject of *The Second Sex* is social through and through, a gendered subject whose freedom is situated, at best always partial, at worst rendered immanent. By the late 1940s Sartre was also beginning to shift ground. As his ideas altered he was influenced philosophically not only (as he acknowledged) by Merleau-Ponty but also by Beauvoir.

Being and Nothingness still lacked a theory that would enable Sartre simultaneously to encompass, on the one hand, individual subjectivity and freedom and, on the other, the general weight of institutions, social struc-

tures, and events. In short, in the late 1940s he could not address the hiatus
he increasingly encountered between his theory of individual freedom and
the profoundly social view of history that his politics now presupposed. It
was not until the *Critique of Dialectical Reason* ([1960] 1976; cited hereafter
as CDR) that he fully came to grips with this problem.

In the *Critique*, Sartre's investigation of history now begins from an account of the subject as an embodied agent of *praxis*. In order to satisfy organic need, this agent must transform nature into those humanized or
worked forms of matter that Sartre calls the "practico-inert." Much of the
book examines the processes through which forms of the practico-inert then
come to function as alienating forces against their human creators. Praxis
might perhaps seem to be simply a new word Sartre has substituted (after
his discovery of Marxism) for being-for-itself. However, this is not the case.
For, unlike being-for-itself, praxis does not involve an absolute freedom. The
practico-inert does not merely impose itself as a series of *external* constraints
on praxis. Through the mediation of others, and in its most intensely alienating forms, it effects a transformation of freedom itself. Sartre now uses the
term "destiny" to describe a praxis in which freedom is so constrained that
its "choices" are pre-ordained!

It is surely not chance that Sartre's fullest discussion of "destiny" concerns a woman, a low-paid woman worker on a production line in a shampoo factory. "Oppression does not reach the oppressed in a particular sector
of their life; it constitutes this life in its totality" (CDR 232), he observes.
Thus, even her so-called inner life, her daydreams and fantasies, are sub-
ordinated to the rhythm of the machine at which she must work. Meanwhile,
outside the factory her low wages preclude the "choice" of motherhood:
"[When] the woman in the Dop Shampoo factory has an abortion in order to
avoid having a child she would be unable to feed, she makes a free decision
in order to escape a destiny that is made for her; but this decision is itself
completely manipulated by the objective situation: she realizes through herself what she is already; she carries out the sentence, which has already been
passed on her, which deprives her of motherhood" (CDR 235).

There is no future she could choose other than the one past praxis has de-
creed. In such a "destiny," and in its moment of subjective comprehension,
praxis is reduced to making oneself the material force through which things
happen. Insofar as it still involves a moment of comprehension, such a praxis
remains a distinctly human force, but it no longer involves the absolute freedom that was being-for-itself. Rather, socially mediated worked matter can
limit freedom to the point where no effective choice is possible, but only a
recognition of what one has been made to do: "the man who looks at his
work, who recognizes himself in it completely, and who also does not recognize himself at all; the man who can say both: 'This is not what I wanted'

and 'I understand that this is what I have done and that I could not do any-thing else' . . . this man grasps, in an immediate dialectical movement, ne-cessity as the *destiny in exteriority of freedom*" (CDR 226–27).

Sartre here recapitulates, but now with regard to the creation of worked matter, those very insights that Beauvoir earlier formulated with regard to the creation of oneself as a "woman": this is not what I wanted to do, but it is what I did; this is not what I wanted to become, but it is what I am; I have made my body something other than myself—yet still "I am my body."

IN exploring these conversations between Beauvoir, Sartre, and Merleau-Ponty, my aim has been to retrieve an account of a self that is embodied and socially situated, a self that can never leap out of its skin. But although this is a self that cannot exist independently of its facticities, it is not reducible to them. This paradoxical quality of selfhood is captured in Beauvoir's no-tion of "becoming" a woman: "to become" can mean to undergo a process of change or formation; and it can also mean to alter oneself. "Becoming" a woman means both.

To become a woman is not freely to choose one's identity or attributes. But neither is it to be the effect of a set of discursive practices. Insofar as post-modern feminism tends to posit "women" as the latter, it is often too one-sided. For it fails to acknowledge the active assumption of gender, with all its practical and ethical implications, that Beauvoir also rightly insists upon. This one-sidedness has its costs for feminism, and gives rise to a set of the-oretical and political difficulties that I have already set out briefly in the in-troduction. I explore these difficulties more fully in the next chapter, where I read Foucault and Foucauldian feminism through and against Beauvoir.

2 Panopticism and Shame:
Foucault, Beauvoir, and Feminism

The best of what "postmodern feminism" has so far developed is a series of radical glosses on Simone de Beauvoir's now classic starting point: "one is not born a woman: one becomes one." Like the work of Beauvoir, postmodern approaches enable us to de-essentialize and de-naturalize the concept of "woman." In particular, creative appropriations of Foucault's genealogical methods have enabled feminist scholars to explore the ways in which representations of "woman" have shifted over time. His insights into the inseparability of power and knowledge, and his explorations of the disciplinary practices that produce "subjectified" subjects, have also made his work a valuable resource for a wide range of feminist analyses of women's subordination.

But there are also difficulties for feminism—and other emancipatory movements—in appropriating Foucault too fully or too uncritically. In reading Foucault both through and against Beauvoir in this chapter, I seek to illuminate and address some of these difficulties. By pointing not only to the divergences but also to the striking complementarities between the two thinkers, I aim to challenge views of Beauvoir and Foucault as exponents, respectively, of "Enlightenment" and "post-Enlightenment" philosophies that are starkly antithetical. For it is not the case that before postmodernism there was only Enlightenment thinking. Nor are we obliged to choose between the unhappy alternatives of a naive Enlightenment "constituting" consciousness on the one hand and the attempt, as Foucault pithily put it, "to get rid of the subject itself" on the other (1980, 117).

What we have indeed learned (or rather relearned) from postmodern theorists is that we should not attribute to consciousness an absolute power to constitute its own world. Subjectivity, they remind us, is never "pure" or fully autonomous. It inheres in discursively shaped and embodied selves. Yet, to acknowledge this does not mean that we must proclaim definitively "the

death of the subject." As Elizabeth Grosz has suggested, we need rather to
investigate the "interconstituency" of consciousness and body. We need approaches that explore the relationship between them at once from "the inside out" and from "the outside in." Grosz uses the helpful metaphor of the
Möbius strip to express this relationship: "the Möbius strip has the advantage of showing the inflection of mind into body and body into mind, the
ways in which, through a kind of twisting or inversion, one side becomes
the other" (1994, xii).

What we have also learned from postmodern theories, such as Foucault's,
is the very real power of discourse and the lack of transparency of language:
there is no returning to a simple realism, or a correspondence theory of truth,
today. Yet, this does not mean that we should abandon realism entirely, to
embrace the kind of hyper-constructivism in which the very category of
"women" dissolves into mere fragment or trace, or can only be asserted "stra-
tegically" (Schor and Weed 1994). For although the relationships between
what Judith Butler has called "anatomical sex" (1990, 137) and sexuality and
gender are not strictly causal, nor are they wholly contingent or discursively
produced. Hence, I want to insist, they are neither indefinitely malleable nor
open to endless possibilities of discursive reconstruction. Here again, we
need to formulate ways of talking about these interconnections that move
us beyond such binaries as causality *or* contingency, realism *or* constructivism, anatomy *or* culture/discourse. As already discussed, Merleau-Ponty's
notions of generality and probability intimate one possible path; Beauvoir's
notion of embodied subjectivity, in which our bodies (each simultaneously
particular and general) are always structuring presences yet never final determinants, indicates another.

In what follows I develop these points by reading Foucault through and
against Beauvoir and by examining the work of Judith Butler as further exemplifying the implications of Foucault's work for feminism. Specifically, I
argue that Foucault's insightful account of the production of subjectified subjects is, as it stands, still inadequate and incomplete. It either remains at the
level of observation and description or else, at an explanatory level, falls into
a version of crude functionalism. In reading Foucault through the lenses of
Beauvoir we can find means more adequately to explain what Foucault describes. I also argue that reading Foucault through Beauvoir enables us explicitly to reintroduce into his theory issues of personal agency and moral
accountability. Foucault claims to deny these any significance, yet his work
still tacitly presupposes them. Via Beauvoir's focus on the ethical aspects of
subjectification, one can bring both greater intellectual coherence and explicit moral import to Foucault's work, as well as to later neo-Foucauldian
feminist theory, such as Butler's.

∽

FOUCAULT'S work is, of course, far from monolithic. In what follows I am concerned with the Foucault of the mid-1970s, that is, with the Foucault whose focus is less on the "care" of the self than on the "anatomo-political" production of the self. For this is the Foucault with whom feminist theory has most pervasively engaged: the Foucault of *Discipline and Punish* (1975), the first volume of *The History of Sexuality* (1976), and the essays and interviews published in English in *Power/Knowledge* (1980), a thinker whose focus is on the inseparability of power and knowledge and on their constitutive role in the production of the "subjectified" self through disciplinary and normalizing practices. This is a Foucault for whom subjectivity is so thoroughly produced "from the outside in," by the micro-practices of power, that to ask questions about the degree to which freedom or moral capacity might be attributes of subjecthood appears simply irrelevant.[1]

It is also the Foucault whose work has a distinctly functionalist, even a teleological, cast insofar as disciplinary practices are said to take on purposive attributes that have traditionally been ascribed to the individuated subject. Discipline is frequently personified or anthropomorphized. It knows what it is doing; it acts in an intentional, goal-oriented, rational manner, to perform necessary social functions. For example, Foucault writes: "discipline *had to solve* a number of problems for which the old economy of power was not equipped. . . . *it arrests or regulates* movements; *it clears up* confusion. . . . *It must also master* all forces that are formed from the very constitution of an organized multiplicity; *it must neutralize* the effects of counter-power that spring from them and which form a resistance to the power that *wishes* to dominate it" ([1975] 1977a, 219; emphases added).

This is not to deny that one can still find reflections on freedom in Foucault's work, but freedom is not an attribute of the subject or of individual agents. Rather, freedom is cast as the "insurrection" of subjugated knowledges (Foucault 1980, 84) or as the emergence of "transgressive" discourse that has a purpose of its own: transgression also has agency but no specific authors. One might talk here not only of a history without a sub-

---

1. The relationship of this Foucault to the later Foucault (not to mention to an earlier one) is, of course, a complex topic. In her discussion of "self-creating selves" in Sartre and Foucault, Morris (1996) has perceptively suggested that there are important affinities between early Sartre and late Foucault. For both, the self is an on-going project of creation (rather than a pre-given "essence") through which a coherent and relatively stable person is produced and sustained by a work of *self*-formation, be it Sartrean authentic choice or (late) Foucauldian "technologies of the self." Morris's reading suggests that the repressed existential postulates, which I argued in the introduction work to undermine Foucault's explicit theoretical claims, finally started to come into their own again in his last work. Here, agency shifts from the impersonal disciplinary practices of *Discipline and Punish* to the conscious practices of the self that he explores in the later volumes of *The History of Sexuality*.

ject, or of a text without a subject, but also of agency and freedom without a subject. As with discipline, Foucault personifies transgression, attributing to it intentional agency rather than attributing such agency to persons. He writes, for example, that "transgression does not seek to oppose one thing to another. . . its role is to measure the excessive distance that it opens at the heart of the limit and to trace the flashing line that causes the limit to arise" (Foucault 1977b, 35).[2]

"WHAT difference does it make who is speaking?" In his essay "What Is an Author?" Foucault suggests that the notion of individual authorship emerged at a particular moment in the history of ideas: a moment when "individualization" came to be privileged. That moment, he argues, has now passed: "it is a matter of depriving the subject (or its substitute) of its role as originator, and of analyzing the subject as a variable and complex function of discourse" (Foucault [1979] 1984, 118).[3] The issue of authorship, then, is part of a wider debate about the status of the subject, about whether human actors are knowing and volitional subjects, and about freedom. But above all, for Foucault (and here we must focus on his particularity) "the subject" in question is the subject of French existential phenomenology. For there is (to psychologize in a way he would have detested) something obsessive in Foucault's relationship to phenomenology: the Sartrean Father has to be killed over and over again. Moreover, the embarrassing evidence of Foucault's own youthful embrace of phenomenology has to be deliberately expunged from the author's presentation of his "work." Thus in an interview published as late as 1983 (the year prior to his death), Foucault referred to *Madness and Civilization* as his "first" book ([1983] 1988, 23). In doing so, this man who claimed he wrote "to have no face" (Foucault [1969] 1972, 17) deliberately (mis)presented his "work" so as to exclude from it his earliest and still phenomenologically influenced book, *Maladie mentale et personnalité* (1954).[4]

2. The most sustained attempt to date to extract a theory of freedom from Foucault is perhaps Dumm's. Dumm makes a strong case that Foucault effectively challenges the "liberal" notion of the "democratic individual" as "the exclusive site of freedom" (1996, 5). His work, however, does not explore issues of freedom raised by an alternative conception of the self, such as Beauvoir's, that does not neatly correspond with the liberal model.

3. This version of the essay "What is an Author?" was originally given at a conference in Buffalo, N.Y., and was initially published in English in Harari 1979. I cite it here from its republication in Rabinow 1984. Foucault had previously published a somewhat different version of the paper in French in 1969, and a translation of that earlier version is published in English in Foucault 1977b.

4. The possibility of the lie is itself an interesting site at which to think about freedom! For lying is an indication of our continued freedom in the face of discursive practices that produce the self, including the "confessional."

Indeed, long after we might have thought phenomenology to be dead in France, Foucault continued to feel the necessity to exterminate it. For example, in an interview I've already cited, he states:

> I don't believe the problem can be resolved by historicizing the subject, as posited by the phenomenologists, fabricating a subject that evolves through the course of history. One has to dispense with the constituent subject, to get rid of the subject itself, that's to say, to arrive at an analysis which can account for the constitution of the subject within a historical framework . . . genealogy . . . is a form of history which can account for the constitution of knowledges, discourses, domains of objects etc., without having to make reference to a subject which is either transcendental in relation to the field of events or runs in its empty sameness throughout the course of history. (Foucault 1980, 117)[5]

This statement opposes as stark alternatives on the one hand a conception of the subject as "constituent" (or constituting), as "transcendental" to history and unsituated, and on the other a conception of the subject as constituted and to be analyzed (through genealogy) as no more than an "effect" of its historical framework. In it we find posed those stark dualities, between humanism and anti-humanism, between "Enlightenment" and "postmodernity," that we need to put into question. In order to account (with Foucault) for the weight of social structures, discourses, and practices in the formation of the subject, and yet still to acknowledge (against Foucault) that element of freedom which enables us also to consider the self as a particular and intentional agent with a degree of responsiblity for its actions, we need a far more complex account of the subject than Foucault would at least appear to grant us.[6]

It is with this in mind that I return to Beauvoir and read Foucault through and against her. For much of her painstaking and detailed account in *The*

---

5. Similarly, in another interview in 1983 he wrote: "Knowledge, reason, rationality, the possibility of elaborating a history of rationality. . . . I would say that here again, we run across phenomenology. . . . Is the phenomenological, transhistorical subject able to provide an account of the historicity of reason? Here, reading Nietzsche was the point of rupture for me. There is a history of the subject just as there is a history of reason; but we can never demand that the history of reason unfold [as] a first and founding act of the rationalist subject" (Foucault [1983] 1988, 23). One could, I suppose, plausibly argue that in the early Sartre a rationalist subject "founds" the meaning of history. But this view crudely travesties the later Sartre, not to mention Merleau-Ponty, Beauvoir, and others. Foucault persistently—and willfully—ignored the nuances and complexities of this long and diverse intellectual tradition in which he was schooled, reducing it to a monolithic, trans-historical, and rationalist account of the subject.

6. Thus James Miller observes, in the preface to his account of Foucault's life and work, that he (perhaps contra Foucault himself) "was forced to ascribe to Foucault a persistent and purposeful self, inhabiting one and the same body throughout his mortal life, more or less consistently accounting for his actions and attitudes to others as well as himself, and understanding his life as a teleologically structured quest" (1993, 7).

Second Sex of the young girl's *formation*[7] and the perpetuation of "femininity" could be re-told in the Foucauldian modes of "the political technology of the body," of "discipline," of "normalization," and of "panopticism." Yet Beauvoir still adheres to a notion of the *repression* of freedom that Foucault would not endorse. However suppressed, however "disciplined," it is still freedom-made-immanent that distinguishes even the most constituted human subject from a trained animal. A real repression—or oppression—of the self always remains possible for Beauvoir. For Foucault—at least as he expressly presents his position—this is not the case. I will pursue this divergence primarily through the notion of "panopticism," of the place of the gaze or look in producing docility, as Foucault and Beauvoir respectively treat it. For Beauvoir, "becoming a woman" also involves subjectification through what Foucault will call panoptic practices. But to understand this process of "becoming" she also explores the ways in which subjectification is lived and taken up by the subject, be it in modes of complicity, of resistance, or both. This "lived" aspect of subjectification cannot be made accessible through Foucault's explicit framework of analysis. Yet his own analyses actually require that we acknowledge and bring to light this suppressed experiential and "existential" dimension.

PANOPTICISM is, according to Foucault, the quintessential form of the "hierarchical observation" that is integral to much disciplinary power. It is a mechanism "in which the techniques that make it possible to see induce effects of power" ([1975] 1977a, 170–71). It is a crucial (though certainly not the sole) component of those modern disciplinary practices which produce the normalized subject, both in formal disciplinary institutions and beyond. In Foucault's account of Bentham's model prison, in which each isolated inmate lives—and *knows* himself to live—under continual inspection from the all-seeing (but anonymous) eye of the guard, the major effect of the Panopticon is "to induce in the inmate a state of conscious and permanent visibility that assures the automatic functioning of power" (210). Interiorizing the scrutinizing gaze to which he (or she) is subjected, the inmate becomes effectively (and efficiently) self-policing: "He who is subjected to a field of visibility, and who *knows* it, *assumes responsibility* for the constraints of power; *he makes them play* spontaneously upon himself; *he inscribes in himself* the power relation in which *he simultaneously plays both roles*; he becomes the principle of his own subjection" (202–3; emphases added).

---

7. The English translator of *The Second Sex*, H. M. Parshley, has unfortunately translated Beauvoir's chapter heading *"Formation"* as "The Formative Years," thus weakening the notion of an active production of the self implied by the French term.

Panopticism is not confined to particular institutions, such as the prison or the asylum. On the contrary, Foucault conceives it to be a general "modality of power" in normalizing societies such as ours. Moreover, women are subject to (and subjects of) what Foucault refers to as "the minute disciplines, the panopticisms of every day" (Foucault [1975] 1977a, 223), in a particularly all-encompassing and complex manner that he does not himself explore. Indeed, Beauvoir's account of how one "becomes a woman" intriguingly anticipates Foucault's later account of panopticism. As she describes it, becoming a woman requires developing an awareness of one's "permanent visibility," learning continually to view oneself through the eyes of the generalized (male) inspecting gaze and, in so doing, taking up as one's own project those "constraints of power" that femininity entails. But becoming a woman is, for Beauvoir, still an intentional process, even if it is enacted within the constraints of power. Thus, questions that Foucault leaves hanging in mid-air concerning *how* this modality of power functions are more adequately addressed by Beauvoir.

Foucault is (to put it politely) sometimes a slippery thinker. His previously cited claim that we need "to get rid of the subject itself" and his affirmations that the subject comes into being as simply the effect of power are tacitly put into question by passages such as the one I just quoted from *Discipline and Punish.* Such passages imply something else: an active and, one could argue, even a quasi-constituting subject; a conscious subject who "knows" that he is visible; one who "assumes responsibility" for the effects of power on himself, and who is active in playing "both roles," that of scrutinizer and scrutinized. But just how and why does the panoptic gaze induce such an active compliance? It is not clear. "Just a gaze," Foucault says. "An inspecting gaze which each individual under its weight will end by interiorizing to the point that he is his own overseer, each individual exercising this surveillance over, and against, himself" (1980, 155). But how and why does an individual interiorize the gaze? What kind of subjectivity is capable of such an interiorization? Or—just as important—of resisting it? For, as Foucault acknowledges, there has also been "effective resistance" to various forms of panoptic scrutiny (162).

But while Foucault's own analyses actually call for an account of the subject as both constituted and constituting, as playing "both roles," his refusal to admit his own existential derivations precludes his acknowledgment of this. Thus his explicit pronouncements that "the subject" is produced through panoptic and other disciplinary "subjectifying" practices, and the more existential postulates still implicit in his account, come to be at odds with each other. Foucault claims that "power relations can materially penetrate the body in depth, without depending even on the mediation of the subject's own representations. If power takes hold of the body, this isn't through its having first to be interiorised in people's consciousnesses" (1980, 186). Yet, we have seen, panoptic power *does* have to be interiorized in a way that engages consciousness, and if its interiorization can be resisted this implies also that, in some manner and to some degree, individuals may choose how to respond to it. Resistance cannot be explained solely as the result of the self-functioning of transgressive discourses or of the deployment of subjugated knowledges (though it might be incited or invited by these). On the contrary, it also involves individual responses that must presume some play of intentional consciousness, and what we might call freedom.

Foucault reverses traditional forms of mind body dualism by privileging the body as the site of the formation of the self, yet he is still caught up in this dualism. If the interiorization of power takes place through "the body," then it can of course bypass that—allegedly—distinct entity called "consciousness." But if, with Beauvoir and Merleau-Ponty, we insist that the body is *not* distinct from consciousness but rather is the *site* of their "interconstituency" (to recall Grosz's felicitous term) and the site of a sentient and intentional relation to the world, then the modalities through which we interiorize and/or resist the panoptic gaze can be explored more adequately.

Judith Butler has suggested that there are ways in which "the body" comes to be a substitute—and an inadequate one at that—for the psyche in Foucault's theories (1997, 94). She rightly argues that Foucault leaves us with the problem of how to understand "not merely the disciplinary production of the subject, but the disciplinary cultivation of *an attachment to subjection*" in the modern self (102). Butler turns to a psychoanalytic framework to address this problem, but in what follows I offer an alternate route. I return to Beauvoir and to her phenomenological explorations of the look, or gaze, in order further to examine some of the issues of complicity and resistance to power that Foucault implicitly raises, yet never adequately addresses.

In Foucault's general discussions of power—of power as capillary and circulating—normalization proceeds through panoptical and other disciplinary practices in which, as subjectified subjects, as both the effects of power and the bearers of power, we are all implicated. As he puts it, "power is employed and exercised through a net-like organisation. And not only do individuals circulate between its threads; they are always in the position of simultaneously undergoing and exercising power. . . . The individual . . . is not the *vis-à-vis* of power; it is, I believe, one of its prime effects" (Foucault 1980, 98).

However, in discussing the generalized masculine gaze, under and through which women become and remain women, Beauvoir suggests that men and women are not subjected to the same forms of power, nor subjected to power to the same degree. At one level Beauvoir agrees with Foucault: the general power of men over women is possessed by no specific individual. Thus, she points out, an individual man who wishes to cease participating in the privileges of masculine power finds that he cannot withdraw from it; it is not his to renounce. "It is useless to apportion blame and excuse . . . a man could not prevent himself from being a man. So there he is, guilty in spite of himself and burdened by this fault he did not himself commit" (SS 723).

Even so, men and women, as socially distinct groups, are differently positioned within generalized networks of power in ways that Foucault does not recognize. Furthermore, as Beauvoir sees very clearly, their differential positionings may easily permit the actual "possession" of power by a particular man over a particular woman. In Beauvoir's France the marriage contract still brought into being a form of "sovereign" power, in which a husband unambiguously controlled his wife's finances, domicile, access to her children, and so on. Beauvoir was acutely aware of the significance of what we might call the institutional dimensions of masculine power, as they mutually enabled and reinforced those more diffuse forms of power that Foucault describes as disciplinary or normalizing. For it was not the case that "power [was] no longer substantially identified with an individual who possesses or exercises it by right of birth" (Foucault 1980, 156). On the contrary, in marriage, right of birth alone still conferred juridical grants of "sovereign" power to husbands in Beauvoir's world. Although such power does not formally exist today, at least in most Western liberal democracies, the institutional dimensions of continuing masculine privilege should not be underestimated.

If we are to understand women's complicity in sustaining those normalizing practices through which their subordinating "femininity" is perpetuated, we will need also to look at juridical, economic, and other institutional arrangements in which women find themselves located. For these often still produce de facto relationships of personal privilege and dependency that make compliance a rational survival strategy for many women. These relationships sometimes give rise to the quite explicit *interests* that women may have in complying with the norms of femininity. For example, for the dependent or low-earning housewife the economic costs of a broken marriage that might result from resistant behavior can be catastrophic. Likewise, refusing docilely to submit to forms of sexual harassment by a male superior at work can jeopardize a woman's career. In some instances, contra Foucault, we may reasonably posit a woman as an interest-maximizing agent, in order to account for her complicity in her own continued personal subordination.

But Beauvoir's woman is not primarily or usually conceived as a rational interest maximizer. Beauvoir's main focus is on the ways in which women become invested in their femininity, less as a material survival strategy than as a mode of lived experience that is integral to the self. It is in exploring these less calculating ways in which women become invested in their femininity that Beauvoir allows us to examine also "from the inside out" Foucault's account of the disciplinarily constituted subject. When discussing the Panopticon, Foucault writes, "we are talking of two things here: the gaze and interiorisation" (1980, 154). However, he does not ever explain how the latter, the interiorization of the gaze, is effected. Nor does he show how it brings into being the complicity of the self-surveilling subject; nor (more generally) does he reveal how the continuous and minute disciplining of the body that he describes produces its correlative "soul."

It is, on reflection, quite remarkable that in the three hundred or so pages of *Discipline and Punish* we get absolutely no sense of what it *feels* like to be subjected to the panoptical gaze; nor do we get any sense of the experiential dimension of becoming a self-surveilling "subject" of panopticism.[8] Foucault's disciplinary subjects do not appear to feel fear, anxiety, frustration, unhappiness. Such emotions, not to mention pain, are strikingly absent from his account. It is here that Beauvoir's analysis adds another necessary dimension to Foucault's. We do not need to posit a Cartesian knowing subject, or a pure constituting consciousness, to understand *how* the practices of power are taken up, or interiorized, by an individual self or "soul" that may inflect, deflect, accept, or resist them in multiple and idiosyncratic ways. However, we do need to posit a subject that is, to some degree, active and intentional. Beauvoir's account of an embodied and situated subject, a subject that, although never an absolute freedom or pure consciousness, has a viewpoint on the world and an intentional relationship with it, offers us what Foucault lacks.

Beauvoir's account of women's diverse interiorizations of the male gaze involves a creative reworking of Sartre's phenomenology of "the look" in *Being and Nothingness*. For Sartre, another's look is always experienced as a threat. For to be seen by another is to become an object in his world; to be aware of myself as being seen by another is to be aware of myself as object-like. The look is thus always experienced as an assault on my freedom: on my ability to define for myself the meaning of my situation.[9] However, for Sartre, I am always free to reaffirm my status as a subject by turning the tables on the other, by in turn looking at him.

We have already seen, in the previous chapter, that Beauvoir radically modifies Sartre's account of self-other relations by insisting that where there are relations of social equality, objectification can be superseded by forms of mu-

8. It is, I think, this omission that Nancy Hartsock has in mind when she observes (following Edward Said) that Foucault is "with power" rather than against it (1996, 36).

9. The French *le regard*, has conventionally been rendered as "the look" in translations of Sartre and as "the gaze" in the case of Foucault. While the two terms carry different resonances in English, these are the function of translation processes and are not present for French readers.

tually validating "reciprocity" (SS xxiii). The look can be a means of expressing friendship or love, of sharing, of validating another: it can, in short, be intersubjective, rather than objectifying. However, in those formal institutions that Foucault characterizes as panoptical—the prison, the asylum, the school, the army parade ground, etc.—surveillor and surveilled are not equally positioned, and the look thus functions irreversibly to objectify. Indeed, in Bentham's design for the Panopticon ([1787] 1995) it is essential that the inmates are illuminated and visible to the inspecting gaze of the guard or overseer, but equally important is that he is not visible to them.[10] Similarly, those assembled for inspection, such as soldiers on the parade ground, may not look back at those who inspect them.

To be subjected to a gaze that one cannot reciprocally return is, indeed, to experience objectification, or an alienation of one's subjectivity. I experience a loss of my immediate, lived subjecthood as I become fixed or immobilized *in my own eyes* as the object that I am (or believe myself to be) in the eyes of the one who looks at me. However, this experience is not *by itself* sufficient to account for the production of docility and of compliant self-surveillance that Foucault attributes to the power of the panoptic gaze.

What is also essential here is what Sartre and Beauvoir call "shame": a relation to oneself, in the presence of another, in which one *evaluates* oneself negatively through the look (or perhaps the presumed look) of the other. Sartre begins his discussion of shame in *Being and Nothingness* with the well-known example of hearing somebody else approaching while, "moved by jealousy, curiosity, or vice," I am peeping through a keyhole (BN 259). The experience of shame in being "caught" in such a circumstance involves not only seeing myself as the object that the other sees but also seeing myself as the other will *judge* me: as reprehensible, faulty, inferior. Moreover, it is not just of my act that I feel ashamed but of my *self*. For suddenly I *am* as I am seen to be: "shame . . . is shame of *self*; it is the *recognition* of the fact that I *am* indeed that object which the Other is looking at and judging" (BN 261). Here we have an initial account of how the power-effect of the look, which Foucault only observes, actually operates. We see how, in interiorizing the shaming look, I become not only the object of my own surveillance but also the judge of myself.[11]

10. That the overseer might also be overseen, or that "anyone" might be the overseer, does not alter the inequality of the relationship of the overseer to the inmates.

11. Vaz has argued, with some plausibility, that Sartre's and Foucault's respective accounts of the function of the look/gaze confirm and complement each other. She suggests that we can perhaps view the Panopticon "as a microcosm of Sartre's infernal social model," in which each lives constantly in a state of being-for-others (1995, 41). Similarly, Sheets-Johnstone observes that "Foucault's 'optics of power' is Sartre's 'the Look' writ large—in broad socio-political script rather than fine, interpersonal hand" (1994, 13). She also points to their common lack of attention to the "corporeal nature" of the optics of power.

But Sartre's account of shame calls out for further elaboration—and Beauvoir offers it in her descriptions of feminine embodied experience. First, I can come to feel shame by virtue of such facticities as my bodily characteristics or my social status without having engaged in any specific act. I may judge myself to be ugly, for example, if my body does not conform to the norms of beauty in my society. Or, if I am a member of a class of people, such as women, that is deemed to be socially inferior, I may judge myself to be inferior.[12] Second, although I may come to judge myself through the look of a single individual, as in Sartre's examples, I may also do so through an impersonal or anonymous, an entirely non-specific, or even in the long run absent other. In the panoptical institutions that Foucault describes, the look is impersonal but presumed present: continuous scrutiny on the part of designated officials is part of the disciplinary regime. But in other instances, the look is generalized or non-specific; "they," "others," "society" judge certain of my characteristics to be signs of my inferiority. And, in its most strongly interiorized forms, the look may become so integral to the self that it functions in a situation of total privacy—as when a woman carefully applies her make-up even if she intends to stay at home on her own the whole day and will be "seen" by absolutely nobody but herself. In these latter cases we might appear to return to notions of panoptical power as circulating and capillary, to Foucault's "minute disciplines, the panopticisms of everyday," in which nobody possesses power. Yet, when we come to look more closely, contra Foucault and as Beauvoir realizes, some are more disciplined, more normalized, and less powerful than others—among them, women.

Woman, as Beauvoir depicts her, is not just man's Other, she is his *inferior* other: "The relation of the two sexes is not like that of two electrical poles, for man represents both the positive and the neutral, so that in French [as in English] one says "men" to designate human beings. . . . He is the Subject, he is the Absolute—she is the Other" (SS xxiv). Whereas Sartre argues that by returning the look one can always turn the tables on the other, Beauvoir suggests that what distinguishes the situation of woman is precisely her *inability* to do so.[13] "No subject," she observes, "immediately and voluntarily affirms itself as the inessential"; thus the question is "from whence comes this submission in women?" (SS xxiv).

12. As we will see in the next chapter, Frantz Fanon also creatively appropriates Sartre's account of shame to address the lived experience of racial objectification and inferiorization.

13. For Sartre, it should be recalled, even a torture victim can turn the tables on the torturer simply by looking at him. I have already discussed Sartre's assumption that qua looks two subjects are always equal, and Beauvoir's tacit challenge to this assumption, in more detail in chapter 1.

In answering this question Beauvoir offers us a series of phenomenological cal descriptions of how women come to exist in the mode of inferiority and to subsume it into forms of "subjectified" feminine subjectivity. If "not every female human being is necessarily a woman" (SS xix), then we need to grasp the processes through which "one becomes one" as not only the exercise of power upon and its transmission through the subject but also as it is interiorized, taken up, and lived. It is here that the panopticisms of daily life and the "interior" experiences of shame they induce are crucial.

Beauvoir begins by describing the multitude of small disciplines to which female children are often subjected and which still today induce passivity, timidity, and physical self-constraint.[14] But she suggests that it is at puberty that more profound experiences of shame usually begin. At that time a girl often becomes the object of stares, whistles, derogatory remarks on the street (and at school in coeducational systems) and, simultaneously, is required to hide from view the newly acquired "secret" of menstruation. In the experience of menstruation (at least in Western society) a young woman's profound sense of herself as not only the other but as the inferior other dramatically develops.[15] She must ensure that she does not appear soiled in public; must learn discreetly to dispose of bloodied pads, tampons, and clothing; is warned that she might give away her "condition" by the smell of menstrual blood should she not keep herself sufficiently clean.[16]

In such ways, a young woman learns how to develop those practices of self-surveillance and self-discipline that Foucault attributes to the panoptic gaze. But they are the effect not directly of the gaze itself so much as of the shame with which it forces her to see "herself"—herself not as a "pure" consciousness but as an embodied subject. Shame, as what we might call a pri-

14. Although girls from most social strata in the United States today are less constrained than were the middle-class women of Beauvoir's France, Beauvoir's observations generally still appear to hold. Iris Young has discussed a range of studies that show that girls (and women) still fail to extend their bodies or to occupy space as fully as boys do; they throw, sit, walk, and carry things in typically timid and constricted "feminine" modalities. Young suggests that these are not merely different from masculine modalities but also indicative of women's oppression: "Women in sexist society are physically handicapped. Insofar as we learn to live out our existence in accordance with the definition that patriarchal culture assigns to us, we are physically inhibited, confined, positioned, and objectified" (Young 1990b, 153).

15. Some girls, Beauvoir notes, greet the onset of menstruation with an initial pride in "becoming a woman." But even for them, the anonymous or generalized gaze (and frequently the specific gaze of male relatives, friends, or schoolmates) from which they are compelled to hide this bodily event rapidly makes of it a matter of shame.

16. An astounding number of products are aggressively marketed today that promise women "protection" against the dread embarrassments of leaks and odors. Deodorant tampons, special cleansers, and other such products abound on supermarket shelves and are heavily advertised.

mary structure of a woman's lived experience, extends far beyond her relationship to menstruation, and it becomes integral to a generalized sense of inferiority of the feminine body-subject. A woman, Beauvoir writes, "*is* her body; but her body is something other than herself" (SS 29). And if in menstruation the experience of shame is so sharply evoked, this is not to say that menstruation is itself the source of shame. For as Beauvoir observes: "In a sexually egalitarian society, woman would regard menstruation simply as her particular way of reaching adult life; the human body in both men and women has plenty of more repugnant needs to be taken care of. . . . her periods inspire horror in the adolescent girl because they cast her into an inferior and mutilated category" (SS 315–16). The conflicts lived out by the adolescent girl continue into adult womanhood: "she knows she cannot become 'grown-up' without accepting her femininity; and she knows already that her sex condemns her to a mutilated and frozen existence . . . wounded, shameful, anxious, guilty, she goes on toward her future" (SS 327).

As Beauvoir's account of women's lived experience proceeds—from early childhood through girlhood, sexual initiation, marriage, childbirth, and motherhood toward old age—shame remains a primary structure of experience. Shame of an embodied self that is always marked as inferior, as defective, is instrumental to women's participation in the multitude of minute daily practices that induce docility and reproduce forms of normalized feminine behavior. The *content* of normalized femininity has, of course, shifted dramatically since Beauvoir's time, especially in the United States. But normalizing demands are no less intense today. Indeed, if the corset once constricted the body from without, today the demands not merely for slenderness but also for a well "toned" body necessitate an ever greater interiorization of discipline (Bordo 1993). Sandra Bartky has suggested, with some plausibility, that women "have their own experience of the modernization of power, one which begins later but follows in many respects the course outlined by Foucault" (1990, 97). As women have achieved more freedom of movement, and as juridical male power over them has diminished,[17] they have become subject to ever more demanding normalizing practices.

17. Gender-based formal, juridical power has certainly not disappeared, however. Rather, it re-emerges in new forms such as "fetal protection" legislation. This has been used to attempt to exclude all women of childbearing age from certain kinds of employment (such as working in contact with lead) that are deemed dangerous to a fetus (Kenney 1992; Daniels 1993; Gonen 1993), to prosecute pregnant women for allegedly harming a fetus through substance abuse, and to require women to submit to medical procedures that are deemed to be in the interest of the fetus (Losco 1989; Daniels 1993; Roth 1993). As Cynthia Daniels observes, the present backlash against women's greater autonomy invokes increasingly direct coercion through the state. She predicts that, "as a tacit respect for masculine authority decays, more coercive and naked forms of power will emerge to take its place" (1993, 147).

Nor does the woman who resists, the would-be "independent" woman whom Beauvoir describes in the final section of *The Second Sex*, escape. On the contrary, the would-be independent woman lives her femininity as a painful contradiction. Brought up (as most girls still are today) to see herself through the male gaze, enjoined to passivity, and to make herself desirable to man, she *is* her femininity. Her being-for-others is profoundly gendered. This is not a facticity that can be ignored, since it thoroughly permeates her being-for-herself. She cannot renounce her femininity, for it is constitutive of her self, even as it undercuts her struggle for self-affirmation.

> For woman to realize her femininity she is required to make herself object and prey, which is to say she must renounce her claims as a sovereign subject. It is this conflict that especially marks the situation of the emancipated woman. She refuses to confine herself to her role as a female, because she does not wish to mutilate herself; but it would also be a mutilation to disavow her sex. . . . To renounce her femininity is to renounce part of her humanity. (SS 682)[18]

The "independent" woman thus lives divided against herself even more starkly than the woman who more fully accepts traditional feminine roles. Committed to affirming her independence and acting in the public domain,[19] she still discovers that "when she is looked at she is not distinguished from her appearance" (SS 683). It is impossible to avoid the fact that one is *seen* as a woman. To flout the norms of femininity is never to escape them but only to take them up in an atypical manner. "A woman who dresses in an eccentric fashion lies when she affirms with an air of simplicity that she dresses to suit herself, nothing more" (SS 683). There is no neutral ground here, and one cannot avoid making a statement that refers to and indirectly reconfirms what is "normal" even by wearing "unfeminine" clothing, refusing to shave one's legs, and so on.[20] Indeed, paradoxically, the more a

18. While Beauvoir is correct that women live divided against themselves, the same is also true for many men. Although not divided from themselves in the same way as women, many men who are members of ethnic or racial minorities or who suffer from physical "abnormalities" also live their bodies as both self and negation of self—a topic taken up more fully in the next chapter.

19. Beauvoir's "independent" woman is the new middle-class professional woman. Even in Beauvoir's France, of course, many working-class women were employed outside the home. But for "factory girls" and those in domestic service, the ideal and expectation was still to leave the paid workforce upon marriage. The "norm" was the housewife, supported by a husband who earned a "family wage." By contrast, peasant women usually continued to engage in agricultural labor after marriage, and Beauvoir suggests that they may well have enjoyed more freedom than many women from wealthier families.

20. Thus, contrary to the claims of much queer theory today, I think Beauvoir would question whether such "transgressive" forms of dress as drag, cross-dressing, or other

woman seeks to escape the traditional domestic role by pursuing success in professional or public life, the more likely she is to have to conform to the norms of feminine comportment—and to put considerable time and effort into the daily disciplines these demand.

Moreover, because woman is not merely man's other, but an inferior other, Beauvoir is keenly aware that individual solutions are not fully realizable. This is not to say that individual women should cease to challenge normalizing femininity. But in challenging it they will disclose the radical inequality of their situation and encounter the limits to what can be individually achieved. Beauvoir is far from affirming the untrammeled capacity for freedom, or "transcendence," of which she is often accused. On the contrary, she would agree with Foucault that it is through subjection to disciplinary and normalizing practices that subjectivity comes into being. The feminine subject cannot simply shed her femininity, for there is no "inner" subject that can, in absolute freedom, transcend its body and its situation; there is no pure constituting consciousness. But to acknowledge this is not to deny freedom to the subject. For most women, a range of choices is still open as to *how* one interiorizes, assumes, and lives normalized femininity. Thus, issues of personal agency, ethics, and responsibility that cannot consistently be posed within Foucault's explicit framework emerge as central for Beauvoir.

Beauvoir posits a continuum of situations. At one end of the continuum, she offers an account of the subject that could be re-cast in Foucault's starkest terms. She talks of the woman who lives in a situation of such extreme subjection that freedom is made immanent and is no more than a suppressed potentiality. Here a woman *is* so thoroughly her situation, so thoroughly its product, that no effective choice as to how it is to be lived is possible. Such a woman is, as Foucault had put it, a constitut*ed*, not a constitut*ing*, subject (1980, 117).

But although immanence marks one end of a continuum of theoretically possible situations, it is doubtful if many women actually live in such a condition. At the other end of the continuum is the "independent" woman, who struggles doggedly against the constraints of her situation and in so doing reveals the impossibility of fully transcending it. Most women, however, live neither in total immanence nor in a mode of continuous revolt. They live somewhere between, embracing various modes of complicity, compromise, or resistance, each of which has both rewards and costs attached to it. Here, we return with Beauvoir to those issues of complicity with subjection, and to questions of individual resistance, that Foucault's account of subjectification tacitly poses but does not adequately address.

---

parodies effectively "destabilize" the norms to which they refer. They are, at the very least, always ambiguous: for if they subvert, they also reinscribe normative gender.

NEAR the end of *The Second Sex* Beauvoir observes that men find in women "more complicity than the oppressor usually finds in the oppressed" (SS 721). The term "complicity" for Beauvoir connotes a moral register, absent in Foucault's account of the subject's "compliance" in disciplinary power. What both Beauvoir and Foucault share is the insight that the subject of disciplinary power actively participates in it: power is not unidirectional nor simply top-down. We have already seen that Beauvoir accounts more fully than Foucault for *how*, through self-objectification and shame, disciplinary power is internalized so that its subject comes also to be its agent. But, beyond the "how," there are also questions of "why." For Beauvoir also suggests that in many instances complicity could be more fully resisted.

The subjectified subject, which takes up those practices of power through which it is both constituted and self-constituting, still enjoys a degree of freedom as to how it assumes them. Here, moral issues begin to arise: for if the subject enjoys a degree of freedom, complicity is not just a fact to be described but also a choice, a project, that is open to moral evaluation. It is a matter of what, following Sartre (BN 47–70), Beauvoir will call "bad faith," "flight," or the choice of "inauthenticity." There is, she suggests, a "fundamental" human tendency toward self-alienation, or self-objectification, since "the anguish of freedom induces the subject to seek for himself in things, which is a kind of flight from self. . . . This is the primary temptation to inauthenticity" (SS 47).[21]

After decades of popular self-help manuals, the term "authenticity" often connotes today a highly psychologized notion of the search for "inner meaning," or of getting in contact with one's "real self." But for Beauvoir—as for Foucault—there is no real or inner self "there" to be discovered, for (as Sartre also argued) the subject can never coincide with itself. Rather, what is at issue here is the choice of a moral stance in the face of one's situation, with all its facticities and indeterminacies. An inauthentic woman affirms herself to be a fixed substance, claiming to be constituted by exterior conditions and forces even when this is not wholly the case. The "bad faith," or self-deception, lies in the fact that one continues to make choices, exercising a degree of freedom and affirming values, while claiming to be unable to do

21. In the introduction to *The Second Sex* Beauvoir sets out woman's temptation to complicity thus: "To decline to be the Other, to refuse complicity with man, this would be [for women] to renounce all the advantages that may be conferred upon them by their alliance with the superior caste. Man-the-sovereign will provide woman-the-liege with material protection and will undertake to justify her existence; along with economic risk she evades the metaphysical risk of a freedom that must invent its own ends without assistance. Indeed, along with the claim of each individual to affirm himself as a subject, which is an ethical claim, there is also the temptation to flee one's freedom and constitute oneself as a thing" (SS xxvii).

so. For to become a woman is not to be sculpted like a lump of clay by exterior force. To claim an analogously inert status, to claim that one is "constituted" through and through, to try to make oneself a "thing," is in bad faith to flee one's freedom.[22] Beauvoir thus insists that, however constrained our situation, we can almost always still take it up in different ways and that we must accept responsibility for our own choices and values.

Today, the details of Beauvoir's portrait of the inauthentic housewife fit few Western women. For this portrait draws mainly from the French middle- or upper-class housewife of the early twentieth century.[23] This woman is not only socially and economically dependent on her husband but also, in bad faith, enjoys the apparent irresponsibility that her dependence permits. For example, she ceases to make judgments for herself and simply assumes as her own her husband's tastes and political views. Or, claiming to stand behind her man, she makes of his life the meaning of her own: his success is hers, and she admits to no other aspirations in life than his.

Yet, although the portrait itself is now outdated, surprisingly many of Beauvoir's insights remain pertinent today. Self-abnegation and denial; deference to the opinions of others and failure to assert one's own; limiting one's goals and ambitions, particularly to fit in with those of a lover or husband: all of these typically "feminine" forms of behavior still endure among a diverse range of Western women. They can, of course, often be explained as rational, even self-interested, strategies on the part of those who are still, to a significant degree, economically dependent on men. In Foucauldian vein, one can also account for them as strictly the effects of those disciplinary and normalizing practices through which women are constituted as subjects. But if neither explanation is false, neither is by itself adequate. For "feminine" behavior is more than either a calculated strategy or a discursively produced effect. It is more than a strategy because being a woman is not an identity that an "inner" self could pick up or shed at will. It is more than a discursive effect because it is interiorized and taken up in ways that are both constrained and yet still indeterminate, and open to moral evaluation.

It is from this indeterminacy that feminism, as a political project, begins. It must start by recognizing that margin of freedom that enables us to struggle,

22. It is also to live in what Beauvoir (following Sartre) calls the mode of the "serious." As she wrote in *The Ethics of Ambiguity*, "the characteristic of the spirit of seriousness is to consider values as ready-made things" ([1947] 1967, 35) and so to refuse to accept responsibility for the values implicit in one's own actions. "The serious man's [sic] dishonesty issues from his being obliged ceaselessly to renew his denial of freedom. . . . The serious man must mask the movement by which he gives [values] to himself, like the mythomaniac who while reading a love-letter pretends to forget that she has sent it to herself" (47).

23. Even in its own times, its class bias made the portrait inadequate as a general depiction of French women—and even less applicable to most women in the French colonies.

not only against institutional dimensions of subordination (such as lack of control over our own bodies, or unequal pay), but also against our own complicity in subordinating and subjectifying practices. It must also recognize its own ethical or value-disclosing import. For any emancipatory project implies an ethical stance. And, indeed, given even the smallest margin of freedom, we cannot avoid affirming values in all that we do. To deny this is to act in bad faith and to claim a condition of irresponsibility that we do not enjoy.

It is also true, of course, that no emancipatory project is entirely innocent. As Foucault has so clearly pointed out, all claims to truth, all affirmations of value, are also productive of power-effects. However, this does not mean that we should endeavor not to affirm our own values lest, in the name of truth, we become yet further complicit with power. Foucault entices us toward a purism that, as I suggested in the introduction, is a potential danger of postmodern theory: toward a preference to say or do nothing, rather than risk dirtying our hands.[24] But the fuller safeguard is to make explicit the values present in our actions while also recognizing our responsibility for the power-effects they produce. Thus to write, with Foucault, "to have no face," to insist that there are not authors (be it of texts or of deeds), to attribute to disciplinary practices their own purposes and intentionality, and to claim that each of us is equally constituted by a power that none possesses amounts finally to a flight into the self-delusional and irresponsible world of bad faith. Foucault, in short, offers us a new version of "the temptation to flee freedom and constitute oneself a thing" (SS xxvii). This is a temptation we should resist, even as we draw on his rich insights into the operations of power and subjectification.

REPLICATIONS of Foucault's more problematic claims often produce similar difficulties in the work of postmodern feminists, and I now turn to the work of Judith Butler as an illustration. Although Butler's views have shifted somewhat over time, I focus on her book *Gender Trouble* (1990) since it has been so tremendously influential for recent feminist theory—not to mention queer theory and performance theory. Certain key Foucauldian problematics centrally structure the argument of *Gender Trouble*. Not only does Butler extensively elaborate on Foucault's argument that any relationship between "anatomical sex" and gender is purely "contingent," but she also goes to great lengths to insist that her account of how subjects come to be constituted, through the repeated performance of stylized gender acts, does *not* pre-

24. Foucault does not explicitly draw this conclusion from his analyses. However, it is the demobilizing consequence drawn from his work by many feminists and other radicals, who fear to speak on certain topics lest they become implicated in power. Silence, we should be remember, can equally implicate one in power.

suppose any intentional, or "interior," notion of the subject. The French existentialists are key protagonists against whom Butler also sets out to argue her case—and she does so with some similarly problematic consequences.

In an earlier article, Butler had argued that there are profound affinities between Beauvoir and Foucault. They both mount a powerful challenge to "feminist positions that maintain sexual difference as irreducible" and, instead, invite an anti-naturalistic "theory of gender invention" (1987, 139). Rather intriguingly, Butler suggests in this earlier article that the affinities between Beauvoir and Foucault reflect their shared roots in the existential tradition! Reading Nietzsche as a key figure in that tradition, she remarks that "Foucault's theory of sexuality and his history of bodies is written against the background of Nietzsche's *Will to Power* and the *Genealogy of Morals* whose method of existential critique regularly revealed how values that appear natural can be reduced to their contingent cultural origins" (141).[25]

But by *Gender Trouble* (1990; cited hereafter as GT) Butler shifts her ground to portray Beauvoir and Foucault—and what each stands for—as in strictly antithetical camps. Now Butler asserts that Beauvoir's analysis of embodiment is premised on "the uncritical reproduction of the Cartesian distinction between freedom and the body" (GT 12). Beauvoir, like Sartre, Butler now claims, often conceives the body "as a mute facticity, anticipating some meaning that can be attributed only by a transcendent consciousness, understood in Cartesian terms as radically immaterial" (GT 129). For Beauvoir, she insists "there is an 'I' that does its gender, that becomes its gender, but that 'I,' invariably associated with its gender, is nevertheless a point of agency never fully identifiable with its gender. That *cogito* is never fully *of* the cultural world that it negotiates, no matter the narrowness of the ontological distance that separates that subject from its cultural predicates" (GT 143). In such a reading, the complexities of Beauvoir's work are ignored, and she is reduced to a Cartesian dualist. She is positioned (with Sartre) as the foil against which Butler can elaborate her neo-Foucauldian account of how the gendered subject is produced: as the effect of stylized, discursively produced performances, repeated endlessly over time and under duress.

In *Gender Trouble*, Butler sets out to argue that, since gender is in no way an expression of anatomical sex but only an effect of performances within "compulsory systems" of discourse (GT 139), gender does not necessarily have to be confined to its normative heterosexual forms. Rather, it should

25. Today Nietzsche is often read (indeed via Foucault) as the locus classicus of postmodern suspicion of the pursuit of truth. But for an earlier generation of scholars (resuscitating him from yet earlier readings that cast him as a proto-Fascist) Nietzsche was read as a key thinker in the existential tradition. Thus Kaufmann wrote in 1950 that "in many ways Nietzsche is close to what one might call the temper of existentialism" ([1950] 1974, 422). See also Barrett 1958; Warnock 1970; and Macquarrie 1972.

be possible to signify and enable a proliferation of genders, such as lesbian, gay, trans- or bi-sexual, hermaphroditic. To insist, for example, on classifying a transsexual as "really" a man or a woman, or to claim that a lesbian is "really" a woman, is to operate within the categories of compulsory heterosexuality. These categories act punitively on those who "do their gender" differently. They also act to ensure that those who do their gender heterosexually continue to conform. For, since gender is not natural, masculine and feminine genders must also be constituted as performances "under duress" (GT 140). For Butler, as for Beauvoir, one is not born a woman (or another gender) but becomes one through a process of becoming that is never definitively completed. How then, we must ask, is Butler's account different from Beauvoir's?

Although Butler criticizes Foucault for elaborating an overly passive conception of the body as the surface of disciplinary inscription (GT 129–31), she shares his insistence that subjectivity, the experience of an "interior" self, is but an "effect." Indeed, in a yet more reductive mode than Foucault's, she claims that any sense of a stable gendered self is not merely an effect but actually an *illusion.* Gender is a set of discrete but repeated stylized acts, publicly performed, that produces the *"illusion* of an abiding gendered self." These enacted styles "produce the coherent gendered subjects who *pose* as their originators" (GT 140; emphases added). Contrary to Beauvoir, Butler views gender as produced through a series of acts that are always "internally discontinuous," rather than knit together in the lived intentionality of a body-subject. Thus, gender is never more than a constructed or constituted identity, and it offers only "the appearance of substance." This appearance is "a performative accomplishment which the mundane social audience, including the actors themselves, comes to believe and to perform in the mode of belief." Because the very notion of "the internal" is, Butler insists, itself but a "surface signification," it is "impossible to embody gender" or to claim that gender is "grounded" in the body (GT 141).

Thus for Butler, as for Foucault, there are only two possibilities: the subject is conceived either as fully constituting or as constituted *tout court.* And like Foucault—at least in his explicit pronouncements on this issue—Butler conceives the subject as entirely constituted. How such a subject then comes "to believe" in the illusions of gender, and whether, alternatively, it could ever engage in doubt about them, are interesting questions she does not choose to address. However, as Beauvoir demonstrates so clearly, becoming one's gender involves a process in which the subject is more than an illusory effect, and in which individual intentionality and agency can be seen to be productive as well as produced.

To recall Grosz's model of the Möbius strip: in becoming one's gender, mind and body, subjectivity and world, intentionality and compulsory performance or practice twist into each other in a fertile "interconstituency." It is only if one assumes, as Butler appears to do here, that no individual agency is possible *except* on the model of the disembodied Cartesian cogito, that one must posit as incompatible alternatives either being constituted through compulsory performance or being free. However, if "I am my body," it is not the case that the stability of the gendered self is *only* an "illusion" produced through repetitive performance.

Butler complains that thinkers such as Beauvoir locate agency in "an 'I' that preexists signification" (GT 143). But what Beauvoir instead suggests is an interactive and continuous process in which previously interiorized significations come to be re-exteriorized as projects and as expressive of the self. Butler insists that gender attributes "are not expressive but performative" since there is no self prior to performance that can "express" itself. But this misses the way in which a personal style, our way of being in the world, emerges both as the sedimented effect of past performance *and* as "the outline of our projects" (SS 34). A self emerges over time that has predispositions, habits, tendencies—an ethos—that are neither strictly necessary nor, as Butler would have it, simply contingent. As Merleau-Ponty observed, probability is a real phenomenon that confounds such distinctions, and my past becomes "the atmosphere of my present" (PP 442). Thus, if the self remains a "point of agency," such an agency is not necessarily, as Butler claims, distinct from gender or other cultural predicates.

However, just as Foucault tacitly attributes more agency to the subject of disciplinary practices than his explicit formulations admit, so too does Butler. For her account *implies* a notion of the subject as more than the illusory effect she claims it to be. To start with, we need to pause at that little phrase in her account of gender performance: "under duress." For if it were the case that the subject is no more than an illusion, brought into being through repetitive gender performance, why would the issue of duress arise? Were subjectivity only an effect of performance, there could be no disjuncture between what one performs and what one believes, desires, or experiences. But if gender is indeed a signifying system produced under duress, this implies, to the contrary, that desires or intentions exceed the signifying processes that allegedly constitute the subject. Butler in fact acknowledges that this is the case: for the "polymorphous perversity" of infantile sexuality includes, she asserts, a bisexuality, the homosexual aspects of which are continuously prohibited and repressed in the enactment of heterosexual gender (GT 57–66). Moreover, there are also implicit normative and political consequences to this claim. For Butler suggests that those gender systems that deny recognition to homoerotic desires are repressive and should be altered. One ought, for example, to be able to perform a lesbian gender without suffering punitive consequences.

Butler, like Foucault, offers us no sense of the experiential dimensions of becoming a subject under duress, or of how it feels to endure punitive consequences if one performs one's gender deviantly. However, she is far more explicit about her political mission than Foucault. She writes as a feminist and queer activist, and she concludes *Gender Trouble* by advocating forms of parodic gender performance that could subvert compulsory heterosexuality and thereby open up a space for new—and preferable—forms of politics. If we can "redescribe those possibilities that *already* exist," she suggests, then "a new configuration of politics would surely emerge from the ruins of the old": the present proliferations of sex and gender might "become articulable within the discourses that establish intelligible cultural life, confounding the very binarism of sex, and exposing its fundamental unnaturalness" (GT 149).

But why, we might ask, should one work to encourage a new configuration of politics? Why struggle to expose the "unnaturalness" of sex? Butler works across the grain of her own values and commitments in insisting that there is no subject except as an illusory effect of performance. It matters to her—and rightly so—that heterosexual sex is constituted as "natural," that non-heterosexual sex is punished. In short, a sentient and suffering (that is, non-Cartesian) subject *is* tacitly presupposed by her normative evaluations and political concerns.

This subject, neither an illusion nor uniquely the effect of signifying systems, perhaps is not so radically different from Beauvoir's embodied subject after all. For if gender performance takes place under duress, and if it can be subverted through parodic repetition, a subject that is both open to oppression and capable of a degree of resistance is implied. The penultimate paragraph of *Gender Trouble* is intriguingly ambiguous. Still affirming the constituting role of discourse, Butler writes: "there is no possibility for agency or reality outside of the discursive practices that give those terms the intelligibility that they have." But she then continues: "The task is not whether to repeat, but how to repeat or, indeed, to repeat and, through a radical proliferation of gender, to *displace* the very gender norms that enable the repetition itself" (GT 148). But who, or what, here is the subject that decides "how" to repeat and to displace? If Butler means that it is discourse that decides to parody itself, then she falls—like Foucault at his worst—into a mode of functionalism that simplistically personifies discourse and implausibly attributes to it motives and rational ends of its own. But if it is the individual human subject that decides how (in parody) to repeat and displace, then Butler implicitly posits a subject that enjoys a margin of freedom within the constraints of gender production—which is what Beauvoir suggested to us over half a century ago!

In the final analysis, like Foucault, Butler operates from suppressed "existential" postulates. For even as she insists on affirming Foucault's binary distinction between constituting and constituted consciousness, arguing like him that we must get rid of any interiority of the subject, she puts this distinction into question. The unintended subtext of *Gender Trouble* is to suggest that feminist theory should not confine itself to analyses of the discursive constitution of gendered subjects alone. Instead, it should explore the complex interplay of constraint *and* freedom through which gendered body-subjects both are constituted *and* constitute themselves. Beauvoir still offers us a framework for such exploration that has not been surpassed.

PART 2

Recognition, Knowledge, and Identity

3   The Politics of Recognition: Sartre, Fanon, and Identity Politics

Questions about "what is to be done" are frequently displaced within feminism today by questions about who "we" are: by questions about the "identities" of women and about how we come to be and to "know" who we are. In this chapter I am less directly concerned with the much debated issues of how identities should best be characterized—whether, for example, they should be conceived as natural givens, social ascriptions, or discursive locations; whether as stable or shifting, unitary or multiple—than with some of the political implications for feminism, and other radical movements, of the present privileging of matters of identity.

I begin by setting out and discussing what I take to be the main propositions of identity politics and briefly surveying some of the feminist debates it recently has generated. Arguing that feminism has not yet "gone beyond" identity politics today, I suggest that we view it as a new version of an older and more universalistic politics of recognition. I next offer an inquiry into the history of the idea of identity politics: I read this history back through the Black Power movement in the United States to the influence of Frantz Fanon on that movement and then, via Fanon, back to Sartre. Through an engagement with Sartre's *Anti-Semite and Jew* (1946) and Fanon's *Black Skin, White Masks* (1952), texts that I argue were key in the historical emergence of the idea of "identity politics," I examine the strengths of a politics that centers on the affirmation of particular identities. But I also argue that it is often limited in its usefulness and can sometimes be self-defeating.

An earlier and abridged form of this chapter appeared as "Fanon, Sartre, and Identity Politics," in *Frantz Fanon: A Critical Reader*, ed. Lewis Gordon, T. Denean Sharply–Whiting, and Renée T. White (Oxford: Blackwell, 1996), 122–33. Reprinted by permission of Blackwell Publishers.

In feminism today, identity is conceived primarily in social, cultural, and/ or psychological terms. It has also come to represent a site of conflict, the place where demarcations among women—by race, ethnicity, class, sexuality, and other criteria—are insistently constructed, deconstructed, reconstructed. The simplistic—and indeed ideological—appeals to sisterhood and solidarity of early second-wave feminism have given way to a concern with differences among women and to a politics of identity within feminism.

By the politics of identity, or "identity politics" as it is more often called, I refer to a politics based on a set of propositions that are only loosely formulated or even tacitly presupposed. There is no one author or text to turn to for a systematic formulation of the tenets of identity politics. However, as much from observation of identity politics in action as from written sources,[1] I believe one can characterize its core propositions roughly as follows: (1) There still exist significant differences of social status and experience (such as those of race, class, ethnicity, gender, and sexuality) that have for too long been obscured by the dominance of the ideas of a hegemonic white, male, upper-class, and heterosexual elite. Under the guise of claiming that there exists a universal human condition, this elite has constructed accounts of reality that serve its own ends. (2) Those groups whose identities have previously been subjugated by this elite should now be privileged as sources of both epistemological and moral authority. (3) Implicit in the first two claims, access to truth and the authority to make moral and political judgments are not universal but are always relative to who one is. (4) To "unmask" or "deconstruct" privileged, universalist readings of reality and make possible the expression of their own identity and truth by the previously silenced and subjugated is not only a valid form of political action, but *the* most important form of political action today. (5) Such a politics of unmasking privilege and enabling the subjugated to "come to voice" urgently needs to be conducted also internally to feminism and other radical movements.[2]

Although I believe all proponents of feminist identity politics would espouse some version of these five propositions, there are also important dif-

1. My most immediate observation of identity politics in action comes from my role as both participant and observer in the heated politics of Oberlin College. Although Oberlin is probably atypical in the intensity of its campus politics, and colleges are certainly not the only sites for identity politics, the ways in which identity is presented and contested in such an institution are not unique. Rather, they are indicative of broader concerns, styles, movements, beyond the confines of this small-college, small-town microcosm. For analyses of the strengths, ambiguities, and paradoxes of identity politics at Oberlin, see Hesford 1999.

2. Although no single author systematically sets out and defends these claims, numerous texts that assert or assume them can be found in anthologies such as B. Smith 1983; Moraga and Anzaldúa 1983; Anzaldúa 1990b; Guy-Sheftall 1995; and García 1997.

ferences in interpretation. As already noted, the very notion of identity is itself open to radically divergent interpretations. These cover a spectrum, from
conceptions of identity as irrevocable essence at one end to postmodern accounts in which identity is held to be not only discursively constructed but
also always unstable and fragmented at the other. For example, at the essentialist end of the spectrum, Deborah King sees identity as constituted by
inborn and ineradicable attributes that define the self. She argues that a black
feminist ideology "acknowledges the fact that two innate and inerasable
traits, being both black and female, constitute our special status in American
society" (1988, 295). Others also view identities as inerasable but treat them
as enduring and stable *social* constructions rather than innate personal attributes (e.g., P. H. Collins 1990); yet others stress the historical mutability
of identities or their multiple, fragmentary, or unstable qualities.

For Chandra Mohanty, for example, identities are fluidly constituted and
re-constituted within the specificities of historical processes and struggles.
She is thus critical of universalizing feminist analyses that seek to depict
women as "an already constituted, coherent group" (1991, 53). Instead, she
argues, it is necessary to demonstrate "the production of women as socioeconomic political groups within particular local contexts" (64). Yet further
emphasizing—and celebrating—the instability of identity, Chela Sandoval
stresses the degree to which "U.S. Third World Feminism" involves a "differential mode of oppositional consciousness." In this mode, the individual
subject continuously shifts and plays among its multiple identities:
"Differential consciousness requires grace, flexibility, and strength: enough
strength confidently to commit to a well-defined structure of identity for one
hour, day, week, month, year; enough flexibility to self-consciously transform that identity according to the requisites of another oppositional tactic
if readings of power's formation require it" (1991, 15).

Weaving through these debates about the nature of identities run other
contentious issues. One set concerns how far identity (whether or not viewed
as ineradicable) also admits of choice: how far can (or should) an identity be
embraced in an affirmative choice of self? How far are even "given" identities open to reformulation or redefinition? Some authors (recapitulating
Beauvoir's account of the ambiguity of "becoming" a woman) argue that
identities are both ascribed and chosen. Shane Phelan, for example, claims
that lesbian identity is both a matter of "ontology" and to be positively
"achieved" through the political strategy of building a lesbian community
(1989, 136). Similarly, Cherríe Moraga, a light-skinned, mixed-race "Chicana"
who can "pass" as white, talks of her Chicana identity as both "birthright"
and political choice (1983, 27–34).

Other debates concern the extent to which knowledge and political capacity derive from identity. Many claim the oppressed are the source of truer

accounts of reality, grounded in particularities of experience to which others simply do not have access. Thus, for example, June Jordan writes:

> I can voice my ideas without hesitation or fear because I am speaking finally about myself. I am black and I am female and I am a mother and I am bisexual and I am a nationalist and I am antinationalist. And I mean to be fully and freely all that I am!
>
> Conversely, I do not accept that any white or black or Chinese man— I do not accept that, for instance Dr. Spock—should presume to tell me, or any other women, how to mother a child. He has no right. He is not a mother. My child is not his child. And likewise I do not accept that anyone—any woman or any man who is not inextricably part of the subject he or she dares address—should attempt to tell any of us, the objects of her or his presumptuous discourse, what we should or should not do. (1995, 408)

In a statement such as this, who one is (one's identity/ies), what one knows, one's right to speak of certain things by virtue of who one is, and the refusal of that right to non-identical others are strongly elided. Consequently, affirming one's identity and engaging in political practice come to be seen as one and the same. In the now classic words of the black lesbian feminist Combahee River Collective: "focusing upon our own oppression is embodied in the concept of identity politics. We believe that *the most profound and potentially most radical politics comes directly out of our own identity*" (1983, 275; emphasis added).[3]

But such claims to ground access to knowledge and to organize progressive politics so directly on the basis of identity, while still common, have also been challenged. Chandra Mohanty, for one, has criticized what she calls "the feminist osmosis thesis," which assumes that "females are feminists by association and identification with the experiences which constitute us as female" (1992, 77). This thesis erroneously conflates *experiencing* oppression with *acting* in opposition to it—a position that A. Sivanandan has ironically encapsulated as the claim: "I am, therefore I resist" (1989, 15). This position also obscures differentials in power and privilege and, as Mohanty and others have rightly warned, attributing "victim status" to all women (or all people of color) obscures this fact.

---

3. Barbara Smith also elides identity and radical politics in the following remarks: "I feel it is radical to be dealing with race and sex and class and sexual identity all at one time. . . . This is why Third World women are forming the leadership in the feminist movement because we are not one dimensional, one-issued in our political understanding. Just by virtue of our identities we certainly define race and usually define class as being fundamental issues that we have to address. The more wide-ranged your politics, the more potentially profound and transformative they are" (Smith and Smith 1983, 126–27).

But such caveats, though important, do not serve to diminish the continuing importance of identity politics. Contrary to some recent claims, I do not believe that feminism has now moved "beyond" identity politics. The assertion that "we are in a post-identity phase" (Dean 1997, 3) is highly dubious. For issues of identity continue to play out compellingly within feminism. There are still good reasons why groups of women remain divided, even over such apparently unproblematic and common areas of concern as improving women's health or organizing to resist violence against women. At a certain point, visions of "post-identity" that engage in too radical a destabilization of identities cease to be useful.

Of course, all group identities become fuzzy at the margins. But this is not to say they lack any basis. For example, black women still face higher mortality rates from certain medical conditions, such as diabetes, than do white women. Thus race may affect how different groups of feminist activists prioritize health-related demands.[4] Likewise issues of "reproductive rights" are often differently conceived by different groups of women. For some minority women, a history of coerced sterilization can make the right to reproduce as pressing an issue as the right not to have to carry an unwanted child, on which white "reproductive rights" activists primarily focus (Ross 1998). Attempts at broad coalition politics around issues of "women's health" or "reproductive rights" cannot afford to ignore such differences.

Forms of coalition or solidarity that go "beyond" identity politics, in the sense of enabling struggles to take place which cut across the boundaries of group identity, remain vital.[5] But it is not helpful to destabilize the notion of identity to the point where those differences that do still de facto divide women's needs and agendas become occluded.[6]

4. In 1991 age-adjusted mortality rates for diabetes in the United States were two and a half times higher for African American women than for white women, and it is the fourth-leading cause of death for African American women (C. F. Collins 1996, 7). Yet white women health activists have rarely flagged diabetes as a feminist issue.

To give another example, although breast cancer has long been a concern of feminist health activists and is the most common form of cancer for black and white women alike, here too priorities might differ by race. Black women have a lower incidence of breast cancer but a higher mortality rate from it than whites (Roberson 1996). This suggests that pushing for better access to early diagnosis and existing forms of treatment might be more important for them than the push for further research into new treatments that white women health activists often advocate.

5. I take up this issue more fully in part 3. There I seek to explore what might be some of the areas of commonality among otherwise different and divided women that could enable forms of solidarity to develop.

6. It is worth noting that theorists to whom Dean refers as exemplifying a sense that we are now in a "post-identity" stage do not include any women of color.

However, their disagreements notwithstanding, diverse advocates of identity politics still share much in common. In a longer-term historical perspective, I suggest identity politics may best be characterized as a comparatively recent and radically new version of what Charles Taylor has called "the politics of recognition." Taylor argues that it was with the collapse of ascribed identities and social hierarchies, that is, with the transition from feudal codes of honor to modern, universalist claims about equal human dignity, that the politics of recognition was born (1991, 46ff.). For with the collapse of the unproblematic, ascribed social identities of pre-modern society, it became necessary to discover, create, or negotiate social and personal identities. With modern notions of dignity, equality, and freedom also emerged the notion of the "authentic" self: that is, the self as a unique and "inner" being that can find its fulfillment only in personal self-expression (Taylor 1991, 61). But since such a self can never in actuality be generated purely inwardly, the importance of the free recognition of the self by others also arose as a pressing need.[7] This authentic self, which demanded recognition from others, was above all a moral self: a self of sentiments, values, and judgments, a self that was the seat of the "soul," and a self that was (and still is) intimately linked to Western individualism.

It was Hegel who most powerfully formulated the demand of the modern self for recognition: to be fully human, to attain full consciousness of self, is possible only through the reciprocal struggle for recognition by the other. Hegel's "master-slave dialectic" was couched in the abstracted terms of a reciprocal struggle between two consciousnesses, and it offered an a-social, primarily ethico-existential, account of the struggle for selfhood. Even so, the demand for free recognition by the other that Hegel described has been fundamental to broad political and social struggles for at least two centuries. It has subtended demands for not only "the rights of man," equality under the law, and adult white male suffrage but also the abolition of slavery, women's suffrage, visions of socialism, and, more recently, the black civil rights movement and wider demands for racial and gender equality. It also remains central to identity politics. Indeed, as Taylor rightly observes: "Not only contemporary feminism but also race relations and discussions of multiculturalism are undergirded by the premise that denied recognition can be a form of oppression" (1991, 50).

---

7. "[I]n the earlier age recognition never arose as a problem. Social recognition was built in to the socially derived identity from the very fact that it was based on social categories everyone took for granted. The thing about inwardly derived, personal, original identity is that it doesn't enjoy this recognition a priori. It has to win it through exchange, and it can fail. What has come about with the modern age is not the need for recognition but the conditions in which this can fail. And this is why the need is now *acknowledged* for the first time" (Taylor 1991, 48).

However, what makes identity politics a significant departure from earlier, pre-identarian forms of the politics of recognition is its demand for recognition on the basis of the very grounds on which recognition has previously been denied: it is *qua* women, *qua* blacks, *qua* lesbians that groups demand recognition. This demand is made irrespective of whether identities are viewed in essentialist terms, as inerasable natural traits, or whether they are viewed as socially, culturally, or discursively constructed. The demand is not for inclusion within the fold of "universal humankind," on the basis of shared human attributes; nor is it for respect "in spite of" one's differences. Rather, what is demanded is respect for oneself *as* different. An earlier advocate of black equality, such as W. E. B. DuBois, argued for the advancement of black dignity, self-respect, and recognition, for a "social regeneration of the negro" ([1903] 1965, 283) through full political participation, education, and entry into Western culture. By contrast, with the slogan "Black is beautiful" and its stress on the value of black culture, the black power movement of the 1960s demanded recognition and respect on the basis of difference rather than admission to a universal humanity. This shift was to become paradigmatic for later forms of identity politics, including those internal to the women's movement.

Several significant reformulations of the assumptions of the older politics of recognition are at work in identity politics. First, identity politics tends toward what I call an epistemology of provenance. By this, I mean it tends toward an epistemological and ethical relativism. As illustrated in the passage from June Jordan cited above, this tendency is grounded in claims about the group specificity of experiences and the exclusive capacity of particular identity groups to evaluate those experiences. Although important in enabling previously marginalized and silenced groups to speak, an epistemology of provenance can also be problematic. For it threatens to undercut notions of shared (or even communicable) experience to such an extent that possibilities for a broadly based emancipatory politics are de facto subverted. This often occurs even as calls for solidarity and coalition across differences are being made.[8]

Second, a pyscho-existential shift has taken place. There is something new about the political *style* of identity politics and of the construction of the self within it. As Todd Gitlin puts it, referring to the late 1960s, the demand for the recognition of difference "was more than an *idea* because it was more than strictly intellectual; it was more of a structure of feeling, a whole way of experiencing the world. Difference was now lived and felt more acutely than unity" (1994, 166). Increasingly, identity politics has become preoccu-

---

8. My concern here is with those who seek to engage in broad coalition politics but whose emphasis on experiential exclusivity often unintentionally sabotages this endeavor. Where explicitly separatist forms of politics are pursued, the difficulties I raise here are not an immediate issue. I address the problems raised by an epistemology of provenance more fully in the next chapter.

pied with the expression of the self in its differences. Thus appearance frequently becomes central to identity politics: how one dresses, what badges one wears, how one's hair is styled become important, as do what one reads, what music one listens to, what one eats, where one "hangs out."[9] In short, acts that display one's being to others are conceived as a form of politics. Such affirmations of the self in its "otherness" can, of course, sometimes be both empowering and potentially subversive of the established order. However, such a politics of identity affirmation has often tended to displace other important, and perhaps more conventional, types of politics: those more oriented toward large-scale institutions and political processes and which center on demands for more equitable distributions of power and material resources.

Perhaps most significantly, this displacement also implies a shift in values and a reconfiguration of what is seen as constituting the domain of the "political." As Taylor suggests, demands for recognition have always been based on the assertion of the moral worth of the self. But in an earlier politics of recognition this led, in turn and over time, to the formulation of clear political demands for redistribution of institutional power at the level of the nation-state: equality before the law, the universal franchise, or the right to equal access to employment. By contrast, in identity politics demands for respect and recognition often remain on a psychological and experiential plane and do not translate into programs for legal or institutional change. The following passage from *Borderlands/La Frontera*, by the Chicana lesbian feminist Gloria Anzaldúa, well typifies this shift:

> Individually, but also as a racial entity, we need to voice our needs. We need to say to white society: We need you to accept the fact that Chicanos are different, to acknowledge your rejection and negation of us. We need you to own the fact that you looked upon us as less than human, that you stole our lands, our personhood, our self-respect. We need you to make public restitution: to say that, to compensate for your own sense of defectiveness, you strive for power over us, you erase our history and experiences because it makes you feel guilty—you'd rather forget your brutish acts. (1987, 85–86)

In this formulation, justice remains a transcendental, if tacit, value: there is to be proper "compensation" for theft and brutish acts; there is to be "restitution." However, restitution is to take place on the pyscho-existential plane: through a public confession of "guilt" and granting of "respect." There

9. At its worst, this runs the risk of degenerating into a politics of consumption. "Niche marketing," which now finely targets minority groups and/or sub-sets of women as consumers, not only turns identity politics into a source of profit for main-stream businesses but can also result in the commodification of identities.

is no demand here for a shift of institutional or material power, no demand here (or elsewhere in the book) for economic restitution. Nor is there here a recognition that racism is a way of advancing material interests. White racism is not just a moral and psychological flaw, born of whites' own "sense of defectiveness," but is also often a politics of self-interest.

Nancy Fraser has recently suggested that one can distinguish between two kinds of contemporary struggle against injustice: those based on demands for recognition, by which she means demands for the positive recognition of different and "despised" identities, and those based on demands for the redistribution of socioeconomic resources (1995). The former, which Anzaldúa well exemplifies, sees cultural domination as the fundamental injustice, whereas the latter sees exploitation as the fundamental problem. Although these two kinds of demands for justice are both necessary and sometimes in practice merge, Fraser suggests there is also a tension between them. As she puts it: "Recognition claims . . . tend to promote group differentiation. Redistribution claims, in contrast, often call for abolishing economic arrangements that underpin group specificity. (An example would be feminist demands to abolish the gender division of labour)" (1995, 74). Moreover, each conceives the domain of political struggle differently: a politics of recognition functions mainly in the sphere of symbolics and cultural representation; a politics of redistribution functions in the sphere of political economy and the state. This is not to say that the cultural or symbolic and the material or economic are distinct, or impermeable, realms. Clearly they are not, and the two kinds of struggles, which Fraser distinguishes analytically, in practice may often overlap.[10]

For example, during the 1960s and 1970s, affirmations of difference by the Black Power movement and the early "second-wave" women's movement often linked together recognition and redistribution, and engaged in counter-institution building in relation to the state and economic organization. The Black Panthers did not just affirm black pride but engaged in a variety of organizational activities. These ranged from armed defense of black areas against state-sanctioned police coercion to breakfast programs for children.

10. Critics have accused Fraser of excessive dualism: of artificially separating those forms of politics that demand recognition from those that demand redistribution. They have also accused her of too rigidly demarcating cultural from material struggles (notably, Young 1997; Butler 1998). For example, Butler points out that homophobia not only is an issue about cultural recognition but also is "material" and has political-economic consequences (1998). Yet it still remains useful to distinguish between struggles that are primarily about redistribution and those, like queer identity politics, that are less immediately so. Actual movements rarely fit neatly into typologies. But the latter still serve as useful frameworks of analysis. They help us to make appropriate judgments about what are the predominant means, styles, and intents, and what are the likely outcomes, of different political struggles.

The early second-wave women's movement also engaged in building its own counter-institutions (illegal abortion referral systems, rape crisis centers that challenged existing legal and cultural conceptions of rape) and challenged forms of state-sanctioned sex discrimination in economic and social life. But since the Reagan and Bush years and beyond, this second kind of politics has increasingly withered, so that today identity politics often remains too preoccupied with the symbolic and cultural domain.[11]

I do not think there is, *in principle,* an irresolvable tension between demanding recognition on the basis of differentiation and demanding forms of material redistribution. But de facto there has been a tendency for movements to privilege one set of demands over the other. While earlier Left politics, characterized by what Fraser calls the "socialist imaginary," frequently ignored demands for the recognition of difference in the name of a de-differentiating politics of redistribution, today contemporary feminist (and other) identity politics, as exemplified in the work of Anzaldúa, tends overly to privilege demands for cultural recognition. As a result, it conceives politics primarily as about the psycho-existential affirmation of the self.

CONTEMPORARY identity politics in the United States recognizably began with the Black Power movement. But this, in turn, drew significant elements of its vision from forms of anti-colonial resistance elsewhere, as well as from earlier U.S. movements such as the Harlem Renaissance. In particular, the *négritude* movement in the French colonies (both African and Caribbean) was an influential precursor to black (and other) identity politics in the United States.[12] Although *négritude* was the movement of an educated elite, and was thus in part parasitic upon colonial culture, it constituted a radically new assertion of the value of the black self and a demand that difference be respected, not assimilated. But what later became even better known in the United States than the poetic glorification of black culture and the black soul, developed by men such as Léopold Senghor and Aimé Césaire, was the far more ambivalent engagement with *négritude* and emphasis on liberation through armed resistance of Frantz Fanon.

---

11. Why this happened is a complex story whose historical sociology I cannot discuss here. But undoubtedly the general shift to the right in U.S. politics since the 1980s has impinged on and broadly shifted the horizons, agendas, and style of Left politics. The focus on single issues, on the local, the micro, as well as on identity, adds up to a less ambitious set of demands for change, perhaps realistic but also indicative of retrenchment.

12. However, the *négritude* movement was, in turn, also influenced by African American writers. In the interwar period Paris provided the meeting point where African American writers and intellectuals and those from the French colonies (both African and Caribbean) met and intermingled, cross-fertilizing conceptions of blackness and visions of Africa (Vaillant 1990, 90–102).

Only a few years after its translation into English (in 1963), Eldridge Cleaver, the Black Panther leader, characterized Fanon's *The Wretched of the Earth* as the "Black Bible."[13] In this book, published in French in 1960, Fanon argued that force was the only form of resistance to colonialism that could reverse the profound psychological damage it had inflicted on the colonized. His call to arms (to which Sartre provided an introduction)[14] was an inspiration not only to the Black Power movement in the United States in the 1960s but also to "Third World" liberation struggles then under way in Asia, Africa, and Latin America, as well as, later, to the Black Consciousness movement in South Africa. Fanon's first book, *Black Skin, White Masks*, was originally published in 1952 and was, in comparison, far less militant in tone. But the phenomenology of black experience Fanon developed in it remained central to the analyses of the later work.

Although the initial impact of *Black Skin, White Masks* was not nearly as wide as that of *The Wretched of the Earth*,[15] over time it has remained the work of more enduring interest, both in the West and in more recent postcolonial contexts. For, as formal struggles for national liberation were (by and large) concluded during the 1970s and as armed revolution ceased to be seen as a viable means of political change by Western leftists, Fanon's analyses of the colonized subject's experiences of non-recognition still continued to resonate. In the United States and elsewhere, these analyses still speak to the on-going struggles for recognition that now frequently constitute identity politics. Indeed, with its focus on the domain of experience and its explorations of the affirmation of black identity, *Black Skin, White Masks* can be read as an inaugural work of identity politics—but it also offers an agonized acknowledgment of its limitations.

Henry Louis Gates has described Fanon as "a Rorschach blot with legs" (1991, 458). National liberation struggles have (for the most part) now been succeeded by struggles about the "postcolonial" condition, and at least in the academy,[16] suspicion has fallen on the naive "humanism" of earlier liberation struggles. Moreover, postcolonial and certain postmodern modes of

---

13. Cleaver began his review of *The Wretched of the Earth* as follows: "This book, already recognized around the world as a classic study of the psychology of oppressed peoples, is now known among the militants of the black liberation movement in America as the 'Bible'" (1969, 18). For an overview of Fanon's immediate influence in the United States and elsewhere, see Gendzier 1985, 263–68.

14. Cleaver refers also to Sartre's introduction as a "masterpiece" (1969, 20).

15. Significantly, although written much earlier, it was translated into English only in 1967, four years after *The Wretched of the Earth* was translated.

16. By "academy" I refer here primarily to the North American and British academy. However, the "Subaltern Studies" movement, which has been highly influential in effecting the shifts I describe, originated among intellectuals in India as well as diasporic Indians.

analysis have increasingly converged, since they share a similar suspicion of the alleged imperializing tendencies of "grand narratives" and of the "totalizing" impulses of earlier visions of human emancipation. In this context, reading Fanon (with the focus now primarily on *Black Skin, White Masks*) has indeed become an enterprise in projection! Thus, for example, Homi Bhabha has offered a (profoundly problematic) profoundly Lacanian reading of Fanon (1990); Diana Fuss has elaborated a "genealogical" reading of Fanon as a theorist of identification who destabilizes sexualities (1995); and Gates himself, after surveying a range of incommensurate postcolonial readings of Fanon, also uses Fanon for his own poststructuralist ends. He happily concludes that we do not have to make evaluations among these readings, since what Fanon teaches us is that we don't after all need "a grand unified theory of oppression" and that "our own theoretical reflections must be as provisional, reactive, and local as the texts we reflect upon" (1991, 470).

What is striking is that the "postcolonial" readings of Fanon are silent about the role that existential phenomenology plays in his work. Gates urges, at the end of his survey of "critical Fanonism," that we read Fanon "with an acknowledgement of his own historical particularity" (1991, 470), but he hardly follows his own advice! Were we to do as he suggests, we would have to consider the intellectual milieu into which Fanon plunged when he came to France to study in 1947. We would consider his avid reading from *Les Temps Modernes*, his wide study of the current philosophical literatures of the time, in which the works of Sartre and Merleau-Ponty were pre-eminent. We would also note that the "psychoanalysis" Fanon develops is not fully grounded in a model of the unconscious. Contra Bhabha's "Lacanian" interpretation (and other neo-Freudian readings), Fanon's approach has strong affinities with Sartre's account of "existential" psychoanalysis, in which neuroses are explained not at the level of the unconscious but as fundamental choices made in responses to concrete situations (BN 557–75).[17] We would also observe that Fanon's account of the racialization of otherness involves a creative appropriation not only of the neo-Hegelian account of "being-for-others" Sartre developed in *Being and Nothingness* but also of Sartre's somewhat later and significantly different analysis of the dynamics of non-recognition in *Anti-Semite and Jew* ([1946] 1976). It is absolutely stunning how "postcolonial" commentators have somehow managed to ignore the

---

17. Fanon's therapeutic methods as a practicing psychiatrist extensively used "milieu therapy," in which small groups of patients and staff in the hospital were organized to form therapeutic communities. Fanon learned such methods initially from François Tosquelles, with whom he did his internship in psychiatry (Gendzier 1985, 63–71; Bulhan 1985, 201–10). Such methods have a strong affinity with the existential emphasis on shifting one's way of being-in-the-world as a means of changing oneself, rather than effecting a cure through bringing the unconscious to light.

embarrassingly large number of references Fanon makes to Sartre in general, and to this work in particular.[18]

Indeed, if we read Fanon in his own context, we must be struck that *Anti-Semite and Jew* itself stands as a pivotal text in the development of identity politics. If we seek to trace the theoretical shifts from the earlier, more universalistic, forms of the politics of recognition to those newer conceptions of recognition that culminate in identity politics, Sartre's role is clearly path-breaking.[19] Reading Sartre today offers us a place wherein to reflect, both at a distance and up close, on dilemmas that continue to shape our times. It is thus to Sartre's work on anti-Semitism and Jewish identity, and then to Fanon's creative and critical appropriation of this text to explore black identity, that I now turn.

SARTRE'S account of non-recognition as a form of oppression, together with his call for those who are oppressed positively to assume their identity, is set out most cogently in *Anti-Semite and Jew* (cited hereafter as ASJ).[20] Of course, the issue of recognition was extensively explored in *Being and Nothingness*, published some three years earlier. There, in his account of "being-for-others," Sartre reworked the Hegelian account of the struggle of consciousnesses to argue that (at least in the present world of alienated human relations) no real *Mitsein* is possible. The other is always a threat to my own experience of self. Not only does the other attempt to reduce me to an object in his or her own organization of the world, but the other's "look" also induces me to flee into *self*-objectification, that is, to apprehend myself as an object. In an experience such as shame the look of the other is internalized as my own.

These forms of objectification and self-objectification are portrayed by Sartre in *Being and Nothingness* as not only ubiquitous but also reciprocal: that is, each can equally objectify others or be objectified. But now, in a highly significant shift, Sartre observes that anti-Semitism is *not* simply "the expression of our fundamental relation to the Other." For in the operation that

18. Fuss is a partial exception. But she fails to notice how Sartre shifts from a Hegelian account of otherness in *Being and Nothingness* to an account of socially structured "over-determined" otherness in *Anti-Semite and Jew*. A few of the essays in Gordon et al. 1996 also acknowledge Fanon's existential orientation.

19. For a perceptive use of Sartrean categories and methods of analysis also to examine anti-black racism, see Gordon 1995.

20. The original essay was published as *Réflexions sur la question juive* in 1946. Parts of it were previously published in *Les Temps Modernes* in 1945: clearly the work was extremely topical in postwar France, where trials of collaborators were in process and French Jews who had survived the Holocaust were returning. What is striking is that Sartre's anti-Semite is not only the German Nazi but also the Frenchman who enabled Nazi extermination of French Jews to take place.

the anti-Semite performs upon the Jew something further is involved, something that precludes the mutuality or reversibility of the objectifying relationship:[21] "the Jew has a personality like the rest of us, and on top of that he [sic] is Jewish. It amounts to a *doubling* of the fundamental relationship with the Other. *The Jew is over-determined*" (ASJ 79; emphases added).[22]

In other words, a reciprocal relation of objectification is not possible between the Jew and other people. For the Jew, in an anti-Semitic world, is never free not to be the Jew, the other, the object. In a passage that all too well captures also the dynamic between white liberals and people of color in the United States today, Sartre writes: "The liberal, when he met a Jew, was free, completely free to shake his hand or spit in his face; he could decide . . . but the Jew was not free not to be a Jew" (ASJ 77).

In explaining the dynamics of this "over-determination," Sartre in significant ways anticipates more recent anti-essentialist accounts of the construction of racial, ethnic, and gender identities. To be a Jew, he argues, is not to be born of a physical race, or even—since many Jews are non-practicing—into a religion. If one asks what it is that Jews have in common, it is no fixed essence but rather the "the identity of their situations" (ASJ 145).

The situation of the Jew in Sartre's account is above all one constituted by the anti-Semite—just as that of women can be said to be constituted by the sexist, or that of people of color by the racist. For, "the Jew is one whom other men consider a Jew . . . it is the anti-Semite who *makes* the Jew" (ASJ 69). To be a Jew is continually to be "*marked*" as the other and to live as such, the yellow star being only the monstrous point of culmination (ASJ 76ff.). The Jew cannot ever avoid this situation, for the hostility of the anti-Semite structures also the relations of Jews with those who would be their friends: "Under the looks of support and compassion [Jews] felt themselves becoming *objects:* objects of commiseration, of pity, of what you will—but

21. This is the shift that (as we saw in chapter 2) Beauvoir urged on Sartre as early as 1940, when she argued against him that not all oppressions are equal and that no freedom is possible in certain situations. In *Anti-Semite and Jew,* Sartre goes as far at one point as to say that no moral blame can be ascribed to the Jew who acts inauthentically (ASJ 93), presumably because he now realizes that in extreme situations there are no other options.

Linda Bell has suggested that Sartre's analysis reveals anti-Semitism to be an oppression of a different kind from that suffered by women, blacks, or workers. For the latter all have a "place" in society assigned to them, even if it is an inferior one; whereas Jews (at least in the context of immediate postwar France) do not. She suggests that the situation of the homosexual today is nearer to that of Sartre's Jew, as being one of placelessness (Bell 1997, 1–20).

22. Sartre's anti-Semite and Jew are unrelentingly depicted as male. There is virtually no consideration in the book of whether anti-Semitism might be differently expressed or differently experienced by women, or whether alternative forms of objectification are brought to bear on Jewish women than men.

objects" (ASJ 76–77). Sartre might be construed as implying here that, since identity is externally created, there would be no Jews (or analogously blacks or women) were over-determination to cease. However, given his objections to a politics of assimilation (discussed below), this is not his claim. Rather, his point is that the *meaning* of this particular facticity would become open, and no longer pre-given, once the subject ceased to be over-determined.

But given that over-determination is a present reality, how does the Jew (or member of another oppressed group) live it? Sartre suggests that the most common way of assuming it is in "flight": the attempt to avoid fully confronting the pain of the situation through a variety of self-evasive strategies that, in *Being and Nothingness*, he described as "bad faith" and that he here more often calls choices of "inauthenticity." Thus, for example, he explains the attraction of many Jews to rationalism as a form of flight: in the abstract life of the mind it would appear that we are all simply "men" and the particularity of the Jew can be transcended (ASJ 111ff.). Similarly, some try to lose their particularity in political movements: Jews in the Resistance would insist they were resisting the Nazis as French and not as Jews (ASJ 96). Yet others engage in different maneuvers of self-detachment, either through ironic humor, "which is a perpetual attempt to see [oneself] from the outside" (ASJ 97), or through various kinds of introspection in which the other is always an internalized witness. Many Jews appear to suffer from an "inferiority complex." But if it exists, Sartre insists it is one for which they themselves are responsible. For "the Jew *creates this complex* when he chooses to live out his situation in an inauthentic manner. He has allowed himself to be persuaded by the anti-Semites; he is the first victim of their propaganda" (ASJ 94).

But such strategies serve only to re-enforce—indeed to perpetuate—the anti-Semite's stereotypes of the Jew. Against them Sartre contrasts the actions of the authentic Jew, the one who demands recognition as the divided and impossible self that he is, rather than seeking in bad faith to deny the painful facticities of his being in situation.[23] Authenticity, as proponents of black pride, gay pride, or gynocentric feminism insist, does not involve the mere admission that one is what others say one is. Rather it involves re-appropriating as a positive value the identity that others have imposed on one. Thus, "The authentic Jew . . . ceases to run away from himself and to be ashamed of his own kind . . . he accepts the obligation to live in a situation that is defined precisely by the fact that it is unlivable" (ASJ 136–37).

23. Thus Sartre's use of the term "authenticity" here, to denote the refusal of bad faith, is not to be confused with the notion of the "authentic self" that Taylor argues is central to the emergence of Western individualism. Authenticity for Sartre (as for Beauvoir) is not a matter of getting in contact with, or giving expression to, a pre-given inner core, since the self does not pre-exist its projects.

Whether an individual assumes it authentically or not, to be a Jew is to live in a situation one has not chosen but which still constitutes part of one's very being. One is not "just" a human being who happens, in addition, to be a Jew—or one might add a woman and/or a person of color. One *is* one's situation. And although one might give to one's being-for-others various meanings, one can never slough it off. Thus, Sartre argues, the old-style abstract humanism of the liberal democrat not merely is inadequate but is also itself oppressive. For it seeks to suppress the particularities of concrete groups and individuals that are, for better or worse, integral to their existence. It is worth quoting Sartre at some length here since he formulates so clearly what is at issue between the liberal universal humanist and the advocate of a politics of difference. The former, says Sartre,

> has no eyes for the concrete syntheses with which history confronts him. He recognizes neither Jew, nor Arab, nor Negro, nor bourgeois, nor worker, but only man—man always the same in all times and places. . . . to him the individual is only an ensemble of universal traits. It follows that his defense of the Jew saves the latter as man and annihilates him as Jew. . . . he wants to separate the Jew from his religion, his family, his ethnic community, in order to plunge him into the democratic crucible whence he will emerge naked and alone, an individual and solitary particle like all the other particles. (ASJ 55–57)

And, Sartre adds, "this is what, in the United States, is called the policy of assimilation."

Liberal universal humanism thus puts "others" in a double bind: it demands that they abandon an identity that, while oppressive, is also constitutive of their very existence. And it also obscures the dynamics of oppression behind the assertion of a universal human essence that "we" all share. Liberal ideology and the Western humanist tradition, as well as "canonical" philosophy and political theory, have indeed all frequently functioned as exclusionary discourses.

However, this is not to say that all universalist values should—or indeed can—be simply dismissed as crass ideology. For, as Marnia Lazreg has observed: "The rejection of humanism and its universalistic character . . . deprives the proponents of difference of any basis for understanding the relationship between the varieties of modes of being different in the world" (1990, 339). We can make sense of difference only by also recognizing a certain oneness to the human condition, a generality that is the horizon against which particularity is configured. Minimally, this is a logical point. But more is at stake. The demand to be recognized in one's particularity or difference is, implicitly, a call for more universal forms of reciprocity and respect. For if one's recognition by the other was not necessary for the integrity of the self, non-recognition per se would not present itself as an injury. A politics of difference needs to navigate between what Cornel West has more recently characterized as an "ethnic chauvinism" on the one hand and a "faceless universalism" on the other (1990, 36). That is, we need to seek for non-exclusionary affirmations of difference and for forms of universalism that can accommodate particularity: no easy task.

It is here that Sartre is helpful. For although he elegantly and presciently formulates the core of a valid critique of abstract humanism, he does not proceed to the stronger and more problematic claim of an epistemology of provenance: that difference irredeemably fractures knowledge, truth, and reality. Instead, Sartre asserts the need to hold together, in tension, both differences and the oneness of the human world. Contrary to an assimilationist vision of oneness that would iron out difference, his appeal is for what he calls a "concrete liberalism," one that grants rights to citizens in conscious recognition of their differences.[24]

However, Sartre also runs up against a troubling disjunction. For his phenomenology gives us access only to the domain of psycho-existential and moral experience, where the need for recognition is *felt* and the demand for recognition is *expressed*. However, this is not the primary domain in which concrete transformations of material and power relations are effected. Sartre realizes that it is important not to elide these domains and is painfully aware of this gap. But he is still unable, in *Anti-Semite and Jew*, to theorize the interplay between these domains. He has portrayed anti-Semitism as above all an existential relation of anti-Semite to Jew, in which the Jew cannot escape the objectifying portrait constructed by the anti-Semite but can choose to live it either less or more authentically, and he has urged authenticity—the active and prideful assumption of that identity—on the Jew. But he also goes on to point out that, although authenticity might permit the affirmation of an existential freedom in the face of oppression, it does not *in itself* address the social situation of the Jew. Although the individual Jew may resist the self-objectifying look of the anti-Semite, authenticity provides no clear orientations toward the elimination of anti-Semitism. On the contrary, with devastating clarity Sartre concludes, "the choice of authenticity appears to be a *moral* decision, bringing certainty to the Jew on the ethical level but in no way serving as a solution on the social or political level: the situation of the Jew is such that everything he does turns against him" (ASJ 141).

The problem that Sartre thus leaves us with is how to bring this realm of existential and moral self-affirmation into practical engagement with the ac-

24. Here Sartre anticipates some recent Anglo-American theory, which seeks to develop visions of citizenship that can recognize and represent difference. See, for example, Young 1990a; Kymlicka 1995; and Phillips 1995.

tualities of a realm of politics that extends far beyond personal experience and expression: the realm of institutions and enduring social structures. For power does not rest on objectification alone. Anti-Semitism is far more than the sum of the actions of a collection of individual anti-Semites. It takes enduring historical and structural forms—in the deployment of state power, in the dynamics of political economy, in the system of public education, in cultural symbolism, in normalizing practices, and so on. Sartre is fully aware of these structural dimensions but still unable to integrate them into his analysis. In *Anti-Semite and Jew* he only notes the hiatus and then tries to bridge it with a hopelessly rationalistic appeal (at the end of the book) for a classless society as the end to all social ills, including anti-Semitism (ASJ 149–51). Suddenly, Sartre becomes guilty of embracing a de-situated and schematic vision of history, an abstract universalism that neglects his own previous insights into the concrete particularities of oppression. Here, recent identity politics takes us beyond Sartre, insofar as it insists on the multiplicity of forms of oppression and refuses to reduce them all to the effects of class oppression.

What hampers Sartre, in coming to grips with the hiatus he points to, is his lack of a grasp of social *mediations,* of the dynamics through which issues of interpersonal recognition and identity pass into (and from) the domain of concrete institutions and social structures. There is no consideration, for example, of the means through which anti-Semitism actually passes into exclusionary legislation against Jews, or how it is that Jews have tended to engage only in particular occupations. Modern identity politics also frequently replicates this failure to consider issues of mediation. Focusing on the politics of difference, it tends to preoccupy itself above all with matters of self-affirmation, with the symbolics of self-presentation and representation. But to affirm one's identity in the face of racism or sexism is not, for example, to address the formation of segmented labor markets that perpetuate low black and female wages; nor does the assertion of gay pride translate easily into a concrete analysis of how homophobia plays out in the emergence of pension plans that discriminate against gay couples.

Later, in the *Critique of Dialectical Reason* (1960), Sartre addresses the issue of mediations head-on and at length. He does not abandon his earlier concerns here, but he shifts from a direct focus on the subject's need for recognition to a focus on the subject as agent. It is as one *acts* in the world, and then finds one's actions returned in altered forms, that one either receives or is denied recognition. In exploring the complex practical and material mediations through which actions return to their agents either alienated or affirmed by the actions of others, Sartre begins to locate the dynamics of self and other in a broader world of social ensembles, structures, and historical forces.[25]

However, it is not the *Critique* but Sartre's earlier work that remains a locus classicus for the emergence of identity politics, with both its attendant strengths and its limitations. It was the analytical framework of *Anti-Semite and Jew* that was creatively taken up and transformed by later thinkers to explore dynamics of identity and oppression. Among others, Frantz Fanon drew on it extensively to examine the black experience of colonial racism.

FANON (1925–61) grew up in the French Antillean colony of Martinique. The child of middle-class parents, he belonged to that small minority of non-white children who received secondary education. The poet, political activist, and advocate of *négritude* Aimé Césaire was one of his high school teachers. Césaire's influence, combined with the impact of the Second World War, helped early to arouse in Fanon keen political sensibilities. One consequence was that he volunteered for the Free French Army as soon as he graduated from high school. His training in North Africa, followed by active service during the liberation of France, brought Fanon face to face with racism in a way that life in more racially mixed Martinique had not: Antillean troops were grossly discriminated against in the army and abused by the civilian population they were helping to liberate. Suddenly Fanon discovered that in spite of his education, fine French, and patriotism, he was not French (i.e., white) but black. It was a shattering experience, one that was to be explored at length in *Black Skin, White Masks*.

Military service entitled Fanon to receive financial assistance to study in France, and he returned there in 1947.[26] After some hesitation, he decided to study medicine in Lyons, completing his initial training in 1951 and a further qualification in psychiatry in 1953. Shortly thereafter, he accepted a senior position in Algeria's sole psychiatric hospital. This enabled him more systematically to study the horrendous psychological costs of colonialism; he rapidly became a passionate activist in support of the Algerian national liberation movement and "Third World" anti-colonial struggles more broadly.

While a medical student, Fanon also read voraciously in existential philosophy. As well as Sartre and Merleau-Ponty, he read Heidegger, Jaspers, and

25. Indeed his account of racism in Algeria (Sartre [1960] 1976, 716–34) comes much closer to connecting the dynamics of recognition and non-recognition with a range of political, economic, and even military processes than did his portrait of anti-Semitism in *Anti-Semite and Jew*.

26. A French colony since the mid-seventeenth century, Martinique became an "overseas department" in 1946, entitling its citizens to receive various kinds of benefits available in the metropolis.

earlier thinkers such as Kierkegaard and Nietzsche. In addition, he attended
Merleau-Ponty's lectures at the university in Lyons.[27] He also read Hegel and
contemporary Hegelian thought and studied Marxism in depth. Fanon was,
moreover, an avid reader of both *Les Temps Modernes* and *Présence
Africaine*, the main periodicals of, respectively, existential Marxism and
négritude.[28] This wide-ranging program of reading was integral to Fanon's
formation as an activist. His intellectual engagement accompanied his intense involvement in the Union of Students from Overseas France (which
he helped to found), as well as support for the numerous worker's struggles
on-going in Lyons at the time.[29] *Black Skin, White Masks* was originally published in 1952 while Fanon was still undertaking his graduate training in psychiatry. In it he drew together his intellectual formation, his politics, and his
own autobiographical experience to develop a powerful phenomenological
analysis of racial oppression.

For better and for worse, the influence of Sartre is pervasive in *Black Skin,
White Masks*. Sartre's account of the dialectics of recognition and non-
recognition deepens and brilliantly mutates in Fanon's hands as it is extended
to issues of racial identity. However, as we shall see, the same tension, between a careful attention to a phenomenology of situated experience and an
abrupt final shift to a universalizing, abstract rationalism, also mars Fanon's
work. But what Fanon also brings to his topic is something that Sartre did
not have: firsthand experience. Whereas Sartre wrote as a progressive, but as
neither anti-Semite nor Jew, Fanon writes as a black man. His work has both
a concreteness and a depth of passion that have rendered it a classic for later
movements for black consciousness. Even though the book focuses on the
experiences of black Antilleans in the 1940s and 1950s, particularly those
male middle-class Antilleans who received education, traveled to France, became intellectuals—such as Fanon himself—it has resonated far beyond
these boundaries of time, place, and identity.

Fanon's starting point in *Black Skin, White Masks* (cited hereafter as
BSWM) is the Sartrean problem of authenticity. Most black men,[30] he ob-

27. Merleau-Ponty was professor of philosophy at the University of Lyons from 1945
to 1949.

28. There were connections between the journals. Sartre contributed a short piece,
"Présence noir," for the first issue of *Présence Africaine* in 1947, and *Les Temps
Modernes* published essays by various figures associated with the former.

29. Biographical information here is drawn from Zahar 1974; Bulhan 1985; and
Gendzier 1985.

30. In *Black Skin, White Masks*, Fanon's oppressed other is, like Sartre's in *Anti-
Semite and Jew*, primarily depicted as male. Fanon argues that the Negro is objectified
above all as a sexual being—and he presents this sexual being, and the threat it presents
to whites, as male. Thus, when Fanon talks of the experience of "the black man," he really does mean the black male. Women are almost absent from his account, with the

serves, are not capable of an "authentic upheaval" today (BSWM 8).[31] They are the victims of a socially produced situation of inferiority that they (like Sartre's Jews) have internalized. They suffer from a "psycho-existential complex" (BSWM 12) that inhibits them from engaging in self- or social transformation. Shame is the fundamental experience of the inauthentic black: "Shame. Shame and self-contempt. Nausea. When people like me, they tell me it is in spite of my color. When they dislike me, they point out it is not because of my color. Either way, I am locked into the infernal circle" (BSWM 116).[32] The black man—the Negro (*le nègre*), as Fanon also frequently calls him—is characterized by a "situational neurosis . . . a constant effort to flee (*de fuir*) his own individuality, to nihilate his own presence (*de néantiser son être-là*)" (BSWM 60; French [1952], 48).[33]

The origin of this neurosis lies initially with the attitudes of white, colonial society to blackness. "Negrophobia" is in many ways a similar phenomenon to anti-Semitism as Sartre depicted it (BSWM 160). But there are also profound differences in how it impacts its object. For the Jew can sometimes be anonymous, but a black man is always visible as such. Taking up Sartre's notion of the "over-determined" otherness of the Jew for his own purposes, Fanon writes: "I am overdetermined from without. I am the slave not of the 'idea' that others have of me but of my own appearance" (BSWM

---

exception of one chapter that discusses the black woman who desires white men. However, in later works Fanon does address the situation of women more fully; notably in *Studies in a Dying Colonialism* ([1959] 1989).

31. Fanon is of course referring here primarily to men of the French Caribbean islands. He makes a point of stating that his observations do not fit as well the inhabitants of France's African colonies and are even less directly applicable to blacks in the United States.

32. As with Beauvoir, shame is here identified as the paradigmatic experience of inferiorized otherness. But although Beauvoir's woman and Fanon's black man both experience shame as a relation to oneself constituted through the objectifying look of the other, the experiences they describe are far from identical. For although blackness and femininity each signifies otherness and lack—and especially lack of reason—Fanon's (male) black is constituted as an active, animal sexuality in the white male imagination, Beauvoir's (white) woman as "prey" or passive nature.

33. I have revised the English translation here, since it loses Fanon's use of explicitly Sartrean terminology. One sees in this passage that Fanon's framework is one closely allied to Sartre's existential psychoanalysis. Neurosis is considered here as a form of "flight": that is, a "bad faith" (if often unavoidable) evasion of an untenable social situation, a project that attempts a nihilation of one's own existence.

Fanon repeatedly emphasizes that black neurosis cannot be explained through conventional Western psychoanalytic frameworks. He insists, for example, that Oedipus complex rarely exists in the Antilles, adding wryly that psychoanalysts such as "Dr. Lacan" will be "reluctant to share my view" (BSWM 152). It is not familial history but racialized social interaction that produces pathology in blacks: "A normal Negro child, having grown up within a normal family, will become abnormal on the slightest contact with the white world" (BSWM 143).

116). In the white unconscious, as well as in white culture, the Negro, even more than the Jew, denotes evil. "Is not whiteness in symbols always ascribed in French to Justice, Truth, Virginity? . . . The black man is the symbol of Evil and Ugliness" (BSWM 180). But the Negro stands not for abstract evil as much as for the threat of uncontrolled carnality and sexuality. The Jew is an intellectual or economic threat, but the Negro "symbolizes the biological danger. To suffer from a phobia of Negroes is to be afraid of the biological. For the Negro is only biological. The Negroes are animals" (BSWM 165). Thus, the experience of alienation in one's body, that self-doubling in which one experiences oneself as a body-for-others, is more profound for Fanon's Negro than for Sartre's Jew or, perhaps, Beauvoir's (white) woman.

The project that Fanon sets himself in *Black Skin, White Masks* is not to account for white Negrophobia but to offer a phenomenology of the lived experience and moral possibilities open to a black man living in a negrophobic world. Like Sartre's Jew, Fanon's Negro most frequently engages in forms of flight; indeed, it would seem almost impossible to do otherwise. For virtually all paths to an authentic self-affirmation are blocked or co-opted. From childhood onwards, exposure to the values of white culture induces—particularly in the educated colonial child, such as Fanon himself was—an inauthentic identification with whiteness. "The black schoolboy in the Antilles, who in his lessons is forever talking about 'our ancestors, the Gauls,' identifies himself with the explorer, the bringer of civilization, the white man who carries truth to savages—an all-white truth. . . . [he] subjectively adopts a white man's attitude. He invests the hero, who is white, with all his own aggression" (BSWM 147). Indeed, Fanon reports, this is so much the case that many Antilleans simply do not think of themselves as black: Antilleans are French; "Negroes" are black and primitive and live far off in darkest Africa.

But once a direct encounter with whites forces on an Antillean awareness of his own personal blackness—when, as Fanon did, he goes to metropolitan France and experiences white fear and hostility as he walks down the street—further forms of inauthenticity are elicited. Having internalized white negrophobia and the belief in the superiority of white "civilization," the Antillean cannot accept his own designation as black. To speak French well, to be educated, are after all signs of being a Frenchman—that is, white. But suddenly there he is, irrevocably marked by his body as the feared and despised other, the threat to "civilization." "Quite literally," Fanon asserts, "I can say without any risk of error that the Antillean who goes to France in order to convince himself that he is white will find there his real face" (BSWM 153, note 16). For many, Fanon included, the response is to internalize the white negrophobe's gaze, to engage in the kind of self-objectification that Sartre described in the inauthentic Jew. "On that day," Fanon writes, "completely dislocated, unable to be abroad with the other, the white man, who unmercifully imprisoned me, I took myself far off from my own presence, and made myself an object" (BSWM 112).[34] This self-objectification is the source of the alleged black "inferiority complex," a complex that has nothing to do with family dynamics or the Oedipus complex but everything to do with what Fanon so aptly calls the "epidermalization" of social inferiority (BSWM 11).

Another response—one that also enticed Fanon—is to attempt to escape into a realm of "universal" humanity through the appeal to reason. Just as the Jew seeks to evade his particular situation through rationalism, claiming that reason makes him a "man" like any other, so too there is a temptation for the black, especially for the black intellectual, to try to escape from his racialized situation by an appeal to reason or other transcendental universals. But this attempt is always thrown back in his face by racism: "this Negro who is looking for the universal. He is looking for the universal! But in June 1950, the hotels in Paris refused to rent rooms to Negro pilgrims. Why? Purely and simply because their Anglo-Saxon customers (who are rich and who, as everyone knows, hate Negroes) threatened to move out" (BSWM 186).

There is yet another strategy, which looks at first sight to be more promising: "I resolved, since it was impossible for me to get away from an *inborn complex*, to assert myself as a BLACK MAN. Since the other hesitated to recognize me, there remained only one solution: to make myself known" (BSWM 115). Here might appear to be the authentic response to racism. This, surely, is what Sartre advocated for the authentic Jew. Here also is the move that distinguishes identity politics from earlier forms of the politics of recognition: the demand to be recognized *as* different. But Fanon is deeply ambivalent, for he sees this as a primarily reactive politics: "what is often called the black soul is a white man's artifact" (BSWM 14).

It is through examining *négritude* that Fanon explores the dilemmas of the affirmation of black identity. *Négritude* is at once untenable and yet necessary. Through extensive citation from the works of Senghor, Césaire, and others, Fanon illustrates that much of its affirmation of black identity rests on a simple reversal, a re-appropriation of white stereotypes of black culture. What is celebrated as authentically "Negro" is rhythm, the magical, the irrational, the emotional, the intuitive—and all of these are saturated with the sexual (BSWM 122–28). Fanon explains the logic that leads to such a reversal: "I had rationalized the world and the world rejected me on the basis of color prejudice. Since no agreement was possible on the level of reason, I

34. Much of Fanon's semi-autobiographical account of the avenues of flight that tempt the black intellectual are set out in the fifth chapter of *Black Skin, White Masks*. This chapter is entitled in the English translation "The Fact of Blackness," a rendering that unfortunately loses the existential flavor of the French original: *"L'expérience vécue du noir."*

threw myself back toward unreason . . . I wade in the irrational. Up to the neck in the irrational. And how my voice vibrates!" (BSWM 123).

There is a distinctly ironic tone to Fanon's presentation of the mythic splendors arrayed by the poets of *négritude*. Yet, however reactive it might be, *négritude* is also necessary. For it does effect a shift in black-white relations. Not only does it offer the black man sources of pride, but the white man suddenly recognizes in the Negro qualities that he now experiences himself as lacking, such as closeness to nature, spontaneity, simplicity. Thus, for the first time, a certain *reciprocity* of recognition emerges. A friend told Fanon, "when the whites feel that they have become too mechanized, they turn to the men of color and ask them for a little human sustenance." Comments Fanon, perhaps not wholly ironically: "At last I had been recognized. I was no longer a zero" (BSWM 129).

But such recognition, even if real, is ephemeral. For white culture still has at its disposal the overwhelming means of devaluing black experience. Although Negro naturalness and emotion are said to be delightful, "History" is still on the side of rationalism, technology, and industry—i.e., Europe. Negro culture thus becomes appropriated as a diversion, as a realm for momentary relaxation. "I will be told," says Fanon, that "now and then when we are worn out by our lives in big buildings, we will turn to you as we do to our children—to the innocent, the ingenuous, the spontaneous" (BSWM 132).

The unkindest cut comes from white progressives who also claim that history is on the side of European society, but now instantiated in the industrial proletariat as revolutionary class. Here, Sartre is Fanon's chief culprit. For just as he rationalistically adduced the classless society as the solution to the Jewish Question, so Sartre argued in *Black Orpheus* ([1948] 1976), his preface to Senghor's anthology of black poetry, that *négritude* as a celebration of difference would, in time, dissolve itself in the world revolutionary movement that transcends both class and race. "In fact," Sartre wrote, "*négritude* appears as the minor term of a dialectical progression . . . it is intended to prepare the synthesis or realization of the human in a society without races. Thus *négritude* is the root of its own destruction" (cited by Fanon, BSWM 133).

Fanon's objection is not that Sartre is in error in asserting that *négritude* is a transitional movement. Sartre's mistake, in fact, is to have told the truth! But the short-circuiting, objectifying, disembodied truth of a *pensée de survol*, which ruptures immediate, lived experience. Using Sartre the phenomenologist to criticize Sartre the rationalist, Fanon points out that "a consciousness committed to experience *is* ignorant, *has to be ignorant*, of the essences and the determinations of its being" (BSWM 134; emphases added). In explaining the transitional social and historical function of *négritude*, Sartre has destroyed its vitality. By dissecting it in the cold light of reason, he "has destroyed black zeal" (BSWM 135). And, Fanon adds, "I needed to lose myself completely in négritude . . . I *needed* not to know . . . at the very moment when I was trying to grasp my own being, Sartre, who remained The Other, gave me a name and thus shattered my last illusion" (BSWM 135 and 137).

Is Fanon saying here that Sartre, as a white man, does not have the right to locate *négritude* in its historical place? I think not. Unlike many later advocates of identity politics, Fanon is not claiming that a person who has not suffered white racist oppression *cannot* understand the meaning of *négritude*. His complaint is exactly the reverse! It is rather that Sartre, who could and should have understood, was guilty of an individual failure of judgment. Sartre made a "mistake," he says. He "had *forgotten* that the Negro suffers in his body quite differently from the white man" (BSWM 134; emphasis added). Sartre failed to consider the effects on others of his utterance, that its meaning would be different for those whose lived, embodied experience was so different from his own. Yet once having given *négritude* its full existential weight, Fanon also seeks for a way beyond its celebration of black difference. Here, he too shifts to an abstract and universalistic key.

In the final chapter of *Black Skin, White Masks*, Fanon develops his own vision of a transition beyond *négritude*. Paradoxically, however, he ends up in as abstract a position as Sartre's. Indeed, his position owes much to Sartre at his most rationalistic. "I have no wish to be the victim of the *Fraud* of a black world," Fanon writes. "I am not a prisoner of history. I should not seek there for the meaning of my destiny" (BSWM 229). He thus criticizes as irrelevant *négritude*'s search for black identity through the retrieval of great African cultures of the past. He also argues that resentment over past injuries and demands for reparations are misguided, for they represent a reorientation toward the past whereas freedom is always oriented toward the future (BSWM 230–31).

Unfortunately, in making these arguments, Fanon draws on the most radically transcendental conception of freedom that Sartre developed in *Being and Nothingness*. He interprets the claim that in authentic freedom "I am my own foundation" (BSWM 231) to mean that one can, after all, through sheer commitment, leap beyond the bounds of historical situation or the present meaning of one's skin color. At the level of authentic freedom, he writes,

> The Negro is not. Any more than the white man. Both must turn their backs on the inhuman voices which were those of their respective ancestors in order that authentic communication be possible. . . . Superiority? Inferiority? Why not the simple attempt to touch the other, to feel the other, to explain the other to myself? (BSWM 231)

Why not, indeed? Earlier in the book Fanon had given us cogent reasons why this is not possible. But, like Sartre, he ends by undermining his own argument. If *négritude*—that "white artifact," that necessary "illusion"—has such a profound existential significance that Sartre should not have cut it short in the name of the universal historical dialectic, then Fanon should not abandon it here in the name of an abstract, universal freedom beyond situation.

Why, we might ask, do Fanon and Sartre both leap so abruptly from nuanced analysis of lived experience to such abstract universalism? What both Sartre and Fanon lack, at least in the works I have been discussing, is an intervening level of analysis that focuses on *mediations*. They lack tools with which to theorize the interconnections between the realm of existential experience, in which the dynamics of non-recognition and self-affirmation are played out, and the broader world of processes and structures, in which the particular dynamics each describes are embedded. Both still lack a conception (and a politics) of mediations that can enable them to examine the articulations between the experiential dimensions of oppression and resistance and the wider social processes in which they are enmeshed.

Later on Fanon, like Sartre in the *Critique*, came to address this problem more fully. As he became deeply involved in the Algerian liberation struggle during the last years of his short life, Fanon came to argue that freedom cannot be sought in the realm of interpersonal affirmation and recognition alone. Thus, in *The Wretched of the Earth*, he did not abandon his earlier concern with the politics of recognition so much as argue that it could only be realized (at least in colonial situations) through engagement in national liberation struggle and the development of a "national culture."

Fanon's specific prescriptions—including the need for armed struggle to bring about territorial liberation and an end to the colonial state—are of course time- and place-specific. They refer to situations where a white minority regime was dominating and exploiting a non-white, "native" majority. Thus, the enthusiastic response they elicited notwithstanding, they were never directly applicable to the situation of ethnic or racial minorities in white-majority societies such as the United States. Nor were they directly relevant to feminism, whose goal is to reconfigure gender relations rather than to establish a female nation. But his message, in *The Wretched of the Earth*, that the affirmation of identity can be liberating *only* in the context of a struggle also to transform wider material and institutional forms of oppression remains profoundly relevant today.

Pre-identarian forms of the politics of recognition passed relatively directly into demands and struggles for the extension of specific rights in the public sphere. Political and civil rights, including the franchise, were demanded and granted on the basis of universal humanist claims. They have, in considerable measure, been extended in the United States to groups other than its original white, male, Christian, and often property-owning citizenry. But, as Sartre contended, and as proponents of identity politics rightly continue to argue, formal equality in the public sphere also tends to obscure and even legitimize other forms of oppression that involve the non-recognition of different others. Thus, in spite of its difficulties, the demand for positive recognition on the basis of differences is, for now and the foreseeable future, necessary. No, we have not yet gone "beyond" identity politics.

However, identity politics continues to be haunted by difficulties we have encountered in the early works of Sartre and Fanon. These concern the integration of a politics that affirms difference and demands its recognition into a wider politics, one more oriented to the traditional public sphere, to the state, and to what Fraser calls redistribution. What, we must ask, are the structures, processes, and practices that mediate between the realm of personal existential experience, in which the dynamics of recognition and non-recognition are played out, and those systemic aspects of politics and history that are not reducible to individual experience and expression?

What is at issue here is the relationship between what is personal, or at most interpersonal, and what is institutional or structural. As I have already suggested, power does not rest on objectification alone. It follows that resistance to objectification, the demand to be recognized and respected in and for one's difference, is not sufficient. To affirm, express, or celebrate one's identity is, as Fanon said, psychologically empowering and thus necessary. It is also, as Sartre said, a desirable moral stance. But to affirm one's identity is not to effect significant structural change.

A liberatory politics must also open up possibilities for the redistribution of material resources and help to increase the capacity of oppressed groups better to resist and/or control the institutions of power in society. But identity politics does not automatically do either of these. For example, the demands for psychological "restitution" that Anzaldúa makes do not automatically or unproblematically extend to include a struggle for material restitution. Nor does redistribution unproblematically follow from recognition. Spanish-language teaching in schools may help to give Chicana/o children access to, and pride in, their own culture, but we should not assume that it will open up wider employment possibilities or more equitable access to formal political power for them. Cultural recognition and redistribution do not necessarily go hand in hand, and they may even at times be antagonistic goals, as Fraser suggests.

To determine when this is the case is primarily a practical, rather than a theoretical, question. But what is certain is that for the two kinds of struggle mutually to reinforce and support each other, attention must be paid both to affirming existential experience and to more explicit agendas for redistribution. What is also certain is that to struggle against those wider social structures and institutions that perpetuate both non-recognition and material inequity, coalitions that can "bridge" differences, and forms of solidarity, are necessary. Groups that espouse particularistic identity politics must also actively seek areas of common ground with others. Thus, as I argue in the next chapter, it is necessary for such groups to seek ways to move beyond the potential divisiveness of an epistemology of provenance, even as they rightly continue to insist on the specificity of their own experiences.

4   Identity Politics and Dialectical Reason: Beyond an Epistemology of Provenance

Second-wave feminism has undergone two marked re-orientations since the late 1970s. The first was a shift away from its earlier demands to minimize distinctions between the sexes and toward a celebratory emphasis on women's differences from men. In gynocentric (or what I will call global-difference) feminism, modern Western culture as a whole has been depicted as fundamentally male in its individualism, competitiveness, and desire to dominate nature; in its denigration of emotions and the body; and in its faith in abstract, disembodied reason. By contrast, women—all women—have been celebrated for their connectedness with nature and with others (particularly through their maternal capacities), for their acceptance of the body, for their more concrete and embodied ways of knowing and judging.

In the second shift, however, the celebration of women's difference has been turned back against global-difference feminism, as critics have pointed out that the grandiose and universal claims made about women's differences from men have obscured profound, and frequently oppressive, differences among women. Just as "humanist" voices, calling since the seventeenth century for the liberation of humankind, have turned out frequently to be speaking uniquely for certain male parts of humankind, so feminist voices turn out to have been speaking for only certain parts of womankind—primarily for white, middle-class, and heterosexual women. They have thus masked power relations and helped perpetuate divergences of interest among different kinds of women. Not only do women have radically different experiences

An earlier version of this chapter appeared in *Hypatia: A Journal of Feminist Philosophy* 10, no. 2 (spring 1995): 1–22. Reprinted by permission of Indiana University Press.

from each other and speak with many different voices, but they may also have widely divergent, or even directly conflicting, interests. In short, there has been a shift toward what I will here call multiple-difference feminism. Such a feminism (as discussed in the previous chapter) emphasizes the multiple identities that often divide women, tending to emphasize identity-based and particularistic struggles.[1]

The double turn toward difference—the recognition of difference as occurring not only between men and women but also among women themselves—has marked an important advance in feminism. Above all, the ideological nature of bold universalistic claims, be they about the nature of "the human self" or "woman's self," about freedom, justice, truth, or progress, has been demonstrated with a thoroughness never dreamed of by Marx. It is not just each ruling class, as Marx said, which has "to represent its interest as the common interest of all members of society" ([1846] 1978, 174). Similarly, those who come to dominate by virtue of sex, race, or other characteristics will tend to represent their own interests in universalistic forms, thus masking oppression and silencing those who are subordinate. The valid goals of much recent multiple-difference feminism, particularly forms of feminist identity politics, have been to expose such ideological maskings within the women's movement itself and to begin to create spaces of various kinds in which the previously silenced can speak.

I have argued that identity politics is still important for feminism. It functions both as a critique of existing power relations and as a project of self-empowerment for marginalized categories of women. Against the hegemonic claims and norms of feminism as a predominantly white, middle-class, and heterosexual movement, multiple-difference identity politics seeks to affirm the validity, indeed even the superiority, of different ways of being and knowing. Black feminist identity politics, along with that of other women of color, has functioned as a particularly powerful attack on global-difference feminism. As Audre Lorde pithily responded to Mary Daly's account of the universality of women's oppression: "The oppression of women knows no ethnic nor racial boundaries, true, but that does not mean it is identical within those differences . . . beyond sisterhood is still racism" (1984, 70).

As a political critique of global-difference feminism, identity politics is indubitably valid. Since women are never women *tout court* but are always situated also as members of a class, a race, an ethnic grouping, a sexual orientation, an age grade, and so on, it is dangerous to assume that the inequities

---

1. Many advocates of multiple-difference feminism have rightly urged that differences among women should be conceived not as discrete and additive but as multiplicative in their effects: "The modifier 'multiple' refers not only to several, simultaneous oppressions but to the multiplicative relationships among them as well" (King 1988, 270).

and power relations that pertain to those other dimensions of social situation will not play out also among women. However, in its attempts to refute falsely universalizing knowledge claims, identity politics sometimes tends to replicate those aspects of global-difference feminism that have stressed the radical incommunicability of women's experience to men. Identity politics tends toward an excessive particularization and partitioning of knowledge, but now along the lines of race or ethnicity, for example, as well as gender. For such experience-based accounts of knowledge posit, be it explicitly or implicitly, what I have referred to as an epistemology of provenance. That is, they presuppose that knowledge arises from an experiential basis that is so fundamentally group-specific that others, who are outside the group and who lack its immediate experiences, cannot share that knowledge. As a corollary, the argument is generally made that outsiders have no basis from which they can legitimately evaluate the group's claims about its knowledge, or those political or moral positions that it takes on the basis of them. In short, only those who live a particular reality can know about it, and only they have the right to speak about it.

Many groups that practice identity politics also advocate a politics of alliance or coalition with others, invoking the ideal of "bridging" differences once they are recognized and respected.[2] Commitments to coalition work, to alliance, to solidarity across groups are vital for any effective progressive politics. However, as previously suggested, the implications of an epistemology of provenance, when consistently pursued, threaten to undercut coalition politics or other forms of solidarity among women. The unintended end point of an epistemology of provenance can be an acute and politically debilitating subjectivism, which belies the possibility of communication and common action across differences. It is this apparent contradiction within feminist identity politics (and other forms of multiple-difference feminism) that concerns me here.

Some identity politics has tended to assert global identities for a particular kind of women, arguing for example that all black women share common culture, experience, and ways of knowing (Brown 1988; P. H. Collins 1990). However, such assertions tend in turn to be challenged as falsely universalistic, and there is thus a tendency for identities increasingly to subdivide. Since nobody can avoid living a plurality of identities, one central dynamic of identity politics is to move toward ever-shrinking identity groups, for

2. For early feminist statements linking identity politics and coalition building, see Reagon 1983; the Combahee River Collective 1983; and many of the writings in Moraga and Anzaldúa 1983. For more recent statements, see essays in Anzaldúa 1990b; Albrecht and Brewer 1990; and Phelan 1989 and 1994. Some advocates of feminist identity politics have taken more separatist positions, but these are not my concern here.

which the logical terminus would have to be not merely subjectivism but solipsism, since no one person's set of experiences is identical to another's.

An alternative tendency is to shift toward a postmodern emphasis on the fragmentary and unstable nature of the self. Although such postmodern notions capture some of the complexities of multiple identity well, they frequently tend to beg the question of how to characterize a "self" that experiences itself as multiple and unstable. Recapitulating the tendency I have previously noted in French postmodern theory tacitly to attribute agency to the subject, postmodern feminist celebrations of multiple identities and mobile subjectivities often implicitly posit what we could call a "transcendental" subject. They presuppose an autonomous subject that is the site of a disembodied and self-reflexive meta-experience of its own existence, one that can contemplate and consciously shift among its multiple identities. For example, Gloria Anzaldúa's statement, "This morning when I got up I looked in the mirror to see who I was (my identity keeps changing)" (1990a, 216), tacitly posits a transcendental "self" that can observe (in the mirror) how its various identities come and go.

Likewise, Chela Sandoval's characterization of a mobile "oppositional consciousness" also tacitly posits a transcendental self, one that consciously decides when to shift its identity. She characterizes the "differential consciousness" of U.S. Third World feminists as enabling them deliberately to switch among identities, "*self-consciously* choosing and adopting the ideological forms best suited to push against [power's] configurations." Using the analogy of the driver of a car, she continues: "As the clutch of a car provides the driver the ability to shift gears, differential consciousness permits the practitioner *to choose* tactical positions, that is, *to self-consciously* break and reform ties to ideology" (1991, 15; emphases added). Such a model of the self presupposes not only a transcendental but also a neo-Cartesian consciousness! For this is a consciousness that contemplates its options and chooses when and how to switch among the identities that it can, apparently, cast on and off at will. The relationship of this transcendental self to its multiple and fragmentary identities remains rather under-explicated in treatments such as Sandoval's and Anzaldúa's. But such accounts seem to have profoundly solipsistic implications, insofar as this transcendental self is depicted as detached from, and as the authoritative negotiator or mediator among, its multiple identities.

Given its solipsistic tendencies identity politics, postmodern or otherwise, threatens to leave us without the possibility that there can be sufficient common knowledge, or that we can form the kinds of collective judgments necessary, for the development of broadly organized feminist coalition politics. To exemplify: some consistent end points of an epistemology of provenance would be to say that those who do not experience domestic violence, or incest, or rape, or unwanted pregnancy, or even unequal pay have no experiential basis from which to evaluate, and so no right to speak about, such issues. Statements such as these, which I think very few feminists would want to endorse, are not of a different propositional order than the statements, commonly heard today, to the effect that white women have no basis or right to discuss the issue of sexism in black heterosexual relationships, or that Western women should take no position on clitoridectomy in Africa or the Middle East.

The challenge identity politics now presents us with is this: to find a way to recognize the power-laden dangers of global-difference feminism and to insist on the importance of the existence of radical experiential differences among women, but to do so without embracing an epistemology of provenance. The problem is to find a way of acknowledging the claims to experiential knowledge of particular identity groups, without thereby wholly denying the possibility that there is a more general basis for knowledge, or that more general visions and projects of emancipation are possible.

To suggest a way out of this impasse I think it helpful to build on some of the insights of feminist standpoint theory, and thus to focus more sharply on how experience and knowledge emerge in and from social practices. In the next section I discuss the work of two theorists, Nancy Hartsock and Donna Haraway. To develop their insights further, I then turn to a later work of Sartre, *Critique of Dialectical Reason.* I argue that his account of practical action, and of the forms of situated knowledge to which it gives rise, enables us to see that there are profound connections between our own particular knowledges and those of more distant, or even antagonistic, others.

LIKE identity politics, feminist standpoint theory, for which the work of Nancy Hartsock (1985) remains paradigmatic, insists on the epistemological validity of the knowledge of a particular oppressed group: women. But it does so while also concerning itself with a *general* human emancipatory project and with the formulation of claims about the world that are accessible and may be seen as valid by others outside the practices and experiences of that particular oppressed group.

Hartsock adopts aspects of a humanistic reading of Marxist epistemology for feminism. Marx had argued that dominant bourgeois accounts of reality are, as Hartsock phrases it, "partial and perverse" (1985, 232) and that the proletariat, through theoretical and political practice, may rid itself of these accounts and formulate an epistemological standpoint of its own. The latter not merely is different from the dominant one but also has an emancipatory potential. In formulating this standpoint, the proletariat may make itself a "universal class," the vehicle not only of its own emancipation but of human emancipation more generally. Similarly, Hartsock argues, women may achieve a feminist standpoint that not only functions as an alternative to, or

a critique of, "abstract masculinity" but which would also involve "[g]ener-
alizing the human possibilities present in the life activity of women to the
social system as a whole" and which would "raise, for the first time in
human history, the possibility of a fully human community, a community
structured by a variety of connections rather than separation and opposition"
(1985, 247).

Hartsock argues that the possibility for the development of such a feminist standpoint is given not in women's subjective experiences per se but
rather in their specific forms of life activity, or practices, within the social
division of labor. She is also careful to distinguish a *feminist* standpoint from
the experiences of women in general, for the latter frequently tend to be
shaped by dominant male views and values, whose hegemony can be exposed
only through a critical and self-critical feminist project. Thus a feminist
standpoint involves more than recognizing and valorizing the *experiences* of
oppression, otherness, marginalization, of which identity politics also speaks.
It involves a work of critical reflection on that experience and on the *social
practices* out of which it is born. It aims to develop a critique of dominant
knowledge claims and an alternative account of social reality on which a
project of *general* human emancipation might be based.

Hartsock's standpoint theory, then, attempts both to show how knowledge emerges from specific *practice*-based experiences and to connect it with
a broader epistemological universe and political agenda. But there are also
difficulties with her work. As critics have pointed out, Hartsock still tends
to operate with an overly global conception of women's practice and experience, and thus to obscure differences and power inequities among women.
As Marlee Kline puts it,

> Hartsock opens herself to the same charge of false generalization that
> she has raised against Marx from the perspective of gender. A feminist
> standpoint, when viewed from perspectives attentive to considerations
> of race, class, ethnicity, religion, sexual identity, physical ability, etc.,
> appears limited and essentialist in the same way the proletariat [*sic*] per-
> spective appears limited from a perspective attentive to considerations
> of gender. (1989, 38)

However, differences among women are not necessarily, or inevitably, excluded from the central concerns of standpoint theory.[3] Because it begins
from the social division of labor and from accounts of social reality that
emerge from different social practices, there is nothing intrinsic to the the-

---

3. Thus I disagree also with Sandra Harding's claim that "the importance of differences in women's politics . . . appears to be excluded from the central concerns of standpoint theories" (1986, 164). See also on this issue Alarcón 1990.

ory that would preclude developing an account of a multiplicity of women's standpoints, which would perhaps overlap in some aspects and diverge radically in others. Thus Hartsock's work can be developed in ways she did not initially undertake herself in order to elaborate an account of multiple feminist standpoints that are neither identical nor yet wholly distinct.[4] As Donna Haraway writes: in her article, "Situated Knowledges: The Science Question in Feminism and the Privilege of Partial Perspective": "There is no single feminist standpoint. . . . But the feminist standpoint theorists' goal of an epistemology and politics of engaged, accountable positioning remains eminently potent. The goal is better accounts of the world, that is 'science' " (1991, 196).

In this significant article, to which I now turn, Haraway filters standpoint theory through certain postmodern sensibilities to argue for the importance of acknowledging a multiplicity of different epistemological locations for a non-dominative feminism. However, she also recognizes the need for objective knowledge—by which I take her to mean knowledge that is at least partially shareable, publicly communicable, and transmissible, about a world that is in some sense "real." Her question, which is also mine, is whether both a respect for different and divergent knowledges *and* some kind of account of objective—thus shareable—knowledge can be sustained at the same time.

Haraway suggests that they can both be sustained if we reconceptualize our notions of objectivity to take account, as feminism (and I would add existential phenomenology) has taught us we should, of the embodied and situated nature of all knowing subjects. Objectivity is not to be confused with the traditional "god-trick" of "promising vision from everywhere and nowhere equally and fully" (1991, 191). Objectivity is not about detachment, she insists, but must emerge through the recognition of "particular and specific embodiment" and is "definitely not about the false vision promising transcendence of all limits and responsibility" (190). Thus, to privilege embodied standpoints is not to embrace relativism or subjectivism. On the contrary, Haraway suggests, "The alternative to relativism is partial, locatable critical knowledges sustaining the possibility of webs of connections called solidarity in politics and shared conversations in epistemology" (191).

4. In her recent essay "The Feminist Standpoint Revisited," Hartsock begins this undertaking herself. "We need to sort out who we really are," she writes, "and in the process dissolve this false 'we' into its real multiplicity and variety. Out of this multiplicity, it should be possible to build an account of social relations as seen from below. . . . I believe that although the phenomenological specifics differ, there are a number of connections to be made and similarities to be seen in the epistemologies contained in the experience of dominated groups. In particular, I want to suggest that white feminists should learn the possibility of solidarity from U.S. feminists of color and postcolonial subjects" (1998, 240–41).

Haraway takes vision as a general metaphor for knowing. She argues that we do not need to conceive of vision as the disembodied and objectifying male gaze, but we can instead use it to remind ourselves that knowing selves are always embodied and that our seeing/knowing is thus always located, partial, and perspectival. But Haraway, like Hartsock, is at pains to stress that not all perspectives are equally valid in the struggle against domination: simply "being" of an oppressed or marginalized group does not automatically give one a privilege in formulating truth. Rather, she argues, "not just any partial perspective will do. . . . We are also bound to seek perspective from those points of view, which can never be known in advance, which promise something quite extraordinary, that is, knowledge potent for worlds less organized by axes of domination" (192). However, such liberatory (my word) "partial perspectives" are not those of a simple identity politics, in which unproblematized, or self-identical, selves claim to present their own direct experience as reality: "Identity, including self-identity, does not produce science; critical positioning does, that is objectivity" (193).

For Haraway, the distinction between asserting an identity and assuming a *critical* positioning involves an awareness of the *mediated* nature of all experience and of the ways that power differentials permeate those mediations. "Vision is *always* a question of the power to see" (192). This power is not equitably distributed across humanity but depends on our differential access to various prostheses or optical technologies: "Vision requires instruments of vision; an optics is a politics of positioning. Instruments of vision mediate standpoints; there is no immediate vision from the standpoints of the subjugated" (193). Thus, she suggests, there is no such thing as "innocent 'identity' politics"—identity politics too is always implicated in power.

This far, I find Haraway's argument helpful. But important questions remain concerning the mediated nature of knowing, to which her answers are less than adequate. Using vision as the metaphor for knowing has the advantage of emphasizing the embodied and situated nature of knowledge; and stressing that vision is never direct, but always mediated by "instruments of vision," has the virtue of pointing out that knowledge is never a simple "given" but is structured—and power-differentiated—by human artifice. But vision per se is also a limited metaphor for knowing, implying that knowledge is rather passively received through the senses and will simply vary according to where we happen to be situated. Thus, to make her metaphor work, Haraway has additionally to introduce the notions of optics and of the *politics* of the production and differential distribution of instruments of vision. But in so doing she actually intimates that we need another account of knowing: one based on social practices. For the questions we must ask about situated knowledges must surely concern the following: How do people come to be situated such that they have different "partial perspectives"? Who makes the instruments of "vision" that enable them differentially to see/ know the world? Who has which instruments, and who controls access to their use and how? We need, in short, a fuller account of the *politics* of the production and distribution of seeing/knowing technologies than can be derived from vision as the primary metaphor for knowing. A theory that links the emergence of knowledges more directly to practice is called for.

Another difficulty concerns the way Haraway characterizes the power-saturated technologies upon which situated knowledges depend. Mixing her metaphors with blithe abandon, Haraway suggests that the instruments, or technologies, of vision are above all semiotic. She says that what she calls a "semiotic-material technology" links "meanings and bodies" (192). But it is never clear in her account what justifies the hyphenated term "semiotic-material." Semiosis could be described as a technology and as involving a "skilled practice" (194). But in what sense is this technology, or practice, "material"? Because it emerges from and affects bodies? Because it uses material analogues of such manufactured objects as the eyeglasses, microscopes, telescopes, or cameras of optics? We are not told. Haraway's insistence on the *materially* mediated nature of all knowledge, including knowledge of the located self, is of prime importance. But her conceptions of the material and of human-material interactions remain far too sketchy. I will turn shortly to Sartre's description of the emergence of the human world as a multiplicity of "practico-inert" totalizations of practices for a way of clarifying and developing her insights.

Although Haraway claims that from "partial perspectives" and "partial connections" there can emerge "webs of connection" and "shared conversations"—that is, forms of objective or partially shareable knowledge—her account never makes clear *how* it is that such connections and communications across difference are possible. What is it that is shared among the viewers of different "partial perspectives"? If we are able to make partial connections, what precisely are the connecting "parts," and why and how do they do the connecting? What needs to be explained is exactly what Haraway takes for granted here: "We do need an earth-wide network of connections, including the ability partially to translate knowledges among very different— and power-differentiated—communities," she writes (187). I fully agree. But what is it that enables knowledges to be even "partially" translatable across radical differences? What enables exit from the solipsistic import of an epistemology of provenance? Haraway points toward a couple of answers but develops neither very far. One is to do with the nature of selves; the other with the kinds of shared, or overlapping, milieux in which selves exist.

The first answer she suggests is that if we cease to view the self as unitary and stable, realizing that it is instead "split and contradictory," we will see that such a split self can join easily with other such selves. For "the knowing self is partial in all its guises, never finished, whole, simply there and original; it is always constructed and stitched together imperfectly, and *therefore* able to join with another, to see together without claiming to be another. Here is the promise of objectivity" (Haraway 1991, 193). It is an attractive metaphor: our rough edges, our seams, our openings perhaps, are the places where we can join with other and different selves. But, we must surely ask, *who* does the stitching together of this self? Is the self a kind of transcendental seamstress who sews her own parts together? If so, this self is perhaps more originative and cohesive than Haraway wants to admit; perhaps the self can even be conceived as a "project," as Sartre would put it.

Alternatively, and with a certain further mixing of metaphors, the stitching together might be construed as an operation taking place on the self from without: automated sewing machines, which can stitch us together, are parts of the "semiotic-material technology." Put less metaphorically, Haraway's second suggestion seems to be that what connects disparate knowing selves is, indeed, the existence of some common dimensions to their otherwise divided lives. Our experiences are never as radically distinct as either identity politics or postmodern notions of fracturing would imply because there are, after all, some elements common to all human lives. These elements make the communicability of experiences across difference possible. Semiosis is one of these elements, but Haraway also gestures to others. She suggests at one point that gender is "a field of structured and structuring difference" (195). Feminism, she also tells us, must critically position itself in "inhomogeneous gendered social space" (195). But to talk of "a field" (even one of "difference") and of "social space" (even if it is "inhomogeneous") is to posit a partially continuous social world that mediates among differently located selves. Such a world is here tacitly assumed to underwrite through the presence of common externalities our ability to communicate.

In order for our partial perspectives to enable situated objectivity to emerge, they must be formulated from our different locations within something that is continuous and in which all of us are embedded, be it field, social space, discourse, or another medium. "Webs of connections" can arise across our diverse standpoints and identities *only* if the world mediates among them in some very general ways. Haraway implies as much, but her discomfort with anything that might be seen as universalizing discourse leaves her reluctant overtly to explore how such general mediations might be constituted. Her project thus remains suspended in mid-air.

Haraway points us in the right direction. She is correct to insist that we need to seek ways of formulating objective knowledges that originate from, rather than obscure, differences and multiple standpoints and which acknowledge embodiment and location. But she offers us neither a sufficient account of situated selves nor a sufficient account of how it is that the world mediates among them.

〜

ENTER the later Jean-Paul Sartre. In the *Critique of Dialectical Reason* ([1960] 1976; cited hereafter as CDR), Sartre develops a theory of situated, practical subjectivity that speaks to the difficulties raised by an epistemology of provenance. What makes this theory of particular interest for feminism is Sartre's concern to defend particularity and difference while still exploring, at least as a heuristic device, the universalistic emancipatory vision of Marx. One of Sartre's main protagonists in the *Critique* is the "orthodox" Soviet-style Marxism that the French Communist Party still espoused in the late 1950s. Such a Marxism, Sartre charged in *Search for a Method*, "is identical with Terror in its inflexible refusal to *differentiate*; its goal is total assimilation at the least possible effort. The aim is not to integrate what is different as such, while preserving for it a relative autonomy, but rather to suppress it" ([1960] 1968, 48).[5] Against such a totalitarian Marxism, Sartre seeks to elaborate a Marxist theory that would privilege differences while still exploring the possibility of a project of worldwide human emancipation.

To emphasize Sartre's sensitivity to difference is not, however, to deny that the *Critique* is still deeply flawed by sexism—it is! In *Search for a Method*, Sartre criticizes orthodox Marxism for failing to recognize the importance of childhood: "Today's Marxists are concerned only with adults. Reading them, one would believe that we are born at the age when we earn our first wages," he writes ([1960] 1968, 62). But, alas, the very same criticism can be leveled against the *Critique*, where both childhood and the various kinds of praxis involved in giving birth to and bringing up children are ignored. Moreover, those rare mentions of sexuality in the many hundreds of pages of the *Critique* treat it almost exclusively from a masculine point of view.[6] Even so, it is useful selectively to appropriate elements of the *Critique*. For my purposes, Sartre's criticism of what he calls "analytic reason" and his development of an account of what, by contrast, he calls "dialectical reason"—a reason that recognizes itself to be situated and to be able to grasp reality only from its own location—are particularly relevant.

Analytic reason (or "positivist reason," as Sartre also sometimes calls it) is the kind of reason that has also been subject to extensive feminist critique, as disembodied, specular, and integral to the domination of women and nature (for example, Lloyd 1984; Harding 1986, 1991; Irigaray 1985). It has also been extensively subjected to postmodern critique as "Enlightenment" thought. It lays the world out as a set of objects for contemplation and dispassionate investigation. Analytic reason thus presupposes a knowing sub-

5. Sartre's *Search for a Method* ([1960] 1968) forms the prefatory essay to the original French version of the *Critique*, but it is published as a separate essay in English.
6. The most extended discussion of sexuality is to be found in the second volume of the *Critique* (Sartre [1985] 1991, 255ff.), published only posthumously.

ject who stands, transcendent, outside the domain he or she investigates. It engages, in short, in Haraway's "god-trick," positing the theorist as the all-seeing spectator, the great panorama of History laid out at his (or her) feet. Against such a conception Sartre had written to Camus some years earlier that "we are up to our eyebrows" in history ([1952] 1965, 77). In short, our vision is always from within or from under, never from without or above. When analytic reason purports to study the world as if the theorist were not immersed in it, it functions ideologically: it serves to mask forms of oppression and exploitation by making the present human condition appear "natural" and thus not amenable to alteration (CDR 820).

Against analytic reason, particularly as it has been used by orthodox Marxists to give a "scientific" account of the "laws of motion" of society, Sartre sets out to develop his account of "dialectical reason." Dialectical reason begins from the situation of an embodied and practically engaged self. It involves an investigation of the human world for which an individual situation is the point of departure. It must begin from "the *life*, the objective being, of the investigator, in the world of Others" (CDR 51).

But what then, we must ask, prevents Sartre also from slipping into relativism and presenting an account of fragmented and incommunicable situated knowledges? If each of us comes to know the world and to theorize about it from our own particular historical and social location, do we not risk embarking, as with identity politics, on an epistemology of provenance that offers solipsism as its worst-case terminus? For Sartre, the answer to such a question is (but only after prolonged consideration) "no." Such particular, situated knowledges are, in principle, communicable and intelligible to others. But this possibility has to be systematically demonstrated, rather than, as in Haraway's work, rhetorically asserted.

The demonstration begins for Sartre from the examination of the purposive and transformative human activity that he calls *praxis*. For (as he and Beauvoir both argued previously) what we become is the outcome of our actions and not of pre-given attributes or essences. Sartre defines praxis as "an organising project which transcends material conditions towards an end" (CDR 734). In its most abstract form, that end is survival, and praxis arises from our existence as organic entities. For unless we can sustain ourselves as living organisms, all other questions about life become moot. As a species, human beings are required to engage in forms of praxis in order to transform nature into those means of survival that will ward off the constant threat of death that assails us.

In its more concrete and complex manifestations, however, this kind of activity generates not only a world of products (of use-values in Marxian terminology) but also many less tangible phenomena. These include aspects of culture, forms of social organization, and even language. In insisting on praxis as the starting point for analyzing human society, Sartre differs significantly from postmodern thinkers who grant constituting primacy to discourse. He also differs from those advocates of identity politics who generally begin not from practices but from shared subjective experiences of denied recognition in order to construct an affirmative identity. For Sartre, it is praxis that constitutes and reconstitutes social identities. He would thus share Chandra Mohanty's critique of an "osmosis theory" of feminism, in which simply *being* a woman is assumed to make one a feminist (1992).

If an adequate social theory must start from what it is that human beings *do* in the world, this has implications for epistemology. Thus Sartre also argues that the specific characteristics of human practical activity must be the point of departure in accounting for the possibility of human knowledge and reason. It is in *doing* (rather than in seeing, or contemplating) that we come (at least initially) to generate forms of knowledge. An adequate theory of situated knowledges, Sartre teaches us, cannot be developed primarily from Haraway's metaphor of vision. For although vision represents a way of accessing the world, it is not by itself a means to transform it.

Although Sartre's examples of praxis tend to involve primarily male actors, the structure of praxis as he describes it is present also in uniquely female forms of activity. Since becoming pregnant, giving birth, and nursing are human actions, and not merely natural functions, they are not fundamentally different in structure from what Sartre calls praxis. Thus Sara Ruddick has argued, in a position highly compatible with Sartre's, that what she refers to as "maternal work" (a set of practices that begins with childbirth and extends to the preservation, nurturance, and socialization of children) gives rise to its own kinds of knowledge and forms of thinking (1989).[7]

Sartre begins his account of dialectical reason at the most abstract point possible, with praxis as an—apparently—purely individual undertaking. However, this individualistic starting point is heuristically chosen in order to be able to demonstrate that human action is in fact social through and through. "Critical investigation," as Sartre also calls dialectical reason, "will set out from . . . the individual fulfilling himself [*sic*] in his abstract *praxis*, so as to rediscover, through deeper and deeper conditionings, the totality of his practical bonds with others and, thereby, the structures of the various practical multiplicities" (CDR 52).[8] Through what might initially appear a thoroughly subjectivist project, the study of one's own situated praxis, ever wider sets of social and historical processes may be made intelligible. It can

7. See also E. Martin 1987 and the essays "Pregnant Embodiment" and "Breasted Experience" in Young 1990b for materials from which to construct a more extended argument that pregnancy, childbirth, and nursing are forms of praxis.
8. Sartre's style in this work (as elsewhere) is consistently masculinist. The English translation of the book, which I use here and in subsequent quotations, has not attempted to render it more gender neutral and neither have I.

be demonstrated that "there is no such thing as an isolated individual" (CDR 677) and that it is possible for us (whoever "we" may be) to understand and communicate about kinds of human praxis radically different from our own.

Examining such abstract, individual praxis, Sartre identifies two sets of analytically distinct but always mutually implicated (indeed dialectical) properties that together account for the fact that praxis is always social. These sets of properties also justify the claim that our situated knowledges can encompass realities that extend beyond the scope of our own direct experience. First, individual abstract praxis comes to discover that it is connected to that of others "in exteriority," through the mediations of what Sartre calls "the practical material field" or the "milieu of action." Second, individual praxis involves "interior" qualities. It possesses a fundamental intelligibility to others because it is intentional. This is to say, no praxis takes place without a purpose, without a project to transform something existing into a future possibility. As such *any* praxis has certain qualities that will enable us, *reciprocally*, to recognize it *as* human praxis. Thus, for example, even when one observes a "foreign" practice whose particular intent one does not understand, one will still understand that for its participants it has intent.

ANY praxis, Sartre argues, must involve a transformation of that segment of the world on which it acts, of its "practical material field." When it acts on the world, however, praxis also produces forms of what Sartre calls the "practico-inert." By the term practico-inert, Sartre refers to forms of worked matter, or externalized solidifications of praxis, that will in turn function to structure or constrain future praxis. These may then be encountered as forms of "exigency," which dictate as necessary certain forms of future praxis. For example, if one cooks and serves a meal, one will then be confronted by the practico-inert exigency that the dirty dishes must be cleared from the table and washed: further specific activities are called forth as a necessary consequence of the initial ones. If the dishes are not cleared, one will soon be unable to serve meals on that table, and if they are not washed disease is likely to ensue. Simply because it cannot take place without the mediation of the material world, praxis always produces something more and other than is intended and that we must then address—be it dirty dishes, waste products, changes in soil fertility through agriculture, or iatrogenic disease in medical practice.

The exigencies of the practico-inert are compounded by the fact that even what might initially appear to be isolated and individual praxis never is, so that altered *social* relationships may also emerge as complex forms of the practico-inert. As Sartre painstakingly demonstrates, individual praxis always takes place situated in a practical material field that mediates between it and other individual praxis. In the process, social entities of various kinds, what Sartre calls "practical ensembles," come into being. The term "practical ensemble" is the most general and neutral one Sartre can think of to cover the diverse kinds of social entities that human praxis can create, whether consciously or inadvertently. While some ensembles are consciously created (a sports team, an orchestra, a political party), others are not. Thus individuals can be members of ensembles even when they are not aware of it, when their praxes indirectly interact, or when they are linked together through the praxis of others.

Moreover, the field in which a multiplicity of praxes take place is generally shaped by scarcities of various kinds. These intensify the exigencies of praxis. Scarcity here does not only mean an objective insufficiency of material goods. It also encompasses the threat or fear thereof (as in the dynamic that can create hoarding) or less tangible lacks—of time, status, affection, or social recognition, for example. Thus a praxis such as child care also takes place in a field of scarcity.

Sartre gives the history of deforestation in China as a simple, paradigmatic example of the material mediation of individual praxis conditioned by scarcity: individual peasants, seeking to increase their arable land, cut down trees. But in the process they *collectively* denuded the land, inducing massive flooding of the Yangtze river and ending by reducing the total amount of arable land available. There was, says Sartre, "no joint undertaking." However, the transformation of each individual undertaking through its unanticipated mediation with other identical undertakings issued finally in a "joint result," which each encountered as the alienation (that is, the making other) of his or her own praxis (CDR 163–64).[9]

An analogue to Sartre's example would be the way that decisions made by individual women in the United States to enter forms of traditionally female employment, such as the "caring" occupations, result in the consolidation of a segmented labor market in which women tend increasingly to be trapped in low-status and poorly paid employment. The demands that fashion places on women offer another example: because employment and promotion (or being "attractive" to sexual partners) often hinge on appearing appropriately dressed, "being in fashion" ceases to be the personal choice of self-adornment it might initially appear and becomes the exigency repeatedly to spend time and money on one's appearance. Furthermore, women who do not participate in this high-level consumption are also conditioned by its exigencies. For being inappropriately dressed can have a significant bearing on one's ability to obtain and hold a job.[10] Here too, individual practices may give rise to

9. One can also think of many environmental examples closer to home that fit Sartre's model, from the dust bowl to the destruction of forests through acid rain.

10. Thus "micro-credit" schemes for poor women in the United States have found that the small loans they provide are often used to buy "interview clothes."

the "joint result," intended by none, of producing increased pressure on all women to conform to fashion norms, often with grave attendant costs.

What is important in each of these examples is that a social ensemble has come into being on the basis of a multiplicity of apparently separate, individual praxes. The Chinese peasants who produce deforestation constitute a practical ensemble even if they are not aware of it—and so do the myriad of Western women who individually rush out to buy the latest fashions from clothing outlets. As his account proceeds, Sartre's examples deal with practical ensembles that are unified by increasingly complex and socially constituted practical material fields, be they a number of people waiting at a stop for a bus that might not have seats for all of them, a collection of people listening to a propaganda broadcast, consumers linked by the market, or workers competing for jobs.

Insofar as such ensembles are constituted through the mediations of the external field, whose practico-inert exigencies react back upon the further praxis of each of its individual members, Sartre describes the relationship of the members of such ensembles to one another as one of "seriality." That is, they are passively and unintentionally unified, each a victim of the unchosen links that alter the outcome of the praxis of each. Sartre uses the term "collective" to describe such an ensemble. By contrast, he uses the term "group" to describe individuals who come together in a more purposive and direct manner, consciously cooperating to achieve shared goals. Thus, in his analysis of the history of the French working classes, he depicts a complex set of dynamics between workers as "collectives"—that is, individual workers who are serialized, atomized, isolated, and placed in competition with each other by the labor market—and workers as "groups." Only the latter involve organized and conscious nodes of resistance of various kinds (ranging from union activity, to spontaneous participation in brief acts of sabotage, to attempted revolution).

Sartre's account of collectives and of the serial relations of their members can help us to address issues about the identity of "women." As Iris Young has also suggested, Sartre's treatment of seriality offers a certain resolution to the vexed feminist debates about essentialism (for example, Fuss 1989; Schor and Weed 1994). For it gives us a means to think about "women" as a general category—still, I believe, a sine qua non of feminist politics—without attributing one fixed essence, identity, or set of attributes to all women. The term "women" rather denotes membership in collectives conditioned by such practico-inert structures as the sexual division of labor, compulsory heterosexuality, or the fashion industry. The identities of individual women, on this view, are constituted in large measure "in exteriority," as members of multiple collectives (for example, as objects of male sexual desire, as consumers of particular kinds of products, as members of ethnic collectives, as pregnant females, as workers in a segmented labor market).[11]

Moreover, the relationship between women and feminism (Hartsock's *feminist* standpoint, Haraway's *critical* positioning) can be clarified by using Sartre's distinction between collectives and groups. That is, we can distinguish between passively mediated ensembles that constitute "women" (series) and intentionally created, goal-directed ones (groups). The latter may form as a project to overcome seriality but frequently collapse back into it again (as did the suffrage movement after the vote was won). Indeed, one could write a fascinating history of feminist movements and their relationships to diverse ensembles of women by adapting Sartre's method of analyzing class as a shifting kaleidoscope of collectives and groups.

However, my main focus here is epistemological. For the fact that individual praxes are materially and serially mediated and are interconnected is a necessary pre-condition for the possibility that critical reflection about one's own praxis can extend to a wider comprehension of other social practices. This is what ensures that the situated knowledge of an individual or a particular ensemble is not self-referential and solipsistic. It is not, however, in itself a sufficient condition. We must thus move on to Sartre's account of other kinds of connections among praxes—those that are "interior" and "intentional."

Co-CONSTITUENT with its multiple "exterior" conditionings and mediations, praxis must also have what Sartre calls an "interior" aspect. Were it to have none, we would be dealing with a blind force of some kind that we simply would not recognize as human action. Although Sartre organizes his account of praxis and its interactions with the world through the *apparently* dualistic categories of interiority and exteriority, these represent mutually implicative, and not alternative, aspects of one and the same process. For Sartre, a human self creates itself and is created through an open-ended chain of in-

11. Young suggests that Sartre's account allows us to avoid using the concept of identity altogether: "Thinking about gender as seriality disconnects gender from identity," she writes (1994, 734). But Young perhaps characterizes the concept of identity a little too simply: as denoting either "who persons are in a deep psychological sense" or as "self-ascription, as belonging to a group with others who similarly identify themselves" (734).

The conception of identity that I have been developing in this book, however, is one that is more complex than either of these definitions allows. Identity emerges both as we act within (what we can now refer to as) the exigencies of serial ensembles and as we intentionally shape ourselves in relation to them (through compliance, resistance, affirmation, etc.). One does in a profound sense "become" one's identity. But although identity is deeply constitutive of selfhood, it cannot be reduced either to a pre-given, "deep," psychological core, or to a self-ascribed choice.

teriorizations of the practico-inert, their exteriorization, and re-interiorization. Grosz's metaphor of the Möbius strip to encapsulate the relation of mind and body (discussed in chapter 2) might also be used here to describe an "inflection" of the practical self and its world into each other, and their "interconstituency" (1994). For Sartre's claim here is not that praxis must be guided by a Cartesian consciousness, existing independently of the world it contemplates—nor indeed by any kind of constituting consciousness.

Sartre's practical subject is not the disembodied propagator of the godtrick. But, as a would-be transformative engagement with the world, any praxis still must involve intentional consciousness, at least at a pre-reflective level. As Merleau-Ponty had also argued, there is an intentionality to human existence that is often prior to consciously formulated goals or knowledge.[12] Sartre's notion of intentionality implies that the practical subject is not, perhaps, as "split" as Haraway's account suggests. There is an embodied intentionality that knits an existence together, integrating its multiple and apparently fragmentary identities, each of which is itself the outcome of its location within a range of collectives and series. What makes possible an integration of the multiple identities that Sandoval, for example, describes in the case of U.S. Third World women is not the presence of the transcendental, disembodied consciousness she tacitly posits. Rather it is the relative stability of an organic, embodied, practical subject, whose styles of behavior and sets of practices sediment over time and are often integrated at the level of a tacit "lived experience."

In *Being and Nothingness*, Sartre had argued (with a certain debt to Husserl) that consciousness is always consciousness *of* something and that it cannot but intend its object. But now, in the *Critique*, where Sartre's concern is no longer with consciousness as a general relation to the world but with consciousness as the "interior" aspect of praxis, intentionality has additionally to do with the purposive quality of our apprehension of that sector of the world in which we are practically engaged. This is not to say that our ends have always to be fully articulated or conscious prior to action. But it does mean that the ubiquity of intentionality is what ensures that the actions of others are amenable to at least a degree of post hoc comprehension.

12. It is also often prior to discourse. Indeed, for Sartre discourse—like any other human artifact—is practically produced. It thus cannot have the constitutive primacy that is accorded to it in most postmodern theory. Overall, Sartre pays insufficient attention to the place of discourse in human affairs in the *Critique*. However, I find the notion of discourse as a form of praxis to be helpful and worth a fuller exploration. To conceive of discourse as a form of praxis that produces its own forms of the practico-inert and of seriality allows us to explain the structuring role discourse often plays in human affairs, without reducing us to discursive effects as do many postmodern accounts. It also enables us to raise questions about the origins of particular discourses that do not self-referentially return us to discourse alone.

For even if I do not fully understand why a person is performing certain actions, I usually can grasp that her actions do have purpose. Indeed, when we cannot recognize any purpose in what somebody does, we tend to say that the person is "mad," connoting that their behavior is not recognizably human to us.[13] But such rare situations apart, we do recognize that an intentional human project is taking place even when we cannot grasp the full import it has for its agent.

Sartre uses the term "reciprocity" to describe this mutual comprehension of each other's projects. It is important to point out that for Sartre reciprocity need in no way denote empathy. It is not a question here of subjective feelings of care, or affective connection among human beings (which I shall explore in the next, and final, part of the book). Reciprocity cannot, says Sartre, "be based on a universal abstract bond, like Christian 'charity'; nor on an *a priori* willingness to treat the human person . . . as an absolute end; nor on a purely contemplative intuition revealing 'Humanity' to everyone as the essence of his fellows" (CDR 109–10). Nor, one might add, can it be based on a mystical or emotional bond of "womanhood," such as one often finds in eco-feminism and other variants of global-difference feminism. Reciprocity lies in no generic essence, feminine or otherwise. It emerges and endures only in the mutual encounter of specific praxes, where the recognition that others are engaged, like myself, in intentional projects of transformation of the practical material field may result in either reciprocal antagonism or reciprocal solidarity, depending on whether our projects threaten each other or are complementary (CDR 112–13).[14]

Moreover, in relations of reciprocity each of us comes to recognize that the praxis of others actually *alters* our own praxis, through the mediations of the practico-inert. For example, the significance of what I have written here will depend not only on what I believe to be its import but also on my situation within the collective of feminist theorists. Through future scholarship others may well return my thoughts to me profoundly altered—for either better or worse—even though this book will remain "my" product. This process of alteration depends, in turn, on such practico-inert structurings of the field of academic production as the marketing and distribution of

13. The project of some alternative psychiatry—notably R. D. Laing's existential analysis (1969) of schizophrenia—is to reveal that there are still coherence and intentionality to what might appear to be non-intentional, and thus unintelligible, behavior on the part of schizophrenics.

14. Thus the denial of recognition to those whose identities are despised (discussed in the previous chapter) must also be conceived as a form of antagonistic reciprocity. It is worth noting that, once again, Beauvoir anticipated Sartre when she argued in *The Second Sex* that (at least among men) forms of reciprocity can relativize otherness in such interactions as "wars, festivals, trading, treaties, and contests among tribes, nations, and classes" (SS xxiii).

books, the positioning of feminist scholarship within the institutions of American academia, and the hierarchies within feminist scholarship. Thus, as Haraway also insists, my relationship to you, the reader, is never one of directly communicating consciousnesses but rather one of *materially mediated* selves.[15] Indeed, material mediations are what enable the relationship to take place at all, and no human interaction is possible in which practico-inert mediations are entirely absent. Even the content of the most deeply "private" fantasy life is, for example, always an interiorization of social symbols, artifacts, and relations.

To make this point more clearly, Sartre now criticizes as idealist Hegel's "master-slave dialectic," which was so central to his own account of human relations in *Being and Nothingness*. Hegel, he now observes, "ignored matter as a mediation between individuals. Even if one uses his terminology, one has to say that while each consciousness is the counter-part of the Other, this reciprocity can take an infinity of different forms, positive or negative, and that *it is the mediation of matter* which determines these forms in every concrete case" (CDR 113; emphasis added).

Such a reciprocal relationship may in some instances involve overcoming seriality to form groups engaged in a common praxis, including forms of common resistance to domination. Indeed, this has frequently been the case in the women's movement, when what were experienced by isolated women as private problems, such as the fear of rape or unwanted pregnancy, have become the basis for group action. But an even more important point here, bearing on the issue of whether partial perspectives can give us "shared conversations" and "objective knowledges," is that in those other instances, where relations of the most profound conflict of interests exist, there must also be reciprocity. As Sartre points out, while denying the humanity of his slaves, an American slave owner still had to recognize that they were, like him, practical subjects. They could choose to put their labor and skills at his disposal, or else plot to revolt or escape. "This is the contradiction of racism, colonialism and all forms of tyranny: in order to *treat a man like a dog*, one must first recognise him as a man" (CDR 111).

The sexism of Sartre's statement notwithstanding, his point is crucial: even in relations of profound antagonism, such as may of course exist not only between men and women but also among women of different races, ethnicities, social classes, sexual orientations, religions, and so on, a reciprocal comprehension of praxis exists. Indeed, if it did not exist, conflict or struggle would not be possible. Whether it be conflict among classes, as in Sartre's

---

15. This would also be the case if you were part of the audience at a conference where I was presenting this material orally, or even if I were telling you my ideas in a one-on-one conversation, although the practico-inert mediations would be somewhat different in each case.

examples,[16] or strife among diverse collectives of women whose unequal power or contradictory interests pit them against each other in relationships of antagonism, struggle is possible *only* because we can reciprocally comprehend each other's praxis as intentional action. Thus the claim to an exclusive domain of knowledge—the core of an epistemology of provenance—is put into question through the very act of asserting that such a domain exists. Moreover, the possibility of objective knowledge—knowledge that is, in Haraway's terms, translatable across "partial perspectives"—is revealed.

To recapitulate, what Sartre suggests is that there are two ways in which the praxis of individuals, and of the various serial ensembles in which they invariably act, are connected. The first of these, linkages through the mediations of practico-inert unifications, ensures that forms of situated knowledge that begin from reflection on one's own practice and practical location do not have to be self-referential or wholly subjective. To the contrary, mediations in exteriority ensure that knowledge rooted in particular praxis can move out beyond it to comprehend ever wider sectors of the practical material field. The investigation of one's own praxis, that is, one's own situated knowledge, may thus develop into wider knowledge of the praxis of others beyond the collectives or groups in which one directly acts.

Second, even when praxis is antagonistic, our ability to recognize that others are engaged in intentionally oriented practice—that is, our reciprocity—also works as a limit on tendencies toward extreme subjectivism or solipsism. Even where there is conflict among different ensembles of women, reciprocity exists as the precondition of that conflict. An epistemology of provenance is thus shown to undermine itself in the very process of asserting itself.

To conclude by returning to Haraway's project, we can now see more clearly why it is indeed possible for the "webs of connections" that Haraway calls both "shared conversations" in epistemology and "solidarity" in politics to be created. If we conceive of the self not only as one of situated (and thus partial) vision but also as a *practical* situated subject, one whose knowledge and whose reciprocal relations with others (be they antagonistic or solidaristic) come into being through praxis and its practico-inert mediations, we avoid the fragmenting tendencies implicit in identity politics, as well as other forms of multiple-difference feminism.

It might sometimes be the case—as advocates of identity politics often claim—that we cannot know the subjective experiences, that is, the "inner"

16. For the most part, members of classes are, alas, male in Sartre's account. The way that gender plays out in the constitution of class identities and interests is not explored in his analyses.

emotions and feelings, of a particular woman or even of an ensemble of women.[17] However, we all engage in a diversity of praxes, mediated through the same or overlapping practical material fields. This means that however different our worlds appear to us, and however antagonistic our interests may actually be, reciprocity and thus the possibility of a mutual comprehension of each other's actions always remain possible. It is out in the world, as we *act*, that we are able to comprehend each other.

And what of Haraway's call for standpoint theories and situated knowledges that are "potent for worlds less dominated by axes of domination"? Can we both value differences and pursue broader political agendas for human emancipation that transcend differences? Epistemology is often political since claims about knowledge usually involve the exercise of power, but politics functions along many other axes than that of knowledge claims and is by no means co-extensive with epistemology. Thus, to establish, as I have set out to do here, that knowledge must be both practical and situated— and that these are the very conditions for the possibility of a knowledge that is both particular and general—does not in itself give us a difference-sensitive yet general emancipatory politics. It is a necessary element of such a politics, but it is not sufficient. Indeed, as I shall argue in the remainder of this book, it must be supplemented by developing other ways that women may come to know each other's experiences and act as groups. These additional ways will require women also to develop affective relationships with one another. At this point, however, the later Sartre will no longer continue to serve us well as a guide.

17. However, it might also be possible to comprehend purely subjective experiences in alternative ways, for example, through poetry, dance, music, or (as I argue in part 3) qualities of embodiment. Sartre's theory does not preclude other such forms of knowledge: he simply does not establish their formal possibility.

PART 3

Experience and the
Phenomenology of Difference

5 Going Beyond Discourse: Feminism, Phenomenology, and "Women's Experience"

Feminists have grown wary of talking about "women's experience." Once regarded as the very bedrock of second-wave feminism, "experience" is today a suspect concept. As second-wave feminism emerged in the late 1960s and the 1970s, women's experience was a touchstone. Against patriarchal ideology in general, and the sex-blind, neo-Marxist analyses of the New Left in particular, the distinctiveness of women's experience was asserted.

Feminist politics, a politics of "sisterhood," was to be built through sharing and "bringing to voice" experience, notably via consciousness-raising groups; feminist theory was to avoid the pitfalls of masculinist rationalism by grounding its analyses in the specificities of women's experience. These claims were epitomized in the 1969 Manifesto of the Redstockings:

> We regard our personal experiences and our feelings about experience as the basis for an analysis of our common situation. We cannot rely on existing ideologies as they are all products of male supremacist culture. We question every generalization and accept none that are not confirmed by our experience.
>
> Our chief task at present is to develop female class consciousness through sharing experience and publicly exposing the sexist foundation of all our institutions. (Redstockings 1970, 113)

Since the late 1970s more complex and nuanced accounts of women's experience have emerged and been used to ground feminist theories. These have ranged from Chodorow's account of how distinctly masculine and feminine selves emerge through divergent infant experiences of separation from the mother (1978) to the claims that women generally experience the world through different moral categories than men (Gilligan 1982), have different ways of knowing (Belenky et al. 1986), or different ways of thinking (Ruddick 1989). In realm after realm, the assertion of the specificity of women's experience has been used to develop critiques of patriarchy and masculinism, and to insist that beginning from women's distinct experiences is the sine qua non of any feminist project of liberation.

The initial feminist critiques of such accounts of experience came from lesbians and then, with increasing urgency, from women of color. Their objections, however, were not to the importance attributed to the concept of experience per se. Rather, their complaint was that their own experiences had been excluded, or occluded, in the name of a "women's experience" that was above all that of white, middle-class, and, usually, heterosexual women. In the work of such thinkers as Lorde (1984), Anzaldúa (1987), or P. H. Collins (1990), experience remains a vital concept but now differentiated by sexual orientation, ethnicity, race, and other specifics. Even so, these critiques cast an enduring seed of doubt on the status of experience itself. For if women's experiences are as radically different, as incommensurate, as such authors have claimed, how helpful can it be to talk of them as a basis for either feminist theory or political activity? Does not the very idea of "women's experience" function as a hegemonic norm that privileges the experience of some by excluding that of others?

The doubts sown by such critiques have increasingly blended with those emerging from the turn toward postmodernism within feminist theory. Earlier concepts of women's experience presupposed the existence of relatively stable "core" selves: selves that were conceived as indubitable authorities about their own experiences. By contrast, postmodern feminist theory, informed by the work of Derrida, Foucault, and others, insists that such selves and their experiences can never be other than discursive effects. The confluence of these two strands of critique, multiple-difference feminism and postmodern feminism, has put into question the continuing relevance of the concept of experience for feminism.

In this chapter, I begin by examining two recent and influential critical reworkings of the concept of experience: those of Richard Rorty and Joan Scott. I do so to demonstrate that even highly thoughtful attempts to account for experience in terms of discursivity alone pose significant theoretical difficulties. For the postmodern feminist project is essentially one of discourse reductionism and—as I argued with regard to postmodernism more generally in the introduction—its procrustean tendencies lead to theoretical incoherence.

In addition, I argue, the explanatory range of discourse analysis is too limited. Its strengths for feminism lie in demonstrating the emergence of those discursive spaces in which it has become possible for narratives of women's oppression and demands for recognition to emerge. But, by itself, discourse analysis is too uni-dimensional to grasp the concrete dynamics through which these demands may give rise to those forms of collective practice that loosely deserve the designation "feminist." In order better to grasp such dynamics, feminist theory must continue to hold onto the concept of experience and must attend to the ways in which experience can exceed discursivity.

In exploring certain dimensions of women's experience that cannot be grasped through discourse analysis alone, I turn to phenomenology. Historically, phenomenology has attempted to grasp the immediacy of certain forms of "lived experience" by using a method of "bracketing," or suspending, the categories and assumptions (be they naturalistic, commonsense, scientific, or now poststructuralist) through which we routinely mediate our descriptions of the world. Since a wholly presuppositionless account of experience is, of course, never realizable, phenomenology is best conceived as a heuristic method. Its strength lies in the fact that (even if they always remain incomplete) such attempts to suspend our "normal" conceptual frameworks often invite into focus valuable aspects of experience that are otherwise occluded.

RICHARD Rorty's aim, both in such general works as *Contingency, Irony, and Solidarity* (1989) and in his essays on feminism, "Feminism and Pragmatism" (1991) and "Feminism, Ideology, and Deconstruction" (1993), is to argue for a radically constructivist and historicist account of the human world. In this account, experience and personhood are said to be exclusively linguistically created. To use his preferred terminology, the ironist, the pragmatist, and the deconstructionist (and a good feminist should be all three) are engaged in contesting "metaphysical" claims that there exist realities, truths, or moral principles beyond our descriptions of them. We do not represent, or even discover, reality, Rorty claims. Rather, we *create* it in the acts of describing and redescribing, for "everything is a social construct" (Rorty 1993, 98). Indeed, he insists, deconstruction persuades "us" that "there is nothing 'natural' or 'scientific' or 'objective' about any given masculinist practice or description, and that all objects (neutrinos, chairs, women, men, literary theory, feminism) are social constructs" (99). It obviously also follows that "there is no point trying to distinguish between the 'natural' and the 'merely cultural' " (98).

Given his radical constructivism, Rorty quite consistently argues that there is nothing *"intrinsically* abominable" (1991, 237) about the subordination of women. Since there are only descriptions and redescriptions, there is no Archimedean point from which we could make such an affirmation. Feminists must drop the claim that they act in the name of principles: they simply struggle to redescribe and to create a new social construct. Like all social visionaries, like "the early Christians, the early socialists, the Albigensians, and the Nazis," feminists are engaged only in "trying to actualize hitherto undreamt-of possibilities by putting new linguistic and other practices into play, and erecting a new social construct" (236).[1] Furthermore, feminists are not engaged in expressing, or bringing to voice, pre-existing women's experiences. For the proper project for feminism is not to try to "express" women's lives but rather to "create" women anew through "the production of a better set of social constructs" (250).

Of course, language is never a neutral medium through which we can capture previously unvoiced experience, and experience is indeed altered in acts of linguistic formulation. But the costs of reducing women's experience to feminist linguistic creation *alone* are high. For personhood then becomes an attribute of linguistic competence and is denied to the silent or silenced. The terminus of Rorty's radical discourse constructionism is a peculiar new version of vanguard theory—the leadership of the linguistically competent.

Not all members of the human species share equally in personhood, according to Rorty. Since human beings do not have "a central and inviolable core surrounded by culturally-conditioned beliefs and desires" (1991, 249), personhood is never an "intrinsic attribute" of all members of the species but rather an *acquisition*, and some—those with the greater power of language—acquire more of it than others. Personhood, Rorty claims, is "something that slaves typically have less of than their masters . . . because of the masters' control over the language spoken by slaves—their ability to make the slave think of his or her pain as fated. . . . [There is no] deep reality which reposes unrecognized beneath the superficial appearances" (244). Where oppression is not voiced, in short, it does not exist.

In spite of his own indubitably great "semantic authority," Rorty does not want to be one of the masters. He happens to believe (although it is not a belief that can be defended in any *principled* way) that more people should be able to attain fuller personhood. The question thus arises, if slaves and other oppressed groups, such as women, blacks, or gays, lack sufficient personhood, how are they to acquire it? Obviously, says Rorty, through the assistance of benign members of the linguistically competent elite, through help from those generous beings who have reached fuller personhood but do not choose to be among the masters. "There is no such thing as the 'voice of the oppressed' or the 'language of the victims.' . . . So the job of putting their situation into language is going to have to be done for them by somebody

1. Rorty's inclusion here of Nazism as simply a "new social construct" is dangerously sanitizing. Such a bland "redescription" cozily protects us from the reek of the densely packed human cargo in the cattle trucks and the mounds of bodies.

else" (1989, 94). And, Rorty adds, "the liberal novelist, poet, or journalist is good at that." So, presumably, is the feminist, who puts the condition of other women into words for them and in doing so creates "women" as an oppressed group.

Rorty's elitism here is predicated upon tacit forms of mind/body and culture/nature dualism that more generally permeate his work. For if there cannot be any personhood-constituting experience outside of language, he has to resort to the expedient of calling those experiences that inconveniently appear to be pre or non-linguistic non-human. Thus, although Rorty goes to great lengths to argue that we cannot distinguish the natural from the cultural, de facto he ends by expelling non-linguistic bodily experience into the realm of nature, as what we share with animals. "The only intrinsic features of human beings are those they share with the brutes—for example, the ability to suffer and inflict pain," he writes (1991, 233). Or, as he puts it elsewhere, "pain is nonlinguistic. It is what we human beings have that ties us to nonlanguage-using beasts" (1989, 94). In contrast to "brute" pain, he suggests that there is a specifically human way of inflicting and suffering pain: humiliation. If there is any bond that holds human beings together it is our common desire to avoid humiliation: "The liberal ironist just wants our *chances of being kind,* of avoiding humiliating others, to be expanded by redescription. She thinks that recognition of a common susceptibility to humiliation is the *only* social bond that is needed" (1989, 91).

Rorty here sunders us into a pain-suffering animal part and a humiliation-suffering human part. Yet again, body/mind, nature/culture are split apart. And, consistent with a long tradition of Western mind/body dualism, mere physical pain is seen as less important than the more "human" suffering of humiliation. In Rorty's comfortable world, we have it seems moved beyond the time when brute pain, and the kinds of cruelty that cause it, need be of much concern. But this is patently not the case in the world at large today, where the "animal" agonies of violent death and mutilation are, if anything, increasing. Nor is it even the case for many within the Western world, the United States included.[2]

Forms of physical violence against women and the infliction of "brute" pain are rife today and are perpetrated against women of all social classes and ethnic identities. Sadly, one of the areas of women's experience that consciousness-raising, and other forms of feminist practice, has most clearly brought to light is the ubiquity of violence against women. Although feminism has indeed recently named some of these forms of violence, such as

2. With remarkable Eurocentrism, Rorty suggests that the ability and desire to prevent the humiliation of others are "rather late" phenomena, associated "primarily with Europe and America in the last three hundred years" (1989, 93).

"date-rape," for the first time, they clearly have pre-existed feminist voicing. They are also experienced by many women today who remain untouched by feminism and who do not know how to speak of what is happening to them. Alcoff and Gray (1993) have argued that this is also so for victims of childhood sexual abuse: they "know" what they have experienced, even though they have no way of putting it into words. They may later re-interpret the experience as they acquire concepts, perhaps feminist concepts, with which to do so. But the original experience precedes such conceptualization.

Similarly, women and other groups who (in Rorty's terms) lack full personhood may experience various forms of suffering that they cannot put into words: fear, frustration, resentment, to name but a few. More positively, compassion, empathy, or affection may also be experienced prior to acts of linguistic creation that name them as such. Rorty argues that solidarity with our fellow humans requires acts of imagination such as we get best from novelists and poets (1989). But, yet again, this claim privileges the linguistically competent and denies a place for forms of experience, including positive affective experience, that may be non-discursive.

The social and ontological dualism that pervades Rorty's account of pain and oppression is symptomatic of discourse theory's more general inability to deal adequately with the issue of human embodiment. If pain is what links us to the brutes, then it is the body, the locus of physical pain, that must form the connecting tissue. Rorty thus implicitly concedes that the body does in some ways preexist or elude social construction. He is unable consistently to uphold his claims that "everything is a social construct" and that nature and culture are indistinguishable.

Similarly, Rorty undermines his own constructivism when he describes the divergent characteristics of male and female bodies as a real but contingent "fact." Masculinism, he argues, is not grounded in "the fact that the people with the slightly larger muscles have been bullying the people with the slightly smaller muscles for a very long time" (1993, 101). But in this statement Rorty is not claiming that muscle size itself is a social construct. Rather, it is a "fact" of nature, but one that properly social-constructionist explanations of masculinism should regard as true but trivial. Yet again, the body is expelled from the realm of the significantly human here.

I certainly do not want, any more than Rorty, to explain masculinism, or other forms of domination, on the basis of muscle size. But neither do I think that we can a priori exclude differences in musculature, or other bodily characteristics, from accounts of what it is like for different groups of people to live, act, and organize in the world. To recall a point Beauvoir makes, although our bodies never define a "destiny," they do significantly shape our way of being in the world, our field of possible actions and experiences. The "coefficient of adversity"[3] in things can differ significantly according to one's physical capacities. For example, the rungs of a ladder are closer together or further apart according to the length of our legs, and whether or not a load is too heavy to carry depends in part on our body size and musculature. Our different experiences of the "same" field of action may be linked to bodily differences that are not wholly divorced from our gender, or even from our sex, implying that discursive construction is not the sole determinant of certain kinds of experience.

∽

IN her essay, entitled simply "Experience," Joan Scott observes that "it is tempting, given its usage to essentialize identity and reify the subject, to abandon [the concept] altogether" (1992, 37). Experience, however, "is so much part of everyday language, so imbricated in our narratives that it seems futile to argue for its expulsion." Why the concept of experience should be so imbricated in our narratives is not a question on which Scott chooses to dwell. But given the self-evident futility of attempting wholly to expel it, she settles for the second best alternative: reworking it. Scott's re-working involves constricting the concept of experience, historicizing it and, like Rorty, demonstrating its always and absolutely discursive nature. Although in many ways insightful, Scott's account, like Rorty's, tends to undermine itself.

Scott's immediate concern is historiographical. For much recent radical history (for which E. P. Thompson's majestic *The Making of the English Working Class* [1963] is paradigmatic) has taken as its main task to reveal the experience of those whose lives historians had previously overlooked—workers, women, ethnic minorities. But Scott's critique of such projects has a wider import. For the arguments she makes against the historian's project of making past experience visible bear also on attempts to grasp present-day experience.

Scott's critique of Thompson hinges on a sharp distinction she makes between "foundationalist" and "historicist" methods of research. Experience, she argues, functions as a "foundational" category for historians (and others), as "the bedrock of evidence" upon which explanations are then built (1992, 25). She describes foundationalism as a method that—erroneously—takes for granted "some primary premises, categories or presumptions," which then are treated as "unquestioned and unquestionable . . . considered permanent and transcendent" (26). By contrast, she claims, historicism wisely "takes all categories of analysis as contextual, contested and contingent" (36). Thus, from a properly historicist perspective, experience should be treated not as "the origin of our explanation" but as "that which we want to explain" (38).

---

3. The phrase is originally Gaston Bachelard's, but I take it from Sartre (BN 482).

But Scott presents us with a false antithesis here. For experience can serve as both a point of origin for an explanation and as the object of an explanation. Whether one chooses to explore it as one or the other—or indeed as both—is a choice that should not be foreclosed a priori. For one's method of investigation may well depend on the reasons why one is undertaking a particular study. For example, we know that many women who are subjected to what is today called domestic violence continue to cohabit for long periods with the men who abuse them. How is one to explain this? There is no one definitive mode of explanation here. Rather, one's mode of explanation may reasonably vary, perhaps depending on whether one poses the question as one of primarily socio-historical interest or else with a political agenda for effective intervention in mind.

Given the former orientation, we may begin by asking about the genealogy of the discursive construction of domestic violence. Through a discourse-constructionist lens we could argue that the experience of being subject to domestic violence is a recent one. It has been constituted by new discourses on the family, violence, and crime (themselves in large measure the effect of second-wave feminist discourse) that now define the use of physical force on women's bodies as a pathology, rather than as the older, legally sanctioned, right of a husband to discipline his wife. Arguably it is only within this new discursive framework that my question, why women stay with men who abuse them, can even be posed. Through textual comparisons we could perhaps also demonstrate that to experience oneself as subject to forms of violence that are now defined as illegitimate is not identical to experiencing oneself as subject to the corporal punishment that it was once a husband's right, or even duty, to inflict upon his wife: discursive shifts have indeed, as Scott claims, altered experience.

But such an account tells only part of the story. For experiences of domestic violence are not only discursively constituted but also lived "from the inside out" (Grosz 1994). Thus, if we want to understand why women today often stay with abusive men, it will make sense also to consider experience as an "origin" here. Women's experience will, indeed, be part of "the bedrock of evidence" for our account. To be able to act in effective support of abused women, those who have not been subjected to domestic violence need (as far as is possible) to have a sense of the lived experience of such abuse.[4] How does it feel to live with the pain, with the continual fear and humiliation? How does one come to experience *oneself* in such a situation? What does one perceive as one's range of possible actions, and what seems beyond possibility?

---

4. I explore the vexed questions of how, and how far, we can experience the suffering of another more fully in chapter 6.

Likewise, for those who suffer domestic violence, it can often be an empowering process for experiences to be voiced and shared. In presenting experiences, individuals may come to realize that their own predicament is part of a wider problem and that forms of resistance they have not previously envisaged might be possible. The fact that experiences are also discursively constructed does not diminish the importance of treating them *in such contexts* as a point of "origin," or even a "foundation," from which to work.

But, in the final analysis, Scott cannot sustain her own sharp distinction between foundationalism and historicism. For her attack on foundationalism spawns its own foundationalist categories: discourse, as well as historicism, become "unquestioned and unquestionable," even "permanent and transcendent," categories in her account of history. Indeed, they have become so established, so a priori that she never raises, even for provisional exploration, the possibility that social life has not been entirely discursively constituted at all times and in all places. Nor does she pause to consider, even critically or as a possible counter-hypothesis, the proposition that there might be some transhistorical or transcultural dimensions to human life that endure across historical differences. The universality of historicism (that is, of non-universality) is taken to be a self-evident, a priori proposition.

No work of explanation (including Scott's own) can proceed without relatively stable concepts and categories through which to make sense of the world. Theoretically informed research requires what we might call "working" or "provisional" foundational categories. For if we try to expunge all foundations we end up deconstructing deconstructed deconstructions in an endless, and ultimately self-defeating, regress. Particular concepts must have a foundational status in relation to *particular* theoretical projects, and it is possible to so use them without naively presupposing they are natural or unproblematic.[5] If all feminist scholars ever did was to write historicist accounts of such pivotal concepts as woman, women, sex, or gender—not to mention such concepts as the self, the subject, or, indeed, experience—we would fail ever to engage in other important projects for which these concepts must provisionally operate as "foundational."

There needs to be a division of theoretical labor, in which not all of feminist theory devotes itself to the potentially interminable deconstruction of concepts and categories. Yes, concepts such as women, gender, or experience

---

5. Thus, for example, Marx simply uses the categories of social class as a "foundation" for analysis in a work such as *The Civil War in France*. Yet in *The German Ideology* and *Capital* he makes an explicit case for the theoretical importance of these categories: he gives compelling *reasons* for analyzing societies in terms of social class and justifies his choice of concepts by the degree of explanatory power they demonstrate. Similarly, the concept of the unconscious is neither "natural" nor unproblematic in Freud's work. Rather, it is carefully developed to do an explanatory job.

are problematic, and they can obscure certain historical and present differences. But we still must use them to develop explanatory frameworks, or a kind of theoretical paralysis threatens to set in. As Jane Roland Martin has observed, "taken to its logical extreme, the argument against general categories like women, gender, mothering, reproduction, and family leaves feminist scholars in the lurch. If categories exist that do not conceal differences, they will be so specific as to stultify intellectual inquiry" (1994, 637).

Scott's anti-foundationalism also requires, like Rorty's, the reduction of experiencing selves, or subjects, to discursive effects. Indeed, one of the main goals of her essay is to refute any claim that the origin or foundation of experience can ever lie in a subject that pre-exists discourse:

> Making visible the experience of a different group exposes the existence of repressive mechanisms but not their inner workings or logics; we know that difference exists, but we don't understand it as constituted relationally. For that we need to attend to the historical processes that, *through discourse, position subjects and produce their experiences. It is not individuals who have experiences, but subjects who are constituted through experience.* Experience in this definition then becomes . . . that which we seek to explain, that about which knowledge is produced. (1992, 25–26; emphasis added)

Although Scott is right that simply making experience "visible" is not in itself a sufficient theoretical project for feminism,[6] it does not follow that experience is *always* discursive or dependent on our subject-position *tout court*. In the passage just quoted, Scott distinguishes between "individuals who have experiences" (that is, the Enlightenment humanist idea of a self-possessing or autonomous self, which she regards as patently erroneous) and "subjects who are constituted through experience" (the poststructuralist idea of the self, which she regards as preferable—"truer"?). Historical processes, she says, "through discourse, position subjects and *produce* their experiences." Experience is, in short, the effect, the passive result, of discourse.

It is here that Scott, perhaps following Foucault too faithfully, again pushes her insights to untenable extremes. Indeed, elsewhere she approvingly quotes Foucault's dubious claim that "one has to dispense with the constituent sub-

---

6. Indeed, when de-linked from critique or feminist politics, an account of experience can be fundamentally conservative. For "given" experience may be accepted as natural and/or desirable when it is in large measure ideologically constructed. For example, if women find pleasure in conforming to fashion ideals, a description of their pleasure is insufficient for a feminist politics: analysis and critique need to follow. Thus, Nancy Hartsock (1985) and other standpoint theorists have argued a distinction must be made between "women's experience" and a "feminist standpoint." The latter is achieved only through reflection on the former and through struggle and critique.

ject . . . to arrive at an analysis which can account for the constitution of the subject within a historical framework" (Scott 1993, 440–41). Scott, like Foucault, posits mutually exclusive alternatives here: either selves are autonomous self-constitutors, or they are discursive effects; either the subject is constituent, or else it is constituted. But, as I have already argued at length, there is no a priori reason to privilege one account over the other. Rather, one might better characterize these accounts as demarcating two dialectically related poles from which knowledge can be produced: one pole explores experience from an impersonal or "third person" stance, its project being explanatory; the other explores it from a "first person" stance, in terms of its personal meaning, as an experience to be grasped or understood rather than explained (Steele 1996).

It is also helpful to think of the relationship of these poles on the model of a gestalt drawing, in which a figure that we foreground functions to occlude another figure, even though through a process of perceptual switching we can come to see that both are present.[7] Depending on which pole we choose to start from, we can render an account of "the same" experience either as a discursive effect or as subjectively lived. And there may often be good reasons for privileging one pole over the other as the starting point for feminist inquiry: it will depend on the nature of our questions and goals. Sometimes the most fruitful theoretical work will involve a process of switching: working back and forth between third- and first-person accounts, between structuralist (or poststructuralist) explanatory modes and those that foreground lived experience.[8]

This point can be clarified by further considering the example of domestic violence. Feminist challenges to previous normative discourse have recently reconstructed women's identities so as to delegitimize, or denaturalize, what we now call domestic violence. Feminist critiques of the once unproblematic distinction between public and private spheres, with which liberal theory traditionally operated, have destabilized the concept of "the home" so that it is no longer defined as an inviolable private space for male action (Okin 1989). With this shift, violence against women in the home has come to be re-described as an issue of public concern. Moreover, women's

---

7. Thus, in one classic gestalt drawing, the figure may be seen as either the profiles of two human faces or the outline of a vase. But one cannot see "both" at the same time.

8. Sartre sketches such a method in *Search for a Method* and then later tries to apply it in his monumental study of Flaubert ([1971–72] 1981–93). The "progressive-regressive method," as he calls it, studies both the social processes that structure the field of action of an individual and action as it is lived. The process of investigation tries continually to bring the two into articulation. The method, Sartre writes, "will progressively determine a biography (for example) by examining the period, and the period by studying the biography. Far from seeking immediately to integrate one into the other, it will hold them separate until the reciprocal involvement comes to pass of itself" ([1960] 1968, 135).

identities have been reconstructed as the bearers of publicly recognized rights to bodily integrity and to protection from domestic violence.[9]

Yet there appears to be a significant discrepancy between these general discursive shifts and their effect on the subjectivities of battered women. Given Scott's argument, one would expect that the discursive shifts would effect a change in battered women so that their subjective self-understandings would be re-constituted as the bearers of rights and as the victims of unacceptable violent crime against which they would demand recourse. But for the most part battered women still appear to see their lot in private and personal terms and to have little sense of themselves as the bearers of rights or as entitled to recourse. Although accounts of "battered woman's syndrome" often overemphasize the victim status and passivity of many women (Downs 1996; De Soto 1997), this disparity still suggests that there are sources of subjectivity that are not primarily discursive. Some of these, I suggest, are connected with embodiment and with experiences of bodily pain and fear that exceed discourse. In order to grasp why it is that battered women so often stay with their abusers, we need also to pay attention to these non-discursive dimensions of experience.[10]

Central to such questions about how far subjectivity is (and is not) discursively constituted lies, of course, the complex issue of agency. Critics of poststructuralism have frequently pointed out that formulations such as those of Scott and Rorty do not enable us to account for the human freedom and agency necessary for resistance. Linda Alcoff's objections are fairly typical. Poststructuralists, she writes, "seem totally to erase any room for maneuver by the individual within a social discourse or set of institutions. . . . In their defence of a total construction of the subject, post-structuralists deny the subject's ability to reflect on the social discourse and challenge its determinations" (1988, 417).

Scott accepts the validity of these concerns but insists that individual agency and choice are not, in fact, excluded by her account. But in the course

---

9. This is, of course, a somewhat idealized account of the discursive shift that has taken place since the 1970s. For in many instances the state continues to evince reluctance to intervene in what is still deemed a "private" affair. Moreover, as Wendy Kozol has argued, media representations of domestic violence tend to undercut this shift by portraying cases of domestic violence as isolated aberrations from a presumed "norm" of harmonious family life (1996). But such caveats aside, we should not under-estimate the significant degree to which feminist discursive practices have, since the 1970s, caused domestic violence to be named and constructed as a new political and legal issue.

10. Other kinds of non-discursive explanations may also be pertinent here. Economic constraints are all too real in preventing many women from leaving an abuser; and the fear that they will be subjected to yet greater violence if they attempt to leave is all too rationally grounded. Men so often pursue and violently attack women who leave them that the term "separation assault" has been coined to describe this phenomenon (Mahoney 1991).

of defending herself from accusations of determinism, she ends by undermining her previous claims. Although insisting that subjects are constituted discursively, Scott says that the presence of "conflicts among discursive systems" and "multiple meanings possible for the concepts they deploy" provide spaces for choice (Scott 1992, 34). Even though subjects are not "unified, autonomous individuals exercising free will," such conflicts and multiple meanings "enable choices" (34). But the assertions that the subject has "agency" and "choice" sit uneasily in Scott's own discourse, and she does not choose to unpack them. Perhaps wisely so, since they put into question her central claim as to the discursively constituted nature of the subject.

For to assert that the subject retains the possibility of "choosing" among contradictory discursive systems, or among the different possible meanings of concepts, is to say that after all the subject has a capacity to evaluate, judge, and decide that is not *itself* structured by discourse. What is tacitly posited here is a notion of a freedom that escapes and transcends discourse and of a subject that, although discursively positioned, still remains capable of rational reflection upon discourse from the perspective of its own freely chosen ends or values. Scott does not elaborate on this notion of the subject, but it is a peculiarly Cartesian notion for such an avowedly post-Enlightenment thinker to embrace. It implies a view of the subject as a *res cogitans* for which the objects of contemplation are now no longer Descartes's *res extensa* but rather the conflicting discursive systems among which, through an act of reflection, evaluations may freely be made. Such a conception presupposes a disembodied, positionless, Cartesian meta-subject that hovers above and contemplates its subject-position(s).

Thus Scott's radical anti-foundationalism and discursivism remain unable to account for individual agency, except by tacitly reintroducing Enlightenment postulates of the very kind she seeks to eliminate. Both she and Rorty replicate those contradictions that I have been arguing, from the introduction onward, are endemic to postmodern theory. What reading both Scott and Rorty teaches us is that, although discourse analysis is a valuable resource for feminism, its scope is too narrow to account in full for women's experiences or for the possibility of feminist agency. When it arrogantly claims to function as an all-encompassing and exclusive method of social or historical analysis, discourse theory ends by tacitly re-instating the most problematic aspects of Enlightenment rationalism: mind-body dualism and the privileging of a disembodied Cartesian subject. It engages, after all, in what Merleau-Ponty called "high-altitude thinking."

IN a more affirmative vein, I now turn to explore what can be gained by starting from a "first-person" pole of investigation and attending phenomenologically to women's embodied, lived experience. I will focus on two areas: First, we can attain a more adequate account of the intentional and volitional aspects of the subject, one that moves beyond the antinomies of "Enlightenment versus postmodern" formulations. Second, we can gain an appreciation of the importance of embodiment as the locus for certain kinds of shared experience between women that may be significant for a politics of feminist solidarity.

If subjects enjoy a degree of freedom and are capable of a degree of individual initiative, yet are not the disembodied "aerial distance" knowers[11] of the Enlightenment ideal, then we must apprehend them as what Merleau-Ponty calls body-subjects. As such, their knowledge will be situated and perspectival, and their forms of cognition and motivations to act will be in some measure sentient and affective. We must acknowledge, in short, that there are ways in which we come to know, think, and act with our bodies. The body is not merely the medium through which discursive effects flow (though it may also sometimes be this). Nor is it, as an alternative reductionism would hold, the site of a biological determinism, even though biology is not wholly irrelevant to human knowing and acting. For, as Maxine Sheets-Johnstone has written:

> the tenets of both postmodernism and sociobiology preclude insights into the essentially corporeal relationship between the personal and the political, thus into those corporeal archetypes that subtend power relations, and into those bodily "I cans" that are the source of our concept of power. In the broadest terms, this is because postmodernism culturizes animate form and sociobiology biologizes gender. (1994, 7)

Thus, beyond these alternatives, we need to recognize that the body has sui generis ways of knowing and acting that have a bearing on what we generally call choice, or freedom.

I begin my discussion of embodied subjectivity by exploring what takes place when a woman "decides" to engage in a feminist practice of some kind. I begin here not to tell individual "conversion" stories nor to imply that feminism comes into being simply as a result of personal choices by individual women. Rather, I want to focus on the role of affectivity in the emergence of such choices, and thus on the importance of embodiment as the site of affectivity. In doing this I want to cast light not only on the inadequacy of discourse reductionism but also on the rationalist dismissal of embodied experience that still runs through some other strands of feminist theory. For feminist theorists who remain more centrally in the Enlightenment tradition also tend, like poststructuralists, to expunge embodied experience from

11. The term is originally George Eliot's and is used by Jane Roland Martin (1996).

analysis. However, they do so by overly privileging reason rather than discursivity. They argue that women turn to feminist action out of an explicit commitment to certain values or principles.

For example, Judith Grant insists that the "choice" to become a feminist arises not from "experience" but rather from a deliberate shift to a "feminist lens." She claims that *"feminism is a choice to view the world differently."* Similarly, she maintains, anti-feminist women are not victims of false consciousness but are also engaged in a political choice: "For whatever *reasons,* anti-feminists do not see feminism as being in their *interests*" (1993, 180–81; emphases added). The feminist lens is oriented above all by certain values, Grant argues: "freedom, equality and universal justice," all of which are presupposed by the key feminist value, "self-determination." Thus "every important feminist issue can be discussed in terms of the importance of self-determination and the ways in which the ideological structure of gender inhibits the same" (186–87).

But our choices are rarely as rational, or as rationally motivated, as Grant here suggests. It may not be the case that anti-feminists have clear "reasons" for their positions or a clear idea of their "interests." Fear, insecurity, anxiety are more likely to motivate them than principled arguments.[12] Nor do feminists, for the most part, conduct their lives, or make their decisions, at the abstract level of values that Grant invokes here. If pushed to say why we act in a certain way we will usually be able to articulate values or state reasoned principles to justify what we do. But "decisions" to engage in feminist practices generally emerge from more cloudy and complex domains, in which values are lived as *affects:* as strongly felt emotions or, as we often say, *gut* feelings. As Alison Jaggar has remarked, "if we had no emotional responses to the world, it is inconceivable that we should ever come to value one state of affairs more highly than another" (1989, 153). It is only when we experience a *sense* of outrage or hurt, a profound *feeling* of injustice, at unequal pay for women for example, that we are likely to decide to act. It is here, in furnishing descriptions of such affects—of the ways in which values are lived by embodied subjectivities prior to conceptualization or rationalization, and the ways in which, as Beauvoir and Sartre put it, we "disclose" values in what we do—that phenomenology has important contributions to make to feminism.

One becomes involved in feminist practices, I am suggesting, in large measure as a response to a range of feelings and emotions. These may well include pain, misery, isolation, frustration, anger, or outrage; these may be experienced with regard to one's own life or that of other women. For such

---

12. One major exception to this is the anti-abortionist position. For pro-(fetus) life women generally operate from very clear (if misguided) theological and ethical principles on this issue.

feelings to be experienced with regard to the lives of others (and I shall argue below that feminism requires such an intersubjective dimension), more positive emotions, such as empathy, compassion, affection, or care, will also often play a part. I talk here of feelings as well as emotions to indicate that there is a *sentient* dimension to emotions. While many simple feelings, such as "pins and needles" in one's hands, may not evoke emotion, almost all emotions are inflected with feeling, or sentience.

My claim is certainly not that feelings alone "cause" women to engage in feminist practices. For it is only in certain discursive (and other) contexts that the emergence of feminist practices becomes possible. There also exist culture- and gender-specific repertoires through which we signify emotions, and thus they are rarely expressed in a "pure" form. For example, when expressing anger, it is more acceptable in modern Western society for men than for women to swear or shout.[13] Moreover, to express an emotion is often to alter it: men's anger may well *be* different from women's in this society because it is permitted different repertoires of expression, and in this sense we can say anger is a function of discourse. But it is important also to recognize that emotions often exceed (or precede) discourse. As the epigraph from Virginia Woolf at the beginning of this book suggests, we often have to struggle to try to express emotions, and we frequently find ourselves unable to do so. To be "speechless," or to "struggle for words," is hardly an uncommon experience. But this inability makes the emotion no less "real." Nor—contra Rorty—does it make it any less "human." Rorty's claim that inarticulate pain, because it is not discursive, is merely "what ties us to nonlanguage-using beasts" assumes what Elizabeth Spelman has called the "Dumb View" of emotions. It conceives them as blind physiological forces that merely disrupt rational judgments and do not involve cognition "proper." (Spelman 1989). Such a view fails dismally to grasp experiences of pain, and to hold such a view is to ignore the profound, but often silent, wellsprings of suffering from which movements such as feminism emerge.[14]

To illustrate, I return to the experience of humiliation, to what Rorty calls the specifically human form of pain. To feel humiliated, or more generally to feel shame, is to undergo an experience not merely of consciousness but also of embodied—and thus gendered—existence.[15] For example, in the face

---

13. There is also more acceptance of the use of physical force on the part of men—no doubt one of the main reasons why almost all heterosexual domestic violence is perpetrated by men on women.

14. Although I make my argument here with regard to feminism, it also applies to other movements for human liberation, such as anti-colonial or anti-racist struggle.

15. As discussed in earlier chapters, both Beauvoir and Fanon draw on and modify Sartre's classic account of shame to emphasize its embodied qualities. Their respective treatments of this issue belie Rorty's disembodied account of humiliation.

of sexist and objectifying remarks made by a passing group of men, a woman is likely to feel acute discomfort with her own body. It is not just that she is visually objectified and sees herself through the objectifying gaze of her humiliators, for whom she is just a nice pair of boobs or a sexy ass. For she also *feels* herself become an object in response to their calls and stares. She tightens, shrinks, turns rigid (thing-like); she feels her face flush, her hands sweat, her stomach knot. The "pain" of humiliation might well be discursively inflicted, but it is viscerally lived. Similarly, if a woman resists such humiliation with anger, this also will be a felt, bodily experience. As she becomes angry, she is aware of her faster pulse, the clenching of her hands and jaw. And if she tosses back a verbal retort, the tone and the bodily gestures that are part of it will "speak" as much as the actual words she emits to her tormentors.

What both discursive and Enlightenment accounts of the subject fail to consider are the lived, corporeal aspects of subjectivity. Sentient, affective, and emotional experiences come to be a vital constituent of cognition, judgment, and speech. Without considering these aspects, we cannot give sufficiently full accounts of experiences such as humiliation, fear, anger, empathy, or care, out of which acts of resistance are often born. Thus, Adrienne Rich subtitled her path-breaking book *Of Woman Born* ([1976] 1986) as *Motherhood as Experience and Institution*, and she begins with her own sentient experience. Her point of departure is the overwhelming bodily exhaustion, the inchoate *feelings* of anger and incipient violence, that drove her to desperation; as well as the sensuality and warmth of the good moments of motherhood.

Rich begins her account with the following extract from her diary: "My children cause me the most exquisite suffering of which I have any experience. It is the suffering of ambivalence: the murderous alternation between bitter resentment and raw-edged nerves, and blissful gratification and tenderness" (21). A bitter taste, the pain of exposed nerve endings, a satiation of desire, a yielding softness—the sensate and erotic resonances of Rich's description of maternal experience speak to the embodied nature of her pains and pleasure. Indeed, it was through a daringly honest phenomenology of her own feelings that she came to break taboos about the "dark side" of motherhood—even to the point of empathizing with the woman, a mother of eight, who one day neatly chopped up her two youngest children on her suburban front lawn (chap. 10). By taking her own experience as "foundational" here, Rich is able to open up a space in which to reflect on motherhood also as patriarchal institution.

Rich reflects on her approach in ways that reveal a striking affinity with phenomenology. In the afterword she writes about the need, as she puts it, "to *think through the body*" (284), adding a few lines later that "we are neither 'inner' nor 'outer' constructed." It is this recognition of selves as embodied, sentient consciousnesses, of selves as constructed neither solely from within nor from without, but as what Merleau-Ponty called "a third genus of being" (PP 350), that is lacking in postmodern accounts of subjectivity (like Rorty's and Scott's) as well as in Grant's rationalism. For feminist resistance, as Rich illustrates, is born of neither discourse nor cognition alone but also of this affective realm of embodied experience.

In his *Phenomenology of Perception,* Merleau-Ponty argues that if we examine our immediate, lived experiences of perception, they put into question how perception has traditionally been explained, through dichotomies between consciousness and matter, mind and body. They also challenge such dichotomies themselves.[16] In the experience of perceiving, I am neither primarily the knowing subject of rationalist philosophy, for whom perception involves the construction of a mental image of an object by consciousness, nor a mere physical receptor and aggregator of external sensory stimuli, as empiricist theories of perception hold. Nor, we could now add to Merleau-Ponty's argument, am I a passive recipient of a discursively produced "reality." Rather, a phenomenology of perception offers us an account of our *sentient* "knowing" of the world and things, an account of our ability to order and make sense of a situation, not as a disembodied consciousness but rather as each a "body-subject" whose intentionality organizes a meaningful world around it.

For example, if I wake up in the night and want to turn on my bedside light, I will not "think" about where I am or where it is, but even half asleep I will "know" in which direction to extend my arm and how to feel for and push the switch. Or (to give a more intersubjective example) if I am walking along the street and I see a small child fall down on the sidewalk in front of me, in one simultaneous rush of perception, bodily motion, and empathetic understanding of her pain and fright, I will rush forward to pick her up and comfort her. I do not first survey the scene and then rationally infer what my course of action should be. Nor do I engage in moral deliberation as to whether I should help her. Rather, my action has *immediate* intersubjective,

---

16. In *Phenomenology of Perception,* Merleau-Ponty treats perception as paradigmatic of sensory experience of all kinds. But feminist critics have pointed out that his focus on perception risks perpetuating the dominating male gaze that so much Western science and philosophy legitimize. As both Butler (1989) and Grosz (1994) point out, the perceiving subject is, for Merleau-Ponty, a male subject. This becomes particularly clear in his treatment of the relation of perception to sexual arousal ("The Body in its Sexual Being," PP 154–73). In his later work, *The Visible and the Invisible* ([1964] 1968), Merleau-Ponty treats touch as the sense most paradigmatic of our ambiguous and reversible relationship with the world. But even here he has been accused of a masculinist bias by Irigaray ([1984] 1993, 151–84). Yet I don't think the masculinism of his specific applications negates his general argument or destroys its relevance for feminism.

moral, and emotional dimensions, in itself disclosing my concern for another.

As this last example suggests, Merleau-Ponty's account of perception also points toward a phenomenology of emotional experience. For emotion is similarly irreducible to intellectual experience, to a simple physiological response, or to a discursive effect. When Rich describes her feelings of "bitter resentment" at her children, she is describing a "taste" that is not reducible either to a mere physical sensation, or to an intellectual experience, or to a discursive construction. Rather, an interconstituency of the physical, the cognitive, and the cultural/discursive is at play in such an experience and the lived body is its site. A poststructuralism that ignores this interconstituency, attributing constituting agency to discourse alone, will fail to grasp the experiential complexity out of which feminist commitments may arise.

My discussion so far has been centered on the experiences of an individual embodied subject. It should already be evident from my illustrations, however, that "individual" experience is always also social. It is social insofar as it comes into being in a humanly created world (be it of light switches, sidewalks, or the institution of motherhood—all forms of what Sartre calls the practico-inert), and it is also social insofar as emotional affects are almost always solicited and cathected in ways that are culturally and interpersonally informed. Thus the issues still to be explored concern the notion of *women's* experience, as opposed to the experience of apparently discrete individuals who are women: Can we talk of "women's experience" as a possible element in a politics of feminist solidarity? Are there kinds of embodied experience that are common to most women in Western society and which might predispose them to engage in those forms of collective resistance to women's subordination that we call feminism? If so, is it also possible to present descriptions of such experiences that do not obscure the profound differences that may also divide women?

Given my account of the lived body, we obviously cannot say that it is the biological body per se that women share as a potential basis for feminist solidarity. Yet there are certain stable biological attributes to the female body, and we should not be too hasty in dismissing them as wholly irrelevant. Although there are exceptions, *in general* women menstruate, have a vagina, clitoris, and womb, are capable of being impregnated, have large mammary glands on their chests, are shorter and lighter in weight and have a higher percentage of body fat than men, and so on. That not all women exactly fit these descriptions, that some individuals have ambiguous genitalia for example, does not invalidate such general statements of fact—any more than the fact that some people have had a leg amputated puts into question the statement that human beings are bipeds, or the fact that some people are born with a sixth finger invalidates the statement that members of the species homo sapiens have five fingers on each hand. The general facts of women's biology are not wholly irrelevant to women's experience in general, even though they do not determine it.

For example, irrespective of the diverse social constructions that are placed upon it, the fact of menstruation, the seeping of blood from her body each month, must be paid attention to by a woman. Furthermore, in virtually no society (Western or otherwise) does the fact that a woman is capable of being impregnated for much of her life not have a bearing on her way of conducting herself and the way she is treated. As Beauvoir put it, a woman's body is not her "destiny," since it determines nothing in any strictly causal sense. But it still remains "one of the essential elements in her situation in the world" (SS 37). Thus, if we seek to explore whether there are some common experiential elements that might predispose a wide range of women to engage in forms of feminist activity, we will need to examine that interconstituency of the biological, affective, cultural, and discursive domains that *is* the lived body. For many women might have in common the meaning and experience of feminine embodiment within a particular national, social, and cultural location, particularly one like the United States that is structured by pervasive, even hegemonic, forms of male domination.

This hypothesis receives confirmation in Emily Martin's anthropological study *The Woman in the Body* (1987), which carefully explores whether women, at least in the contemporary United States, share certain common embodied experiences that cut across race and class differences. Martin found that the organization of society into public and private spheres was lived as a fragmenting clash of bodily and social experiences by all the women she interviewed, irrespective of race or class. The bodily temporality of menstruation, for example, is incommensurable with the "normal" time requirements of the modern working day and even the school day—as are pregnancy and breast-feeding. Similarly, "dealing" at menopause with the hot flashes that are deemed publicly taboo is experienced as a divisive clash between bodily self and social world. Such experiences of fragmentation can, however, be taken up in different ways. Most of the women Martin interviewed expressed resentment, but others engaged in forms of questioning and self-affirmation (1987, 197–200).

In another illustration, Iris Young's phenomenological studies of gender differences in motility and spatiality suggest that there are profound differences between masculine and feminine body comportment in advanced Western industrial society. Although body comportment is also expressive of class, race, and other dimensions of identity, Young also suggests that the feminine "types, modalities, styles of existence" she describes are not exclusive to white, Anglo, middle-class women such as herself, and can "resonate" with the experiences of "differently identifying" women (1990b, 16–17). In comparison with men, women rarely extend their bodies fully or with confidence. They usually sit, stand, walk, and carry parcels in an inhibited fashion that minimizes the amount of space they occupy. A girl, Young suggests, "learns actively to hamper her movements" (154). Living under the objectifying male gaze of patriarchy, and faced with the ever-present threat of bodily invasion, she learns not to be expansive but rather to close in on herself. Young ends her essay by offering the intriguing—and surely highly plausible—"intuition" that "the general lack of confidence that we frequently have about our cognitive or leadership abilities is traceable in part to an original doubt of our body's capacity" (156).

Commonalities of feminine embodied experience, such as Martin and Young point to, certainly are not sufficient to justify claims for "sisterhood" among women, even within a specific national context. Yet neither should we be too hasty in dismissing their importance. Such minimal commonalities of women's embodied experience still remain significant for feminist politics. *Solidarity* between women, that is, support for other women where one's own immediate well-being is not at issue, is a necessity for feminism, yet is always fragile. Even though common experiences of feminine embodiment do not offer a basis for "sisterhood," I believe they can furnish what I will call an *affective predisposition* to act on behalf of women other than and different from oneself: a predisposition toward forms of feminist solidarity.

For example, I have never been motivated to struggle for the rights of the blind or to act in support of the demands of the Aboriginal peoples of Australia. But, even though I have never been abused myself, I have spent considerable time and energy in helping to establish and maintain a shelter for battered women. Why? This was not because I feared I might one day need the use of a shelter myself, or because I carefully diagnosed domestic violence as the most pressing problem for women, or because I believed I had a stronger moral obligation to offer support to battered women than to anybody else. In short, I did not *dispassionately* choose, according to moral principles or rational criteria, where to put my energies. If, as I have suggested, it is when we *feel* outrage, or anger, or pain that we are most likely to act, then we are most likely to do so when we are able to experience a degree of affinity with others for which our own embodied experience predisposes us. In the case of battered women, similarities of feminine embodiment and my awareness of the susceptibility of all women's bodies, my own included, to male violence offered such predisposing factors.

My claim here is a fairly modest one, for obviously I cannot enter fully into the worlds of other women by way of such commonalities of embodiment. And indeed, the greater the social differences there are between me and them, the less will I be able to enter their worlds—or they mine. Here the search for wider knowledge about others becomes an important issue. For the more we make an effort to learn about women whose lives are radically different from our own, the more do bonds of affinity become possible. But wider knowledge is not a substitute for our capacity, through our own embodied experience, to engage affectively with the experience of others; rather, it may enable us, if we so endeavor, to extend our affectivity across wider divides.

By insisting on the role of embodied experience as an affective basis for solidarity among women, I do not mean to argue that women have a greater capacity to "care" than men. Care is an orientation to be achieved, and it is neither automatically present in the lives of women nor irrelevant to the lives of men.[17] Nor am I referring to pity or charity for women more oppressed than oneself, for such responses (as I discuss in the next chapter) would involve forms of objectification. Rather, what I am talking about is a *direct* experience of affinity among women that is possible (though never guaranteed) because I can recognize as also "mine" the embodied experiences of another woman, even while knowing that she and I are in other ways very different.

Thus, contrary to the claim that to seek for commonalities in women's experience is to essentialize women or to deny difference, I argue that giving attention to commonalities of experience, even to the minimal ones of feminine embodiment, is one of the most important ways that we can become open to others different from ourselves. An exclusive focus on the discursive construction of identities risks occluding, in the name of pre-given categories of difference, concrete embodied experiences that we well might find we share. For feminism to endure as a movement that can encompass differences among women without reifying them, it is urgent that we explore areas of possible common experience: notably those of the lived feminine body.

To conclude, solidarity among women is certainly not automatic or "natural." But if we are ever to struggle toward wider forms of feminist solidarity, we will do so by being attentive to one another as embodied and affective subjectivities and not only as discursively constructed subjects. Nothing is guaranteed here, however. Thus in the next (and final) chapter, I further explore some of the conditions in which affective bonds and forms of solidarity among women may—or may not—become possible.

17. Tronto persuasively argues that an "ethic of care" should not be gender-specific or confined to the private sphere, and that the boundaries between ethics and politics would shift radically were practices of care seen to be of general political import. As she concludes: "Care is not a parochial concern of women, a type of secondary moral question, or the work of the least well off in our society" (1993, 180).

6 Phenomenology and Difference: On the Possibility of Feminist "World-Travelling"

The heady days of "Sisterhood is Powerful" are long over. Today, feminists tread warily as they negotiate the minefield of diverse identities that divide women, not merely in terms of their experiences but also by degrees of privilege and power. Attention to such differences is critical, yet while effecting a crucial shift in feminist consciousness, it can also present its own pitfalls. If automatic sisterhood was problematic, so also is a vision of feminist politics as a set of shifting coalitions among women of radically different identities, formed only from fear or necessity. In her much-cited talk "Coalition Politics: Turning the Century," Bernice Johnson Reagon, for example, distinguishes between "home," a protecting space, a "barred room" where one feels comfortable because it contains only people like oneself, and "coalition" (1983, 357–59). Coalition is not to be confused with home: it is not where women give one another comfort or sustenance. On the contrary it is "uncomfortable," even "terrible" (362). One enters coalition with people who are not like oneself as a matter of survival. "The 'our' must include everybody you have to include in order for you to survive. . . . That's why we have to have coalitions. Cause I ain't gonna let you live unless you let me live. Now there's danger in that, but there's also the possibility that we can both live—if you can stand it" (365).

Reagon offers a clear-eyed critique of naive notions of sisterhood, and her no-nonsense affirmation that power dynamics operate within feminism is to be heeded. However, I think she presents us with overly polarized options. Diverse groups of women need sometimes to open the barred rooms of "home," or choose to venture forth from them, for reasons other than the sheer necessity that Reagon sees as the basis for coalition. A view of feminist politics as coalition-work based above all on fear, or the need for survival, is too Hobbesian in import. It implies that there are no bases for forms of positive recognition and relation among differently located women and that feminism is not informed by any ethical impulse. An efficacious feminism must be more than a mere alliance for survival. Though "sisterhood" certainly cannot be assumed as its pre-given starting point, yet something to which the term sisterhood gestures surely remains an aspiration, a vision to be struggled toward. If not sisterhood, then at least solidarity—by which I mean an action-oriented concern for the well-being of others where one's own survival is not directly at issue—must be integral to any effective feminist movement.

The solidarity I am concerned with here is not that of the "standing shoulder to shoulder" variety, among those who already perceive that they share a common subjection to a pre-given wrong—for example, trade union solidarity against a wage cut.[1] Although this kind of solidarity can be important, it is a different kind that I examine here. My concern is with solidarity in situations where an injury to others does *not* directly injure oneself (or one's own group), for this is often vital for a heterogenous movement such as feminism.[2] Such solidarity requires an act of generosity—a gratuitous giving of attention, time, effort, resources to others. In addition, it requires a generosity that respects its recipients. Otherwise it risks degenerating into charity and reducing them to an objectified victim status.

My purpose in this final chapter is thus to explore some possible grounds from which what I will call a "respectful recognition" of other women—women with whom one does *not* share certain core elements of identity, or even perhaps any direct interests—might develop. By respectful recognition, I mean a relationship in which one is deeply and actively concerned about others, but neither appropriates them as an object of one's own experience

1. Jodi Dean has usefully distinguished between various kinds of solidarity. She refers to this trade union style as "conventional solidarity" and suggests it is "based on our common interests, concerns, and struggles" (1996, 39). She contrasts it to "affective solidarity," which is based on feelings of care or concern but which she believes must remain very small-scale and particularistic. Beyond these alternatives, she defends and develops a model of what she calls "reflective solidarity," based on a Habermasian model of "communicative engagement" with others that respects differences. In terms of Dean's typology, my project here is to explore the possibility of expanding "affective solidarity" beyond the limited and particularistic boundaries Dean unnecessarily attributes to it. Dean's own neo-Habermasian project, to develop a model of reflective solidarity grounded in communicative action, is I think problematic. For it tends to assume that diverse participants are equally positioned in debate and that they all have equal communicative skills—assumptions that risk effacing significant differences in power and privilege.

2. For example, on a strict self-interest model, there is no reason for heterosexual women actively to support lesbian and gay struggles for domestic partnership rights, etc. Either one has to assert a (surely highly problematic) pre-given unity of interests between *all* women in order to urge straight women to participate in such a struggle, or else (more plausibly) one must appeal for an act of solidarity that is based not on direct self-interest but rather on ethical and/or what I will refer to as affective grounds.

or interests nor dissolves oneself in a vicarious experience of identification with them. Such a relationship allows others space of their own and recognizes a distance between us that is not the distance of unconcern. Are there, I want to ask, certain grounds that might generally predispose women toward a mutual and non-appropriating recognition of other women, even when their life experiences and degrees of power and privilege are radically different? For white, middle-class, heterosexual feminists, such as myself, attentiveness to such differences self-evidently arises as a pressing concern, and we must always be aware that our own privileges may make it difficult for us to recognize others on their own terms. But it is also arises for other groups. For example, as some feminists of color have observed, although all women of color are subject to white racism, they are also often inequitably positioned with regard to other axes of privilege. Differences in sexuality or social class, for example, may often divide them.

As I tried to delineate my area of inquiry, several different formulations of the central question initially came to mind: how is it possible to have sympathy with, or compassion for, radically different others? Or, how does one develop empathy, or perhaps a sense of affinity, with women significantly different from oneself? Whatever term we choose (and all of them are fraught and ambiguous), is it possible to develop a respectful but concerned *affective* relationship of recognition with others significantly different from oneself?

The term "affect," implying a relationship strongly inflected with sentience and emotion, is important here. I take it as my starting point (as argued in chapter 5) that affective relations are desirable, even necessary, for a viable feminist movement precisely *because* of our differences. Because women do indeed have different degrees and kinds of privilege and power, and because their immediate interests are often not only divergent but also positively conflictual, forms of recognition that rely on shared interests alone are insufficient for feminism. Nor are those forms of recognition that rely on abstract moral principles that "ought" to transcend divergences of interest, or on appeals that we take the stance of "the generalized other," sufficient.[3] For a politics grounded in principle alone usually lacks sufficient passion to be efficacious.

To sustain any kind of a long-term or broad feminist movement in the face of a multiplicity of distinctions in power and privilege among women, forms of recognition that are grounded in *affect* are also necessary. *Feelings* of concern for others must develop, and forms of intersubjective embodied experience that are not discursively thematized may be important in the development of such feelings. I do not want to claim that these are necessarily

3. See Benhabib 1987 for an attempt to integrate the "generalized other" into the project of a more concrete feminist ethics.

more important than discursive relations. But I do claim that intersubjective embodied experiences—the ways we tacitly "know" the experience of others through our bodies—warrant far fuller consideration than they generally receive (or indeed can receive) within the discourse-oriented, postmodern paradigm that now predominates in feminist theory. For, as Richard Kearney has put it with regard to transformative politics more generally, "the deepest motivational springs of political involvement are located in the capacity to *feel* needs for others beyond our most immediate circle of family and friendship" (1998, 234).

None of the terms I have mentioned—sympathy, compassion, affinity, empathy—quite conveys my theme, though all of them approximate it. I seek to explore some of the ways that women's affective experiences of embodiment may facilitate the emergence of forms of recognition of (and among) significantly different others that are both respectful and engaged—and also to consider when this might become difficult or unlikely. In what follows, I explore the possibility of such recognition in a phenomenological vein: What, I ask, are some of the most fundamental qualities of the experience of encountering radically different others? In particular, since concern with the suffering of other women may be a crucial affective impetus for feminist politics, how does one experience the suffering, physical and otherwise, of others? Are there situations where one can do so without either objectifying the other or losing oneself in excessive identification?

SOME years ago now Maria Lugones coined the notion of "playful 'world'-travelling" to describe a process of entering the experiential domain of others (1990). Drawing on Marilyn Frye's distinction between the "arrogant eye," which in perceiving "arrogates" another as an object, and the "loving eye" which recognizes and values the independence of the other (Frye 1983, 52–83), Lugones advocates world-travelling as a way to enter the world of another in a non-objectifying manner. World-travelling can be achieved, she claims, through an attitude of "loving playfulness" that can enable one to "identify" with another and enter her world. For this to be possible one must eschew a fixed conception of oneself and refuse antagonism or competitiveness.[4] Instead of defending boundaries, one must endeavor to be open to ambiguity and surprises, to accept being a fool and having oneself and one's own world continually reconstructed (1990, 399–401). "Travelling to someone's 'world' is a way of identifying with them . . . because by travelling to their

---

4. Thus "play" here does not mean the engagement in agonistic, rule-bound competition integral to such "games" as football or chess. Lugones notes how different her notion of play is from that of such masculine theorists as Huizinga or Ricoeur (1990, 399–400).

'world' we can understand *what it is to be them and what it is to be our-selves in their eyes*. Only when we have travelled to each other's 'worlds' are we fully subjects to each other" (401).

Lugones makes a strong claim here that in world-travelling the self shifts not merely perceptually or cognitively but ontologically: "The shift from *being* one person to *being* a different person is what I call 'travel.' . . . One does not pose as someone else. . . . Rather one *is* someone who has that per-sonality or character or uses space and language in that particular way" (396; first two emphases added). As a vision of feminist relationality that can tra-verse radical differences, I find Lugones's account appealing. But on closer scrutiny it also begs difficult questions. Some of these concern the possi-bility of doing what she advocates; others concern its desirability, particu-larly for women who are in positions of privilege.

Most Western women do, of course, live between two, or more, "worlds" and shift existential modalities as they move between them. For example, almost all women are employed in waged or salaried work for at least a part of their lives,[5] and most of us are aware that we alter our speech, body com-portment, dress, and so on when we go "out" to work, departing from where we are "at home" with family or friends. When going "out" involves also a shift into the language, or cultural style, of others who are dominant along axes such as language, class, race, and/or ethnicity, this process becomes in-creasingly demanding and even painful. Such is the case for a Latina, like Lugones, who must function in an Anglo world. However, this process of shifting does not mean that Lugones can literally become, can assume the being of, an Anglo when she enters an Anglo world. Nor is it to say that even if I, as an Anglo,[6] learn to speak Spanish and endeavor, in good faith, to world-travel "lovingly and playfully" into her world, I will ever actually assume the *being* of a Latina. Our experience of attempting to enter the world of oth-ers is both more complex and less complete than Lugones assumes in de-scribing the process of "identification." For we cannot shed our own weighty identities as freely and playfully as she suggests. As Susan Bordo has put it with reference to other celebrations of "mobile" and "playful" selves, Lugones ultimately offers "a new imagination of disembodiment: a dream of being *everywhere*" (1990, 143).

I would add that were full identification with others in their worlds even possible, it would not be desirable. For the fact remains that the privileged

5. This is also increasingly becoming the case for many non-Western women.
6. The term "Anglo" is, of course, itself problematic. I am an Anglo for the purposes of Lugones's distinction. However, I am a first-generation immigrant to the United States, having grown up in England. Although I am thus a "native" English speaker, I find I frequently miss social cues and am misunderstood in U.S. Anglo society: Anglo identity itself is far from unitary.

world-traveller (be she white in a world of women of color, young in a world of the aged, financially well-off in a world of the poor, heterosexual in a world of the lesbian) still has the option of returning to her "own" world and its privileges. To obscure this fact by too strong an identification with others permits us to deny the responsibilities that are born of our own location. For example, when reading works by feminists of color, numerous white students in my women's studies classes so strongly identify with the material that they express outrage at racism, as if they were not themselves structurally implicated in it. It is as if they are personally exonerated from white racism by virtue of the depth of their empathy. Their identification is so intense that they no longer have to deal with the realities of their own social location. In short, they have vicariously "become" women of color; but in so doing, they have entered a world of fantasy.[7]

These concerns about strong identification not withstanding, Lugones's paper still stands as an important benchmark in feminist struggles with the issue of difference. More recently Christine Sylvester has taken up and endeavored to flesh out Lugones's notion of world-travelling, developing an account of what she calls "empathetic cooperation" (1995). Sylvester is an American political scientist who does research in Southern Africa. Thus, although she emphasizes the ways African women also world-travel as they negotiate with the complex postcolonial worlds at home or abroad, for her the main challenge is to world-travel from a position of privilege—as the outsider, the Western "expert"—without objectifying the women she studies. As she points out, the dangers to be avoided are manifold: one must avoid the objectifying stance of the tourist, who consumes African women as exotica. One must also avoid objectifying African women by casting them in the role of victims of oppression, such that their own agency is effaced. Finally, one must avoid objectifying them as research objects, as mere sources of data to answer one's own pre-determined questions.

Unlike Lugones, Sylvester does not endeavor to enter the world, to assume the very *being,* of another through empathetic cooperation. Rather, she suggests, one "relies on empathy to enter into the spirit of difference and find in it an *echo of oneself as other than the way one seems to be. . . .* [one studies] 'the other' as *a familiar resonance*" (1995, 946 and 948; emphases added). Sylvester borrows the notion of "relational autonomy" from object-relations theory to describe this dynamic. Relational autonomy is not the masculinist "reactive" autonomy of the rigidly bounded male ego that, Nancy Chodorow has argued, is formed when a boy establishes his identity

7. Fantasy surely has a place in feminism, in the much-needed formulation of feminist utopias. However, it is not a good basis for working out relationships among different women in the here and now.

by sharply splitting himself from his mother and positing her as an object in opposition to himself (1978). Rather, the "empathetic identities" that Sylvester suggests are possible through relational autonomy "exist separately and yet inform and draw on each other. . . . As one travels, one encounters few aliens out there at the same time that one appreciates the many nuances of 'women' " (1995, 946). But, as she rightly warns, women are not automatically empathetic: world-travelling must be "willfully" embraced (948).[8]

Empathetic cooperation demands similar qualities of the self to those Lugones discusses: a "mobile" subjectivity, rather than the parading of fixed identity positions, and thus, flexibility, a commitment to juggling, an embrace of ambiguity and irony. In terms of the politics of research, what is required is a "cooperative researcher-'subject' coalition," a democratic and participatory process in which research agendas are reoriented by their "subjects" and in which the researcher is flexibly open to shifts and surprises. Although her main concern is with the politics of research, Sylvester's account also suggests a model for cooperative coalitions in feminist politics more generally. *Pace* Reagon, coalition might not always be hell but might sometimes be a process in which one "encounters few aliens" and "appreciates the many nuances of 'women.'" However, Sylvester's model cannot be fully transferred from research to politics. For the researcher is a temporary visitor in the world of her "subjects," whereas in domestic feminist politics, because we are all here to stay and have long-term interests, much more is at stake in our conflicts and in the successes and failures of empathetic cooperation. Moreover, Sylvester's account remains peculiarly abstract. Although she offers a powerful exhortation as to how we should endeavor to act, she conveys very little of the *feel* of attempting to develop such empathetic cooperation, of the dimensions of intersubjective experience it requires, or of the experience of encountering their limits.

A more experientially concrete account of what is involved in respectful and affective relations of recognition among radically different others is initiated, however, by Sandra Bartky. In her essay "Solidarity and Sympathy: On a Tightrope with Scheler" (1997), Bartky draws on the work of the German phenomenologist Max Scheler (specifically *The Nature of Sympathy* [1913]) to explore a range of ways of relating to the experience of others. Scheler examines and rejects what in English we would call "sympathy," arguing that it involves "a heightened commiseration bestowed from above

8. In relation to this "willful" project, Sylvester also cautions against excessive postmodern destabilization of the subject. For empathy must presuppose a subject with a degree of stability. Although postmodern critiques of overly centered subjects are valid, she argues that the subject cannot be allowed to evaporate entirely into the play of shifting discursivities. How, she asks, "does empathy emerge if there is no subject to empathize from and with?" (1995, 953).

and from a standpoint of superior power and dignity" (Scheler, cited in Bartky 1997, 181). He also rejects "empathy," by which he means an emotional "identification" with another which is so intense that one loses one's own ego boundaries in an illusory merging with him (or her). Akin to Sylvester's notion of empathetic cooperation based on relational autonomy is Scheler's notion of *Mitgefuhl*, "fellow-feeling" as it is rendered in the English translation (Scheler [1913] 1954) or, as Bartky more exactly renders it, "feeling-with" another. In this relationship, one neither objectifies the other person nor dissolves one's own subjectivity in his or hers.

Bartky suggests that Scheler's phenomenology of feeling-with offers feminists a helpful framework for addressing experiences of difference among women. She takes as her focus (as I also shall) the problem of encountering the suffering of other women. For, as she argues, the question of with whom we choose to act in solidarity is largely connected to our responses to particular kinds of suffering (1997, 180). In attempting to feel-with those who suffer, we must not reduce them to passive victim status nor to mere objects of sympathy, or even pity. But neither can we actually experience their suffering ourselves. Instead, "genuinely" to feel-with another "presupposes that awareness of distance between selves which is eliminated by identification" (184): to feel-with somebody is not the same as to feel what they actually feel.

Bartky gives as an example of feeling-with her response to reading Nawal El Saadawi's autobiographical account of how, as a small girl, she was dragged from her bed at night and subjected, with no previous explanation, forewarning, or anesthesia, to a clitoridectomy.[9] As she read the account, Bartky did not engage in identification: that is, she did not picture *herself* as the terrified, suffering child. Nor did she reduce El Saadawi's experience to her own by trying to render an account of it inferentially, extrapolating from her own memories. With Scheler, Bartky suggests that we do not have to have undergone an experience ourselves, or even something very similar, in order to feel-with another who is undergoing it. Feeling-with is sui generis, in the sense that it is not reducible to any other form of experience. It is immediate, and it is not indirectly built up by extrapolation from our own memories or by otherwise deliberately projecting from our own experiences. As Scheler writes, "a person who has never felt mortal terror can still understand and envisage it just as he can also share in it" (Scheler, cited in Bartky 1997, 186). But even so, some contextualization, some degree of mediating "background" information, as Bartky puts it, still is necessary in order for us to

9. In *The Hidden Face of Eve*, Nawal El Saadawi, an Egyptian feminist and physician, begins her account of the lives of girls and women in the Arab world with this searing personal story (1982, 7–8). It should be clear that Bartky is not taking a political position on the practice of clitoridectomy here. She is simply describing her immediate reactions to reading an account of one.

feel-with another's terror. Arguably, we can increase our capacity to feel-with another woman by choosing to learn as much as we can about her world. For the more sense we have of her world, the more easily may we feel-with her, the more possible is an immediate apprehension of her experience.

Feeling-with thus requires what Bartky, paraphrasing Scheler and echoing Frye, calls "a loving orientation," and what I have previously called "respectful recognition," toward another.[10] That is, it requires a concern for the other in her own selfhood, as neither an object of pity nor one whose experience I vicariously appropriate as my own (1997, 186). In such an orientation, the distinction between undergoing an experience and feeling-with the one who undergoes it is *not* obliterated. Nor, I would add, are our differences in social location, which may well include significant differences in privilege and power, eradicated. Yet these differences do not impinge on the immediacy of feeling-with another, and indeed our relationship is momentarily one of equals. For at the moment of embodied affective experience, as is clear in Bartky's example, social distinctions do not play a significant role. When I feel-with the pain of another, the immediacy of the experience temporarily suspends our social differences. I remain subliminally aware of them, insofar as I am still aware that I am not the other, but they remain at the periphery of my attention and do not directly color my relation to the other.

As Bartky remarks, feeling-with takes place rather infrequently today. In the face of ubiquitous and horrendous human suffering on every continent of the globe many of us tend simply to shut down, to inure ourselves to the television images and news reports and go about our "normal" daily business with a shrug of our shoulders. For as Shoshana Felman points out, with regard to teaching United States students about the Holocaust, to allow oneself to feel-with those undergoing trauma is itself traumatic (Felman and Laub 1992, chap. 1).[11] Of course, not all of the experiences of other women that we might feel-with are traumatic. Indeed, to feel-with the pleasures of women different from oneself can also be vital to an affective recognition of

10. I have been treating such terms as loving perception and loving orientation as roughly synonymous with my term, "respectful recognition." However, I prefer to use the latter term because *respect* acknowledges a distance between selves that is important here. It intimates a concern that includes a willingness to let the other be, whereas love can potentially be far more demanding of the other. Love can imply a much higher degree of identification and bonding than is, I think, either possible or perhaps desirable in relationships among different collectivities of women.

11. There are, of course, many explanations one can offer as to why people refuse to feel-with others. These range from psychoanalytic explanations concerning sadism, to socio-biological hypotheses about innate aggression, to the fear of otherness, to crude self-interest. But simply not wanting to know, not wanting to subject oneself to the pain of being aware of the pain of others, might be the most plausible general explanation. As the psychologist Lauren Wispé notes: "the most difficult question to answer about sympathy is 'Why?' Why would people willingly make themselves unhappy?" (1991, 135).

radically different others. It is also perhaps as hard to achieve. The difficulty of feeling-with others, whether in their suffering, their anger, or their joy, requires us more carefully to explore what is involved in the experience. But here my focus will remain on the issue of suffering.

Bartky suggests that the ability to feel-with others has several preconditions. First one must desire to engage in it—or at least not refuse to do so. That is, there must be an ethical impulse, however implicit, to affirm the value of the other. For if one refuses such an affirmation, feeling-with others is instantly precluded. One can cite numerous instances of refusal. These include those where, rather than feeling-with the physical suffering of other women, women have condoned or even participated in it. One can think of wives of American slave owners who would order, and apparently watch with equanimity, the flogging of women slaves; Nazi women who expressed no remorse at the physical suffering of Jewish women; more recently, gangs of Hindu fundamentalist women in India who have participated in beating up Moslem women; or women in certain "right to life" groups in the United States who condone violence against women seeking abortions. Indeed, in some circumstances it appears to be as easy to objectify other women's physical suffering, perhaps even to take pleasure in it, as to feel-with it. This is especially so where differences of race, religion, or other highly charged dimensions of otherness are an issue.

Even so, as members of an inherently social species, human beings do generally find that their own well-being is intimately connected with that of at least some set of other persons about whom they care. As Adam Smith observed in the first paragraph of *The Theory of Moral Sentiments:*

> However selfish soever man [*sic*] may be supposed to be, there are evidently some principles in his nature, which interest him in the fortune of others, and render their happiness necessary to him, though he derives nothing from it, except the pleasure of seeing it. Of this kind is pity or compassion, the emotion which we feel for the misery of others, when we either see it, or are made to conceive it in a lively manner. ([1759] 1976, 9)

Smith is arguably right that it does matter to most of us whether "others" are happy or are suffering, and we do frequently suffer (though in a different manner from the sufferer) at the sight of another's suffering. But Smith's statement operates at a level of universality of which we have correctly learned to be suspicious. For the questions are: About the fortunes of *which* others are we concerned? Whom do we include and exclude from our concern?[12] Indeed, the issue of feminist solidarity can be posed as a set of ques-

---

12. Thus, as Arendt pointed out in her discussion of the "banality of evil," Adolph Eichmann could be a devoted and caring family man while also organizing the mass ex-

tions about the breadth of that set of others: whether, to what extent, and in what situations might others, who are significantly different from ourselves and with whom we are not "at home," belong to it.

Beyond this ethical impulse, beyond our willingness to feel-with others, Bartky also rightly emphasizes the key role of imagination in enabling us to feel-with others. And, as she incisively points out, "imagination" in this context does not just involve the ability, as the term unfortunately suggests, to invoke *images*. Feeling-with involves an imagining that is not just "an internal seeing" but also a *feeling* (Bartky, 1997, 192). Imagination cannot take place in a vacuum, however. It needs ways to mesh into a world. Thus Bartky also emphasizes (with Scheler) that it is not possible to feel-with another (or others) unless the condition of adequate "background information" about their world is met. However, as with Lugones's and Sylvester's accounts of world-travelling, Bartky's account of the nature of such background information remains rather underspecified. It is here that I now focus my attention: on the place of sentience and on our pre-conceptual ways of "knowing" through our bodies (bodies that are both anatomically sexed and deeply gendered) as important sources of background information conducive to feeling-with others.[13]

My method here will be loosely informed by Merleau-Ponty's phenomenology.[14] For such a phenomenology explores individual "lived" experience as indicative of, and as a way of enabling us to clarify, more *general* structures of human experience. This is not to say that strict universality is necessarily claimed for phenomenological descriptions but rather that it is possible to generalize short of universality. Descriptions of what Maxine Sheets-Johnstone has called "tactile-kinesthetic invariants" of the human body—such as having "two legs of a certain form, teeth of a certain kind, a tongue of a certain shape" (1990, 368)—do have a near-universal dimension: that is, they describe norms of human embodiment that are deviated from only in cases of severe illness or deformity. However, although invariant in their basic qualities, they are also *indeterminate* in that they are culturally

---

termination of others whom he deemed to be beyond any claim to his care or respect (1963).

13. Although I agree with Sylvester that the term "empathy" is not necessarily appropriative or condescending, it still often carries those connotations. Thus I continue using Bartky's translation of Scheler's term "feeling-with" as I proceed with my discussion.

14. Although Merleau-Ponty's own descriptions of embodied subjectivity tacitly presuppose a male body and have rightly been criticized by some theorists for this, his approach to lived bodily experience has still proven to be one feminists can creatively appropriate. Not only did Beauvoir draw vital insights from him (as we have seen in part 1), but so have a range of more recent feminist theorists. I have found the work of Young (1990b), Sheets-Johnstone (1990, 1994), Bigwood (1991), and Grosz (1994) particularly helpful.

colored: *styles* of walking, chewing, talking can vary from culture to culture—and also, of course, by gender.[15]

Iris Young has usefully explained the relationship of particular to general in phenomenology in aesthetic terms: "I think of the description of experiences as being like musical notation; it is the 'same' for each instance of its performance. But the music exists only in its particulars, and the particular performances vary in innumerable ways" (1990b, 16). Of course, some postmodern feminists would want to question the stability of the body implied by the metaphor of musical notation. But such a degree of stability is plausibly defended in terms of the constraints and possibilities, what Merleau-Ponty calls the "I cans," of embodied human existence. These include the capacities and limits that are given with our size, strength, sensory range, and so on, and that distinguish humans as a species. Some of these are also differentiated by sex: male "I cans," for example, do not include gestation, giving birth, or lactation. As Beauvoir observes in *The Second Sex*, "there will always be certain differences between man and woman; her eroticism, thus her sexual world, having a particular character of their own, cannot fail to engender a particular sensuality, or sensitivity" (SS 731).

But, of course, the variations in the performance of the basic notation can also be immense. Thus Young suggests, in her phenomenology of "breasted experience," that although having breasts must mean that all women's experience of being in the world is different from that of men, *how* it is different will be culturally specific. She thus sets out to disclose experience that is specific not to all women but only to women living in "capitalist, patriarchal American media-dominated culture, in which breasts are fetishized [and] valued as objects" (1990b, 191).

In what follows, I offer a series of phenomenological examples, some my own and some borrowed from other authors, to propose that there are certain stable notations, certain "invariants" to feminine embodiment, and that these may enable women to feel-with the visible physical suffering of other women more easily than that of men. I also go on to offer some caveats, however, and to suggest that, although the experience of feeling-with others is vital for feminist solidarity, it is never in itself a sufficient ground for feminist politics.

IT has been argued that a unique characteristic of pain is its noncommunicable character. Hannah Arendt, for example, writes that "the experience of great bodily pain, is at the same time the most private and least communicable of all" (1958, 50–51). This is because pain has no object in

---

15. Thus, Bigwood uses the felicitous phrase "an indeterminate constancy" to describe the lived human body (1991).

the world and a body in pain is wholly self-referential. As Arendt also observes, "pain and the concomitant experience of pain are the only sense experiences that are so independent from the world that they do not contain the experience of any worldly object" (114). In *The Body in Pain*, Elaine Scarry builds on Arendt's insights to argue that physical pain is unshareable and actively "language-destroying" (1985, 19). This is so much the case, she asserts, that my relationship to another who claims to be in pain is quintessentially one of doubt. In a strikingly Cartesian vein, she claims that:

> for the person in pain . . . "having pain" may come to be thought of
> as the most vibrant example of what it is to "have certainty," while for
> the other person it is so elusive that "hearing about pain" may exist as
> the primary mode of what it is "to have doubt." . . . Whatever pain
> achieves, it achieves in part through its unsharability, and it ensures
> this unsharability through its resistance to language. (4)

In one sense Arendt and Scarry are correct: the discursive representation of pain is extremely difficult to achieve, and, insofar as pain cannot be described to a non-sufferer, one may easily choose to doubt, or even deny, its existence. Scarry argues that such denial is integral to the structure of torture, in which the torturer reduces his victim to speechlessness while turning pain into the insignia of power (1985, 57). But if pain is language-destroying, this does not mean that it lacks all qualities of communicability. On the contrary, bodies in pain do, to varying degrees, express their condition, and through our own sentience we can also directly feel-with the pain of others. Indeed, it is this non-linguistic character of the communication that, perhaps paradoxically, actually enables it to take place in situations where people do not share the same language or culture. We can "speak" a certain lingua franca through our bodies.[16]

In her account of feeling-with the small girl undergoing a clitoridectomy, Bartky points out that she does not only *see* the scene in her imagination: there is also a sentient dimension. "I must imagine not only the sight of the knife but what she *feels* as it cuts her flesh" (1997, 192). This account points toward the importance of sentience as a vital background condition for feeling-with others and, indeed, for imagining more generally. But however hard she tries to imagine what the girl felt, Bartky does not, of course, literally feel the same.

Feeling-with another's physical pain and directly feeling a pain in one's own body are not identical. Indeed, even imagining a pain in one's own body

---

16. Contrary to Rorty's claim (discussed in the previous chapter) that pain is what "ties us to nonlanguage-using beasts," the body in pain can be the site of extremely wide and profoundly human forms of communication. It is not evident that other animal species communicate their pain to each other as we do.

and actually undergoing the painful event are different. For example, the "pain" I feel in anticipation of having a shot and what my body feels as the injection actually takes place are not identical, even if this is a repeat shot so that I "know" from previous experience what it will feel like. So what then is involved in Bartky's (or my, or your) feeling-with the physical pain of another?

I will begin with a personal, "face-to-face" example. I used to work as a volunteer at a "battered women's" shelter in London. One day I arrived and a woman I had not met before was in the kitchen. Her left eye was bruised and closed, her cheek grazed, her lip gashed. As I greeted her, I did not feel bruising around my own eye, or a graze on my own cheek, or a gash in my own lip. But I did feel physical pain. I was, of course, also aware that the woman was in the shelter because the bruises on her face had been intentionally caused by an abusive male partner, and that in Britain "domestic violence" is the most common source of the kinds of injuries I was seeing. I was also aware, from her clothing and her physiognomy, that the woman was Nigerian (a member of a relatively new immigrant group to Britain at the time), thus that her life experiences were radically different from mine. They must have included cultural dislocation, poverty, and subjection to racism that I had never undergone. But these diverse cognitive realizations, though still subliminally present, remained at the periphery of my consciousness. In the immediacy of feeling-with this woman our social differences were temporarily suspended for me, and what remained central was my sentient and affective response.

As I imagined the blows raining down on the woman's face, what they must have felt like as they impacted, and how much her face must still ache, my own stomach knotted and I felt nauseous: common physiological responses to fear and pain. Thus, while my primary attention was on her suffering and I could feel-with her pain, I was also sharply aware of my own body as discrete. In a certain doubling of embodied awareness, my body was a locus of pain that was distinct from hers, and yet my body was also connected to hers since my (dissimilar) pain was engendered by feeling-with hers. We are, my example suggests, capable of an immediate intersubjective apprehension of another's experience of pain. This apprehension takes place in the dimension of sentience and is not primarily a function of conscious evaluation or discourse. Moreover, this immediate apprehension does not involve an appropriation of the other in which I claim her suffering as my own or an identification in which I claim I can fully enter into her experience.

In *The Psychology of Sympathy*, Lauren Wispé reviews a body of experimental evidence to conclude that what she calls "sympathy"—which she defines as both a heightened awareness of another's suffering and an urge to alleviate it (1991, 68)—does involve forms of immediate embodied response to others, as well as evaluative and imaging activities. In seeing—or even just imagining, as in Bartky's example—another in pain, or one who is visibly unhappy, we often undergo, for example, changes in skin conductivity or heart rate. We also engage in a process of "muscle mimicry," in which we contract our own muscles as if in pain, and in doing so induce an unpleasant mood change and shift of affect in ourselves (Wispé 1991, 135–55). If we conventionally say that depressed people are depressing or, conversely, that happiness or laughter is "infectious," we are right: feeling-with another involves not simply an act of imagination, or a rational reconstruction of "how I would feel if I were them," but also a directly physiological and affective response.[17]

The evidence that Wispé reviews, however, does not consider gender as a factor. In my example, the person in pain was, like myself, a woman. That she was a Nigerian woman whose physiognomy, speech, life experiences, and social status were very different from mine did not interfere with my ability immediately to feel-with her pain. To clarify the place of gender here it is useful to ask a further question: Do I also feel-with the pain of a man whose face has been smashed? A bruised eye and a split lip certainly communicate another's pain to me irrespective of the gender of the sufferer, yet generally I do find that my affective response to a man's pain is weaker. This is surely because, although I share with him those key invariants that make us both sentient human beings, my lived body is also significantly different from his. As I see his bruises and cuts I see them in the context of a body that is not only differently socially located from mine but also organized differently from my own in significant ways.

In *Phenomenology of Perception,* Merleau-Ponty writes of the lived, sentient body that "my whole body for me is not an assemblage of organs juxtaposed in time and space. I am in undivided possession of it and I know where each of my limbs is through a *body image* in which all are included" (PP 98). But one must add to Merleau-Ponty's remark that we also experience ourselves as more than an undivided set of limbs: we experience ourselves as sexed and gendered.[18] My body image includes breasts, a vagina from

17. "[S]ympathy . . . must refer to the sharing of the negative affect of another person despite the fact that the sympathizer and the sufferer are separate entities with no physical connection between them. . . . The sympathizer's experience of pain derives from the distal stimulation of visual and auditory receptors, and from imaginal processes, while the sufferer's pain sensations come from the pain receptors and neural transmitters within the body in which they are experienced" (Wispé 1991, 58).

18. There are, of course, also other differentiae that may be central to one's body image: race is one, as Fanon's account of black embodiment, in *Black Skin, White Masks,* makes clear. Age and physical disablement also radically structure body image. Merleau-Ponty treats the latter instance in part 1 of *Phenomenology of Perception.* In his discussions of the injured soldier, Schneider, Merleau-Ponty argues that his dysfunctions cannot

which I seep and bleed, smooth facial skin. I do not experience as full a recognition of my own body image in seeing another person who is male; thus the background conditions for feeling-with his pain are somewhat less strongly fulfilled for me, though certainly not absent.

Moreover, there are also forms of pain that are directly sex-specific, and it seems plausible to suggest that our ability to feel-with others might be affected by this consideration. To explore this possibility further, I take up a counter-example to Bartky's: one in which, in reading, I encountered limits on my ability to feel-with the pain of another. In Nelson Mandela's autobiography, *Long Walk to Freedom*, he describes the process of "becoming a man," the circumcision rite that all young Xhosa males must go through. Circumcision is conducted publicly on a group of initiates, each of whom must prove his manhood by not flinching. Mandela describes the actual moment as follows:

> before I knew it, the old man was kneeling in front of me. I looked directly into his eyes. He was pale, and although the day was cold, his face was shining with perspiration. His hands moved so fast they seemed to be controlled by an otherworldly force. Without a single word, he took my foreskin, pulled it forward, and then, in a single motion brought down his assegai. I felt as if fire was shooting through my veins. The pain was so intense that I buried my chin into my chest. Many seconds seemed to pass before I remembered the cry, and then I recovered and called out, "Ndiyindoda" [I am a man]. (1994, 24)

In reading this passage, I can feel-with Mandela in his excitement and anxiety—but not, even if I wish to, in his pain. I cannot imagine the pain of the assegai slicing through Mandela's foreskin in the same way that I can imagine the blade slicing through El Saadawi's clitoris. Nor does my own body experience pain with Mandela's pain, as it does with El Saadawi's (or with the bruised Nigerian woman I met at the shelter), although "intellectually" I know that his pain was probably as acute as hers. Of course, the meaning and structure of the two events are very different. El Saadawi was six, unaware of what was to be done to her, unaware even afterward of what was done or why, feeling only pain, powerlessness, betrayal, and a vague sense that this was all to do with being female; whereas for Mandela, although painful and daunting, circumcision was a much desired and publicly celebrated entry to manhood. But even so, more is at issue in my differing responses than can be explained by my evaluation of the meaning of the two events.

---

be explained on an organic basis alone but involve profound disturbances of his body image.

I do not know, phenomenologically speaking, what it is to possess a fore-skin. I have no feel for its sensations, for its tenderness or its sensuality. I do not know how it feels to roll or pull it, or to wash it, or how it feels as it surrounds either a flaccid or an erect penis, or as another person touches it. I have, in short, no lived experience of its pleasures or its pains, nor of how these might radiate to other parts of a man's body. If there are some tactile-kinesthetic invariants in human experience that are constant irrespective of sex, there are also some that are sex-specific, and it would seem that we are condemned to a degree of sexual solipsism.

Indeed, this sexual solipsism may be one factor (among others) in accounting for the prevalence of rape as perpetrated by men on women. It is often argued that rape is motivated by hatred of women and the desire to dominate and humiliate them. These may often be the motives, but I suggest that there is, to use Arendt's term, also a more "banal" explanation in many instances. There may be a simple failure to consider the effect on another of what is pleasurable for oneself; that is, a total failure to world-travel. Lacking female genitalia, and the experiences of feminine embodiment of which they are in part constitutive, a man cannot directly feel-with the pain and humiliation of forced vaginal intercourse, and a woman's suffering can seem trivial or even non-existent in comparison with his own pleasure.

Conversely, to return to my central theme, those invariants of the lived body that are specific to women may enable us more easily to feel-with the pain of women who are, in other ways, radically different from ourselves: women raped in Bosnia, women of all ethnicities in U.S. cities enduring backstreet abortions without anesthesia, women subject to forced sterilization, or laboring through multiple births without analgesia in any number of places. Even if we have not lived through such experiences ourselves, we are able to feel-with women undergoing them.

An interesting historical example of a feminist politics that emerged in significant degree from such direct apprehension of invariant feminine embodiment can be found in the work and writings of the nineteenth-century British feminist Josephine Butler. Butler, an educated and middle-class feminist, battled tirelessly for repeal of the Contagious Diseases Acts. Under these acts, prostitutes (and other working-class women who had to use the streets as they went about their daily tasks) were routinely arrested, subjected to humiliating, specular gynecological examinations, and, if found to have venereal disease, incarcerated in "lock" hospitals. These measures, popular with the general (i.e., male) voting public, were alleged to be necessary to prevent the spread of venereal disease, particularly in garrison and naval towns. In a letter about the cruelty of the Acts, Butler writes as follows:

All the evidence I have, or most, is from the *victims* of the Acts, the suffering women. . . . I should believe the female prostitutes, and not the
male doctors—simply because I am a woman. I know my own make,
and I know that women who, by the hundreds tell me the same tale, do
not lie to me. And I could say this, too, that in merely listening to their
accounts I have a pain in my back and loins from the very sympathy I
feel. They may call this fancy, but pain is pain." (Cited in Wilkinson
1870, 22)

We know our "own make," and it enables us to feel-with the suffering of
others, even to the point of ourselves feeling pain—not the actual pain of the
speculum for Butler any more than the pain of the blade cutting El Saadawi
for Bartky, but rather the distinct and distinctive pain of the apprehension
of the pain of others. In Butler's case, such feeling-with helped to motivate
an efficacious politics in solidarity with women who, in late Victorian
Britain, lived literally in a world apart from her own.

Modern feminist historians have rightly criticized Butler for condescension toward her socially inferior "sisters" and for a tendency to cast them—
particularly colonized women who were subjected to the Acts in India—as
passive victims of male brutality (Ware 1992, 154–59). Nonetheless, one finds
expressed in Butler's comment a direct, sentient connection with other
women radically unlike herself. This immediate feeling-with others unlike
herself helped here to motivate an efficacious political campaign to reduce
their suffering, a campaign that also successfully challenged male, state control over women's bodies. However, Butler's politics was deeply paradoxical:
at once an effective intervention to end abusive practices against a group of
highly vulnerable women, and yet an often condescending representation of
"fallen women" as passive victims and a reinscription of the class hierarchies of late Victorian Britain.[19]

19. Butler and the Ladies National Association, which she headed from its formation
in 1869, were not solely responsible for the final repeal of the Contagious Diseases Acts
in 1886. But their role in changing social attitudes to the Acts was of enormous significance (Walkowitz 1980, chap. 5).

Walkowitz points out, moreover, that the Association members were not uniformly
condescending or appropriating. Even though they frequently used images of mothers
(older, middle-class, "respectable" women) rescuing younger, "fallen" daughters from
abuse and sin, they also sought to empower the prostitutes themselves: "They sought
out subjected women in the hospitals, low streets, and workhouses . . . they worked with
these women largely on their own terms—providing legal advice and defense along with
moral uplift. They taught them how to fight the arbitrary actions of the police, and in
some cases to elude the law. They treaded a thin line between providing legal and tactical advice and encouraging the women to commit civil disobedience and resist legal authority" (1980, 138–39).

I HAVE been arguing that aspects of shared feminine embodiment may offer us a basis for feeling-with other women and that such affective relationships may be pivotal for the development of relations of respectful recognition among women: relations that can bridge differences among women in ways that involve neither objectification of others nor over-identification with them. But, as the example of Josephine Butler also intimates, caution is needed. The line between respectful recognition and Scheler's "heightened commiseration bestowed from above," between solidarity and charity, can be a fine one. And indeed, several other caveats and qualifications are now in order.

First, in many situations, a direct, embodied feeling-with the pain of others, such as I have been describing, is not possible. The examples I have been using involve situations where not only has acute pain been inflicted on women's bodies, but there are also visible or tangible (or at least reported or imagined) signs that it has been inflicted. These examples involve what Elaine Scarry has called "analogical verification" (1985, 13ff.), where a weapon (such as a knife) or signs of the use of force on the body (such as bruising caused by a fist on the face) offer to another an analogue of the pain the body is undergoing, a form of immediate, sentient "evidence." But other forms of physical suffering are less immediately apprehended. For example, if my colleague tells me she has a dreadful headache, I may well dismiss her claim even though she tells me the pain is really disabling. Whereas if I see a huge bruise on her forehead from walking into an open cabinet drawer, I will have no doubts about her claim that her head hurts.

Although the most extreme forms of domination to which women's bodies are subjected do usually produce signs that invite analogical verification, still much of the suffering that women endure (physical and otherwise) is relatively intangible or invisible. For example, even with a goodwill intention to world-travel, it is not easy for me (or for Christine Sylvester) to feel-with the chronic back pain that many rural African women endure from carrying heavy loads on their heads, or with the wrist pain experienced by women working on certain high-speed assembly lines in the United States. I "know" about their pain, yet I do not feel-with it in the way I felt-with that of the Nigerian women in the battered women's shelter. Thus, it is not surprising that it has been much easier to mobilize women and build feminist organizations in the United States around such issues as rape and domestic violence than around, for example, injurious work conditions in sectors of predominantly female employment.

A feminism that restricted itself to addressing only issues involving direct and visible bodily harm to women would, of course, fail to engage with many other insidious forms of women's subordination. But such a politics may be an important starting place. For feeling-with other women's visible suffering may enable further, perhaps less immediate, forms of imaginative access to the worlds of others to develop. For where sentience does not offer us an immediate feeling-with others, the project of world-travelling will require that we develop alternative ways of connecting with them.

Ironically, at those very moments when the immediacy of embodiment no longer enables us to feel-with others, language also often fails us. Although I think Arendt and Scarry overstate the case for the non-communicability of pain, not only is it easy to dismiss my colleague's verbal complaint about her terrible headache, or that of an assembly-line worker about her (invisible) wrist pain, but it can be positively difficult to feel-with the experiences they tell us about or that we "know" intellectually they must be undergoing. The less visible or tangible forms of suffering are, the greater the risk of indifference on the part of others, *even* when pain enters the domain of discourse and is spoken about.

Thus, in order to offer solidarity, we will need more deliberately to build up for ourselves an account of others' worlds, seeking out the kinds of information that our imagination can mesh into. To do so will require a more explicit commitment to an ethic of simultaneous concern and respect for others. But even then, as our connections with others become less immediate, the risks of objectifying them are also heightened. For as Lorraine Code has observed, the more we are in the stance of an outside spectator, and thus the more we have to try to construct for ourselves the experiences of others, the greater is the "imperialist potential of declared empathy" (Code 1995, 130). There is no easy solution to this problem. But a willingness to enter imaginatively into the worlds of others, tempered by a persistent commitment to respectful recognition, in which we accept that there are limits to world-travelling and acknowledge that we cannot know exactly what another feels, may help to diminish such tendencies.

Another complex set of issues concerns the transitions between our immediate, affective responses to others and our more considered political choices and actions. Although I have been arguing that feeling-with the suffering of other women is a powerful, and indeed necessary, predisposing factor in the development of an egalitarian politics of feminist solidarity, it does not in itself tell us what the specific content of such a politics should be in any particular instance. Between the immediate affective impetus to action that arises as we feel-with the pain of others and the formulation of political positions and movements lie many and complex mediations. These raise vexing issues of power, inequality, identity, culture, discourse, knowledge, values, and so on.

For example, although I think any woman reading El Saadawi's account of her clitoridectomy will, like Bartky, immediately and shockingly feel-with her pain, this experience does not *in itself* offer up a clear political agenda.

Some Egyptian women might read the account and, while feeling-with El Saadawi's pain, perhaps reliving their own painful memories of the operation, still affirm it to be necessary; others might take El Saadawi's book as a call to resistance and join the growing movement in Egypt against clitoridectomy. For Western feminists (of any complexion), questions of whether or how to act from one's immediate feelings here are even more complicated. Colonial histories, and the continued economic and cultural imperialism in which the West is implicated, raise difficult questions as to whether or not, irrespective of the suffering indubitably produced by the procedure, it should be our affair to pass judgments. I do not want to engage with this issue here[20] but only to point out that, although I have been arguing that the kind of affective bond with the suffering of others engendered by El Saadawi's account can be conducive to mobilizing women to action in solidarity with others, it does not by itself guide us through the minefield of different possible political positions.

This leads me back to Josephine Butler, to the fine line between solidarity and charity, and to the risks of transmuting feeling-with into the condescending "commiseration bestowed from above" that Scheler called sympathy and others have called pity. Although our immediate feeling-with the suffering of others involves, even in Butler's case, respectful recognition, the temptation increases, as we move from the immediacy of affect toward deliberation and action, to cast sufferers as "victims," whom out of a pure kindness of heart we will "help." Such a move toward objectification is by no means inevitable, however.

Moreover, it is not *necessarily* condescending or appropriating to act on behalf of others. We should not automatically assume that oppressed groups are always able to speak or act for themselves better than others can do it for them. In the case of the Contagious Diseases Acts, prostitutes could endeavor individually to evade regulation, but as marginal women—impoverished, uneducated, and socially stigmatized—in a society where all women still lacked the vote and were marginal to national political processes, the possibility that they themselves could have mounted the campaign that was to lead to the actual repeal of the Acts was about zero. Educated and "respectable" women, who could write, speak in public, had the resources to travel around the country and organize, and had personal contacts with men of the political classes, were much better positioned to be effective agents of change. As Linda Alcoff has argued, to retreat from speaking for others (or, I would add,

20. Questions about whether Western feminists should take an evaluative stance toward clitoridectomy, and (if so) what it should be, are hotly debated. See, for example, Gunning 1992; Walker and Parmar 1993; and Winter 1995. For a good recent overview and evaluation of such debates, see James 1998.

acting on their behalf) for fear of "appropriating" their voices is sometimes, de facto, a form of irresponsible complicity with the status quo. As she notes, "even a complete retreat from speech is of course not neutral since it allows the continued dominance of the current discourses and acts by omission to reinforce the dominance" (1995, 242).[21] Sometimes (though certainly not always) a weaker group does need and want a more powerful one to speak and act on its behalf.

The questions then, particularly for more privileged women, are not necessarily about whether, *in principle,* one should or should not act from one's concern for others but rather about *when* and *how* to do so: Is it possible to act on behalf of more oppressed groups without rendering them as passive victims, or otherwise objectifying them? If so, in what situations? In her essay "Changing the Subject: Studies in the Appropriation of Pain," Elizabeth Spelman is not sanguine on this point. Considering the nineteenth-century history of white abolitionist women's support for and simultaneous appropriation of the suffering of slave women in the United States, she argues that this support was always contradictory: it both undermined or destabilized racism and also sustained it. Like Alcoff, Spelman concludes that it is important sometimes to speak for others. Indeed, she notes, slaves often wanted others to understand their suffering and do something about it (Spelman 1995, 184). But the way in which white abolitionist women spoke on their behalf often appropriated slave women's experience. That is, they used it as a means of talking about "all" women's suffering, thus erasing its specificity and claiming to share a suffering that was not theirs.

Spelman's discussion is structured around a particular historical example, where expressions of concern for less privileged women were politically important in the struggle against slavery, yet were made in objectifying and appropriating ways. Presumably Spelman is implying through this example (for why else consider it?) that present-day attempts to extend feelings of concern to others more oppressed than ourselves are equally likely to end in similar contradictions. However, it may not necessarily or always be so. What we need are careful, case-by-case, analyses of specific situations. A general prohibition on speaking or acting for others can be dangerously demobilizing.

Spelman is correct that concern for the pain of others can take the form of a condescending pity, where one sees the other as distinct from and inferior to oneself in her suffering. It can also take the form of an empathetic identification that is an imposition on the sufferer. As Spelman points out,

21. Alcoff also points out that to claim to speak only for "oneself" is not a solution either. Such a claim is based on an illusory liberal notion of the autonomous self, but "there is no neutral place to stand free and clear in which one's words do not prescriptively affect or mediate the experience of others, nor is there a way to decisively demarcate a boundary between one's location and all others" (1995, 242).

the claim, made on the basis of asserted empathy, that "I am you" can be wholly one-sided. It can be a thoroughly inegalitarian and unwelcome imposition of oneself on an objectified recipient (1995, 191–92). However, I have been arguing that there is yet another option. For also possible is a respectful recognition of another, such as I have been describing in the experience of feeling-with her suffering. Such an experience involves a doubled awareness: both an immediate affective response to another's pain and a simultaneous awareness that my response is *not* the same as the other's suffering. This response acknowledges that I am not you; we are connected, and your pain concerns me, yet I recognize that the pain is yours and not mine. My solidarity must admit of the difference between us, even as we share a bond of sentience.

I HAVE not been arguing, however, that the commonalities of feminine embodiment *ensure* a bond of sentience, let alone that they guarantee the possibility of those less immediate forms of connection necessary for practices of solidarity. Far too often neither is the case. But if we choose (and I submit we are selves that are capable of choosing) to struggle for forms of difference-respecting solidarity, such commonalities are an important place from where to begin. For they can inaugurate in us a concern for others that may extend far beyond the immediate, embodied experiences that I have been describing. They invite us to endeavor respectfully to travel to the worlds of others in fuller and more ambitious ways.

But here two other elements must increasingly come into play. First, what Sylvester refers to as the "willful" embrace of world-travelling, a moral choice, however tacit, is necessary. For, as we have seen, it is also very easy to refuse the attempt to world-travel. We can withhold recognition by deliberately objectifying those whom we despise. Or, more commonly, we can withhold it through indifference, by simply refusing to grant others our attention at all. We can also grant others attention in ways that make them objects of our pity or that annex them to ourselves through excessive empathy and identification ("I am you").

Second, the endeavor "willfully" to enter another's world requires that we engage ourselves in it imaginatively while simultaneously acknowledging the limits to our imagination. Imagination involves an intentional reaching out toward others, a generous or gratuitous giving to them of our attention. Such a use of imagination may enable us to grasp a sense of others' lived experiences and needs, and thus better to act in support of their struggles. But a non-imperialistic imagining must always recognize what is different about other worlds, as well as what it finds familiar, and it must acknowledge its own limits. We must also remember that, just as I am aware that my pain at another's pain is not identical to hers, so too our more willful imaginative

entry into the world of others does not actually give us access to their experiences. No, we cannot feel how others feel. We cannot, as Lugones wishes,
"become" another nor fully travel to her world. But, if we so choose, we can
feel *enough* to be able to offer others forms of respectful, non-appropriating
recognition and solidarity.

But here, I leave the last words to Simone de Beauvoir. For as usual, she
has said it first. At the end of *The Second Sex*, she writes of a relationship in
which, "mutually recognizing each other as subject, each will however remain for the other *an other*" (SS 731). Beauvoir is talking here about possible future relations between men and women. But her vision, of an intersubjectivity that can acknowledge and accept otherness, one that can respect
difference, also encapsulates the project of feminist world-travelling at its
best. It also points us back—and forward—toward a powerful vision of the
subject: an embodied subject that, although not the site of an untrammeled
freedom, is more than the plaything of social and discursive forces; a subject
that creates and that affirms values, though never ex nihilo. As we begin this
new and perilous century, feminists need urgently to retrieve such a vision.

Bibliography

Alarcón, Norma. 1990. "The Theoretical Subject(s) of *This Bridge Called My Back* and Anglo-American Feminism." In *Making Face, Making Soul/ Haciendo Caras: Creative and Critical Perspectives by Feminists of Color*, ed. Gloria Anzaldúa, 356–69. San Francisco: aunt lute books.

Albrecht, Lisa, and Rose M. Brewer, eds. 1990. *Bridges of Power: Women's Multicultural Alliances*. Philadelphia, Pa.: New Society Publishers.

Alcoff, Linda. 1988. "Cultural Feminism versus Post-Structuralism: The Identity Crisis in Feminist Theory." *Signs: Journal of Women in Culture and Society* 13 (3): 405–36.

——. 1995. "The Problem of Speaking for Others." In *Overcoming Racism and Sexism*, ed. Linda A. Bell and David Blumenfeld, 229–53. Lanham, Md.: Rowman and Littlefield.

——. 1997. "The Politics of Postmodern Feminism, Revisited." *Cultural Critique* 36 (spring): 5–27.

Alcoff, Linda, and Laura Gray. 1993. "Survivor Discourse: Transgression or Recuperation?" In *Signs: Journal of Women in Culture and Society* 18 (2): 260–90.

Anzaldúa, Gloria. 1987. *Borderlands/La Frontera*. San Francisco: aunt lute books.

——. 1990a. "Bridge, Drawbridge, Sandbar or Island, Lesbians-of-Color Hacienda Alianzas." In *Bridges of Power: Women's Multicultural Alliances*, ed. Lisa Albrecht and Rose M. Brewer, 216–31. Philadelphia, Pa.: New Society Publishers.

——, ed. 1990b. *Making Face, Making Soul/Haciendo Caras: Creative and Critical Perspectives by Feminists of Color*. San Francisco: aunt lute books.

Arendt, Hannah. 1958. *The Human Condition*. Chicago: University of Chicago Press.

——. 1963. *Eichmann in Jerusalem: A Report on the Banality of Evil*. New York: Viking Press.

Ascher, Carol. 1981. *Simone de Beauvoir: A Life of Freedom*. Boston: Beacon Press.

Bair, Deirdre. 1989. "Introduction to the Vintage Edition." In *The Second Sex*, vii–xviii. Trans. H. M. Parshley. New York: Vintage Books.

Barnes, Hazel E. 1990. "Sartre and Sexism." *Philosophy and Literature* 14 (2): 340–47.

——. 1999. "Sartre and Feminism: Aside from *The Second Sex* and All That."
  In *Feminist Interpretations of Jean-Paul Sartre*, ed. Julien S. Murphy, 22–44.
  University Park: Pennsylvania State University Press.
Barrett, William. 1958. *Irrational Man*. New York: Doubleday Anchor Books.
Bartky, Sandra. 1990. *Femininity and Domination*. New York: Routledge.
——. 1997. "Sympathy and Solidarity: On a Tightrope with Scheler." In
  Feminists Rethink the Self, ed. Diana T. Meyers, 177–96. Boulder, Colo.:
  Westview Press.
Beauvoir, Simone de. 1944. *Pyrrhus et Cinéas*. Paris: Gallimard.
——. 1945. "La Phénoménologie de la perception." *Les Temps Modernes* 2
  (November): 363–67.
——. [1960] 1962. *The Prime of Life*. Trans. Peter Green. Cleveland, Ohio: World
  Publishing Company.
——. 1964. *Force of Circumstance*. Trans. Richard Howe. New York: Putnam.
——. [1947] 1967. *The Ethics of Ambiguity*. Trans. Bernard Frechtman. New
  York: Citadel Press. Originally published as *Pour une morale de l'ambiguïté*.
  Paris: Gallimard.
——. [1949] 1989. *The Second Sex*. Trans. H. M. Parshley. Preface by Deirdre
  Bair. New York: Vintage Books. Originally published as *Le Deuxième Sexe*.
  Paris: Gallimard. Original English edition, New York: Knopf, 1952.
——. [1990] 1992. *Letters to Sartre*. Trans. Quintin Hoare. New York: Arcade
  Publishing.
Belenky, Mary Field, Blyth McVicker Clinchy, Nancy Rule Goldberger, and Jill
  Mattick Tarule, eds. 1986. *Women's Ways of Knowing: The Development of
  Self, Voice, and Mind*. New York: Basic Books.
Bell, Linda A. 1997. "Different Oppressions: A Feminist Exploration of Sartre's
  Anti-Semite and Jew." *Sartre Studies International* 3 (2): 1–20.
Benhabib, Seyla. 1987. "The Generalized and the Concrete Other: The
  Kohlberg-Gilligan Controversy and Feminist Theory." In *Feminism as
  Critique: On the Politics of Gender*, ed. Seyla Benhabib and Drucilla Cornell,
  77–95. Minneapolis: University of Minnesota Press.
——. 1995. "Feminism and Postmodernism: An Uneasy Alliance." In *Feminist
  Contentions: A Philosophical Exchange*, 17–34. Introduction by Linda J.
  Nicholson. New York: Routledge.
Bentham, Jeremy. [1787] 1995. "Panopticon Letters." In *The Panopticon
  Writings*, ed. Miran Bozovic, 29–95. New York: Verso.
Bergoffen, Debra. 1997. *The Philosophy of Simone de Beauvoir: Gendered
  Phenomenologies, Erotic Generosities*. Albany: State University of New York
  Press.
Bhabha, Homi. 1990. "The Other Question: Difference, Discrimination and the
  Discourse of Colonialism." In *Out There: Marginalization and Contemp-
  orary Cultures*, ed. Russell Ferguson, Martha Gever, Trinh T. Minh-ha, and
  Cornel West, 71–87. New York and Cambridge, Mass.: New Museum of
  Contemporary Art and MIT Press.
Bigwood, Carol. 1991. "Renaturalizing the Body (With a Little Help from
  Merleau-Ponty)." *Hypatia: A Journal of Feminist Philosophy* 6 (3): 54–73.
Bordo, Susan. 1990. "Feminism, Post Modernism, and Gender-Scepticism." In
  Feminism/Postmodernism, ed. Linda J. Nicholson, 133–56. New York:
  Routledge.

——. 1993. *Unbearable Weight: Feminism, Western Culture, and the Body.* Berkeley: University of California Press.

Bourdieu, Pierre, and Jean-Claude Passeron. 1967. "Sociology and Philosophy in France since 1945: Death and Resurrection of a Philosophy without a Subject." *Social Research* 34 (1): 162–212.

Brooks, Ann. 1997. *Postfeminisms: Feminism, Cultural Theory and Cultural Forms.* London: Routledge.

Brown, Elsa Barkley. 1988. "African-American Women's Quilting." In *Black Women in America: Social Science Perspectives,* ed. Micheline R. Malson, Elisabeth Mudimbe-Boyi, Jean F. O'Barr, and Mary Wyer, 9–18. Chicago: University of Chicago Press.

Bulhan, Hussein. 1985. *Frantz Fanon and the Psychology of Oppression.* New York: Plenum Press.

Burstow, Bonnie. 1992. "How Sexist Is Sartre?" *Philosophy and Literature* 16 (1): 32–48.

Butler, Judith. 1987. "Variations on Sex and Gender: Beauvoir, Wittig, and Foucault." In *Feminism as Critique: On the Politics of Gender,* ed. Seyla Benhabib and Drucilla Cornell, 128–42. Minneapolis: University of Minnesota Press.

——. 1989. "Sexual Ideology and Phenomenological Description: A Feminist Critique of Merleau-Ponty's *Phenomenology of Perception.*" In *The Thinking Muse: Feminism and Modern French Philosophy,* ed. Jeffner Allen and Iris M. Young, 85–100. Bloomington: Indiana University Press.

——. 1990. *Gender Trouble: Feminism and the Subversion of Identity.* New York: Routledge.

——. 1997. *The Psychic Life of Power: Theories in Subjection.* Stanford, Calif.: Stanford University Press.

——. 1998. "Merely Cultural." *New Left Review* 227 (January/February): 33–44.

Chanter, Tina. 1998. "Postmodern Subjectivity." In *A Companion to Feminist Philosophy,* ed. Alison M. Jaggar and Iris M. Young, 263–271. Malden, Mass.: Blackwell.

Chodorow, Nancy. 1978. *The Reproduction of Mothering.* Berkeley: University of California Press.

Cleaver, Eldridge. 1969. *Post-Prison Writings and Speeches,* ed. Robert Scheer. New York: Random House.

Code, Lorraine. 1995. *Rhetorical Spaces: Essays on Gendered Locations.* New York: Routledge.

Collins, Catherine F., ed. 1996. *African-American Women's Health and Social Issues.* Westport, Conn.: Auburn House.

Collins, Margery, and Christine Pierce. 1973. "Holes and Slime: Sexism in Sartre's Psychoanalysis." *Philosophical Forum* 5 (1/2): 112–27.

Collins, Patricia Hill. 1990. *Black Feminist Thought: Knowledge, Consciousness, and the Politics of Empowerment.* Boston: Unwin Hyman.

——. 1998. *Fighting Words. Black Women and the Search for Justice.* Minneapolis: University of Minnesota Press.

Combahee River Collective. 1983. "The Combahee River Collective Statement." In *Home Girls: A Black Feminist Anthology,* ed. Barbara Smith, 272–82. New York: Kitchen Table: Women of Color Press.

Daniels, Cynthia. 1993. *At Women's Expense: State Power and the Politics of Fetal Rights.* Cambridge, Mass.: Harvard University Press.

Davies, Howard. 1987. *Sartre and "Les Temps Modernes."* Cambridge: Cambridge University Press.

Dean, Jodi. 1996. *Solidarity of Strangers: Feminism after Identity Politics.* Berkeley: University of California Press.

———. 1997. "Feminist Solidarity, Reflective Solidarity: Theorizing Connections after Identity Politics." *Women and Politics* 18 (4): 1–26.

Delphy, Christine. 1995. "The Invention of French Feminism: An Essential Move." *Yale French Studies* 87: 190–221.

Derrida, Jacques. [1962] 1978. *Edmund Husserl's Origin of Geometry: An Introduction.* Trans. John P. Leavey, Jr. Stony Brook, N.Y.: Nicolas Hays.

———. [1980] 1983. "The Time of a Thesis: Punctuations." In *Philosophy in France Today,* ed. Alan Montefiore, 34–50. Cambridge: Cambridge University Press.

———. 1999. *La Parole.* Paris: Éditions de l'Aube.

Descombes, Vincent. 1980. *Modern French Philosophy.* Trans. L. Scott Fox and J. M. Harding. Cambridge: Cambridge University Press.

De Soto, Paris. 1997. "Feminists Negotiate the Judicial Branch: Battered Woman's Syndrome." In *Feminists Negotiate the State: The Politics of Domestic Violence,* ed. Cynthia Daniels, 53–64. Lanham, Md.: University Press of America.

Diprose, Rosalyn. 1998. "Generosity: Between Love and Desire." *Hypatia: A Journal of Feminist Philosophy* 13 (1): 1–20.

Downs, Donald A. 1996. *More Than Victims: Battered Women, the Syndrome Society, and the Law.* Chicago: University of Chicago Press.

DuBois, W. E. B. [1903] 1965. "The Souls of Black Folk." In *Three Negro Classics,* 207–389. New York: Avon Books.

Dumm, Thomas. 1996. *Michel Foucault and the Politics of Freedom.* Thousand Oaks, Calif.: Sage Publications.

El Saadawi, Nawal. [1980] 1982. *The Hidden Face of Eve: Women in the Arab World.* Trans. and ed. Sheriff Hetata. Boston: Beacon Press.

Evans, Mary. 1987. "Views of Women and Men in the Work of Simone de Beauvoir." In *Critical Essays on Simone de Beauvoir,* ed. Elaine Marks, 172–84. Boston: G. K. Hall.

Fanon, Frantz. [1952] 1967. *Black Skin, White Masks.* Trans. Charles Lam Markham. New York: Grove Weidenfeld. Originally published as *Peau noire, masques blancs.* Paris: Editions du Seuil.

———. [1959] 1989. *Studies in a Dying Colonialism.* Trans. Haakon Chevalier. London: Earthscan Publications.

———. [1960] 1991. *The Wretched of the Earth.* Trans. Constance Farrington. New York: Grove Weidenfeld.

Felman, Shoshana, and Dori Laub. 1992. *Testimony: Crises of Witnessing in Literature, Psychoanalysis, and History.* New York: Routledge.

Flax, Jane. 1987. "Postmodernism and Gender Relations in Feminist Theory." *Signs: Journal of Women in Culture and Society* 12 (4): 621–43.

Foucault, Michel. 1954. *Maladie mentale et personnalité.* Paris: Presses Universitaires de France.

———. [1969] 1972. *The Archaeology of Knowledge.* Trans. A. M. Sheridan Smith. London: Tavistock Publications.

———. [1975] 1977a. *Discipline and Punish: The Birth of the Prison.* Trans. Alan Sheridan. London: Penguin Books.

———. 1977b. *Language, Counter-Memory, Practice: Selected Essays and Interviews.* Trans. and ed. Donald F. Bouchard. Ithaca, N.Y.: Cornell University Press.

———. 1980. *Power/Knowledge: Selected Interviews and Other Writings, 1972–1977,* ed. Colin Gordon. New York: Pantheon Books.

———. [1979] 1984. "What Is an Author?" In *The Foucault Reader,* ed. Paul Rabinow, 101–20. New York: Pantheon Books.

———. [1983] 1988. "Critical Theory/Intellectual History." In *Michel Foucault. Politics, Philosophy, Culture: Interviews and Other Writings, 1977–84,* ed. Lawrence D. Kritzman, 17–64. New York: Routledge.

———. [1968] 1989. "Foucault Responds to Sartre." In *Foucault Live (Interviews, 1966–84),* 35–43. Trans. John Johnston. New York: Semiotext(e).

Fraser, Nancy. 1995. "From Redistribution to Recognition? Dilemmas of Justice in a 'Post-Socialist' Age." *New Left Review* 212 (July/August): 68–93.

Frye, Marilyn. 1983. "In and Out of Harm's Way: Arrogance and Love." In *The Politics of Reality: Essays in Feminist Theory,* 52–83. Trumansburg, N.Y.: Crossing Press.

Fullbrook, Kate, and Edward Fullbrook. 1994. *Simone de Beauvoir and Jean-Paul Sartre: The Remaking of a Twentieth Century Legend.* New York: Basic Books.

Fuss, Diana. 1989. *Essentially Speaking: Feminism, Nature, and Difference.* New York: Routledge.

———. 1995. "Interior Colonies: Frantz Fanon and the Politics of Identification." In *Identification Papers,* 141–72. New York: Routledge.

García, Alma M., ed. 1997. *Chicana Feminist Thought: The Basic Historical Writings.* New York: Routledge.

Gates, Henry Louis, Jr. 1991. "Critical Fanonism." *Critical Inquiry* 17 (3): 457–70.

Gendzier, Irene L. 1985. *Frantz Fanon: A Critical Study.* New York: Grove Press.

Gilligan, Carol. 1982. *In a Different Voice.* Cambridge, Mass.: Harvard University Press.

Gitlin, Todd. 1994. "From Universality to Difference: Notes on the Fragmentation of the Left." In *Social Theory and the Politics of Identity,* ed. Craig Calhoun, 150–74. Cambridge, Mass.: Blackwell.

Gonen, Julianna S. 1993. "Women's Rights vs. 'Fetal Rights': Politics, Law, and Reproductive Hazards in the Workplace." *Women and Politics* 13 (3/4): 175–90.

Gordon, Lewis R. 1995. *Bad Faith and Antiblack Racism.* Atlantic Highlands, N.J.: Humanities Press.

Gordon, Lewis R., T. Denean Sharpley-Whiting, and Renée T. White, eds. 1996. *Fanon: A Critical Reader.* Oxford: Blackwell Publishers.

Grant, Judith. 1993. *Fundamental Feminism: Contesting the Core Concepts of Feminist Theory.* New York: Routledge.

Grosz, Elizabeth. 1994. *Volatile Bodies: Toward a Corporeal Feminism.* Bloomington: Indiana University Press.

Gunning, Isabelle R. 1992. "Arrogant Perception, World-Travelling and Multicultural Feminism: The Case of Female Genital Surgeries." *Columbia Human Rights Law Review* 23 (2): 189–248.

Guy-Sheftall, Beverly, ed. 1995. *Words of Fire: An Anthology of African-American Feminist Thought.* New York: New Press.

Habermas, Jürgen. 1991. *The Philosophical Discourse of Modernity.* Trans. Frederick G. Lawrence. Cambridge, Mass.: MIT Press.

Harari, Josué V., ed. 1979. *Textual Strategies: Perspectives in Post-Structuralist Criticism.* Ithaca, N.Y.: Cornell University Press.

Haraway, Donna. 1991. "Situated Knowledges: The Science Question in Feminism and the Privilege of Partial Perspective." In *Simians, Cyborgs and Women: The Reinvention of Nature,* 183–202. New York: Routledge.

Harding, Sandra. 1986. *The Science Question in Feminism.* Ithaca, N.Y.: Cornell University Press.

——. 1990. "Feminism, Science, and the Anti-Enlightenment Critiques." In *Feminism/Postmodernism,* ed. Linda J. Nicholson, 83–106. New York: Routledge.

——. 1991. *Whose Science? Whose Knowledge? Thinking from Women's Lives.* Ithaca, N.Y.: Cornell University Press.

Hartsock, Nancy. 1985. *Money, Sex, and Power: Toward a Feminist Historical Materialism.* Boston: Northeastern University Press.

——. 1987. "Rethinking Modernism: Minority vs. Majority Theories." *Cultural Critique* no. 7 (fall): 187–206.

——. 1990. "Foucault on Power: A Theory for Women?" In *Feminism/Postmodernism,* ed. Linda J. Nicholson, 157–75. New York: Routledge.

——. 1996. Community/Sexuality/Gender: Rethinking Power." In *Revisioning the Political,* ed. Nancy Hirschmann and Christine DiStefano, 27–49. Boulder, Colo.: Westview Press.

——. 1998. *The Feminist Standpoint Revisited and Other Essays.* Boulder, Colo.: Westview Press.

Heinämaa, Sara. 1997. "What Is a Woman? Butler and Beauvoir on the Foundations of Sexual Difference." *Hypatia: A Journal of Feminist Philosophy* 12 (1): 20–39.

Hekman, Susan. 1990. *Gender and Knowledge: Elements of a Postmodern Feminism.* Boston: Northeastern University Press.

Hesford, Wendy S. 1999. *Framing Identities: Autobiography and the Politics of Pedagogy.* Minneapolis: University of Minnesota Press.

hooks, bell. 1990. *Yearning: Race, Gender, and Cultural Politics.* Boston: South End Press.

Howells, Christina. 1992. "Conclusion: Sartre and the Deconstruction of the Subject." In *The Cambridge Companion to Sartre,* ed. Christina Howells, 318–52. Cambridge: Cambridge University Press.

Hyppolite, Jean. [1946] 1974. *Genesis and Structure of Hegel's Phenomenology of Spirit.* Trans. Samuel Cherniak. Evanston, Ill.: Northwestern University Press.

Irigaray, Luce. 1985. *Speculum of the Other Woman.* Trans. Gillian C. Gill. Ithaca, N.Y.: Cornell University Press.

——. [1984] 1993. *An Ethics of Sexual Difference,* Trans. Carolyn Burke and Gillian C. Gill. Ithaca, N.Y.: Cornell University Press.

Jaggar, Alison M. 1989. "Love and Knowledge: Emotion in Feminist Epistemology." In *Gender/Body/Knowledge*, ed. Alison M. Jaggar and Susan Bordo, 145–71. New Brunswick, N.J.: Rutgers University Press.

James, Stanlie M. 1998. "Shades of Othering: Reflections on Female Circumcision/Genital Mutilation." *Signs: Journal of Women in Culture and Society* 23 (1): 103–48.

Jameson, Fredric. 1995. "The Sartrean Origin." *Sartre Studies International* 1 (1/2): 1–20.

Jordan, June. 1995. "A New Politics of Sexuality." In *Words of Fire: An Anthology of African-American Feminist Thought*, ed. Beverly Guy-Sheftall, 407–11. New York: New Press.

Kaufmann, Walter A. [1950] 1974. *Nietzsche: Philosopher, Psychologist, Antichrist*. Princeton, N.J.: Princeton University Press.

Kearney, Richard. 1984. *Dialogues with Contemporary Thinkers: The Phenomenological Heritage*. Manchester: Manchester University Press.

———. 1998. *Poetics of Imagining: Modern to Post-Modern*. New York: Fordham University Press.

Kenney, Sally. 1992. *For Whose Protection? Reproductive Hazards and Exclusionary Policies in the United States and Britain*. Ann Arbor: University of Michigan Press.

King, Deborah K. 1988. "Multiple Jeopardy, Multiple Consciousness: The Context of a Black Feminist Ideology." In *Black Women in America: Social Science Perspectives*, ed. Micheline R. Malson, Elisabeth Mudimbe-Boyi, Jean F. O'Barr, and Mary Wyer, 265–95. Chicago: University of Chicago Press.

Kline, Marlee. 1989. "Women's Oppression and Racism: A Critique of the 'Feminist Standpoint.' " *Socialist Studies/Etudes Socialistes: A Canadian Annual* 5:37–64.

Kojève, Alexandre. [1947] 1962. *Introduction to the Reading of Hegel*. Trans. J. H. Nichols, Jr. New York: Basic Books.

Kozol, Wendy. 1996. "Fracturing Domesticity: Media, Nationalism, and the Question of Feminist Influence." *Signs: Journal of Women in Culture and Society* 20 (3): 646–67.

Kristeva, Julia. 1981. "Woman Can Never Be Defined." In *New French Feminisms: An Anthology*, ed. Elaine Marks and Isabelle de Courtivron, 137–41. Trans. Marilyn A. August. New York: Schocken Books.

———. [1974] 1984. *Revolution in Poetic Language*. Trans. Margaret Waller. New York: Columbia University Press.

———. [1979] 1986. "Women's Time." In *The Kristeva Reader*, ed. Toril Moi, 187–213. New York: Columbia University Press.

Kruks, Sonia. 1987. "Simone de Beauvoir and the Limits of Freedom." *Social Text* 17 (fall): 111–22.

———. 1990a. "Sartre's First Ethics and the Future of Ethics." In *Writing the Future*, ed. Andrew Benjamin and David Wood, 181–91. London: Routledge.

———. 1990b. *Situation and Human Existence: Freedom, Subjectivity and Society*. New York: Routledge.

———. 1991. "Simone de Beauvoir: Teaching Sartre about Freedom." In *Sartre Alive*, ed. Ronald Aronson and Adrian van den Hoven, 285–300. Detroit: Wayne State University Press.

———. 1992. "Gender and Subjectivity: Simone de Beauvoir and Contemporary Feminism." *Signs: Journal of Women in Culture and Society* 18 (1): 89–110.

Kymlicka, Will. 1995. *Multicultural Citizenship.* Oxford: Clarendon Press.

Lacan, Jacques. [1955] 1966. "Le Séminaire sur «la lettre volée»." In *Ecrits,* 11–61. Paris: Editions du Seuil.

———. [1957] 1966. "L'Instance de la lettre dans l'inconscient ou la raison depuis Freud." In *Ecrits,* 493–528. Paris: Editions du Seuil.

Laing, R. D. 1969. *The Divided Self.* New York: Pantheon Books.

Lamont, Michèle. 1987. "How to Become a Dominant French Philosopher: The Case of Jacques Derrida." *American Journal of Sociology* 93 (3): 584–622.

Lauretis, Teresa de. 1987. *Technologies of Gender.* Bloomington: Indiana University Press.

Lazreg, Marnia. 1990. "Feminism and Difference: The Perils of Writing as a Woman on Women in Algeria." In *Conflicts in Feminism,* ed. Marianne Hirsch and Evelyn Fox Keller, 326–48. New York: Routledge.

Le Doeuff, Michèle. 1980. "Simone de Beauvoir and Existentialism." *Feminist Studies* 6 (2): 277–89.

———. 1991. *Hipparchia's Choice: An Essay concerning Women, Philosophy, Etc.* Trans. Trista Selous. Cambridge, Mass.: Blackwell.

———. 1995. "Simone de Beauvoir: Falling into (Ambiguous) Line." In *Feminist Interpretations of Simone de Beauvoir,* ed. Margaret A. Simons, 59–65. University Park: Pennsylvania State University Press.

Lévi-Strauss, Claude. [1962] 1968. *The Savage Mind.* Chicago: University of Chicago Press.

Lloyd, Genevieve. 1984. *The Man of Reason: Male and Female in Western Philosophy.* London: Methuen.

Lorde, Audre. 1984. *Sister/Outsider.* Freedom, Calif.: Crossing Press.

Losco, Joseph. 1989. "Fetal Abuse: An Exploration of Emerging Philosophic, Legal, and Policy Issues." *Western Political Quarterly* 42 (2): 265–86.

Lugones, María. 1990. "Playfulness, 'World'-Travelling, and Loving Perception." In *Making Face, Making Soul/Haciendo Caras: Creative and Critical Perspectives by Feminists of Color,* ed. Gloria Anzaldúa, 390–402. San Francisco: aunt lute books.

Lundgren-Gothlin, Eva. 1996. *Sex and Existence. Simone de Beauvoir's "The Second Sex."* Trans. Linda Schenck. Hanover, N.H.: Wesleyan University Press/University Press of New England.

Lyotard, Jean-François. 1954. *La Phénoménologie.* Paris: Presses Universitaires Françaises.

———. [1979] 1984. *The Postmodern Condition: A Report on Knowledge.* Trans. Geoff Bennington and Brian Massumi. Minneapolis: University of Minnesota Press.

Macey, David. 1993. *The Lives of Michel Foucault: A Biography.* New York: Pantheon Books.

Macquarrie, John. 1972. *Existentialism.* Philadelphia, Pa.: Westminster Press.

Mahoney, Martha. 1991. "Legal Images of Battered Women: Redefining the Issues of Separation." *Michigan Law Review* 90 (1): 35–75.

Mandela, Nelson. 1994. *Long Walk to Freedom.* Boston: Little, Brown.

Martin, Emily. 1987. *The Woman in the Body: A Cultural Analysis of Reproduction.* Boston: Beacon Press.

Martin, Jane Roland. 1994. "Methodological Essentialism, False Difference, and Other Dangerous Traps." *Signs: Journal of Women in Culture and Society* 19 (3): 630–57.

——. 1996. "Aerial Distance, Esotericism, and Other Closely Related Traps." *Signs: Journal of Women in Culture and Society* 21 (3): 584–614.

Marx, Karl. [1846] 1978. "The German Ideology." In *The Marx-Engels Reader*, ed. Robert Tucker, 146–200. New York: Norton.

Mathy, Jean-Philippe. 1995. "The Resistance to French Theory in the United States: A Cross-Cultural Inquiry." *French Historical Studies* 19 (2): 331–47.

Merleau-Ponty, Maurice. [1945] 1962. *Phenomenology of Perception*. Trans. Colin Smith. London: Routledge and Kegan Paul.

——.[1948] 1964. *Sense and Non-Sense*. Trans. Hubert L. Dreyfus and Patricia Allen Dreyfus. Evanston, Ill.: Northwestern University Press.

——. [1956] 1964. "From Mauss to Claude Lévi-Strauss." In *Signs*, trans. Richard C. McCleary, 114–25. Evanston, Ill.: Northwestern University Press.

——. [1960] 1964. *Signs*. Trans. Richard C. McCleary. Evanston, Ill.: Northwestern University Press.

——. [1964] 1968. *The Visible and the Invisible*. Ed. Claude Lefort. Trans. Alphonso Lingis. Evanston, Ill.: Northwestern University Press.

——. [1947] 1969. *Humanism and Terror*. Trans. John O'Neill. Boston: Beacon Press.

Miller, James. 1993. *The Passion of Michel Foucault*. New York: Simon and Schuster.

Mohanty, Chandra Talpade. 1991. "Under Western Eyes: Feminist Scholarship and Colonial Discourse." In *Third World Women and the Politics of Feminism*, ed. Chandra Talpade Mohanty, Ann Russo, and Lourdes Torres, 51–80. Bloomington: Indiana University Press.

——. 1992. "Feminist Encounters: Locating the Politics of Experience." In *Destabilizing Theory: Contemporary Feminist Debates*, ed. Michèle Barrett and Anne Phillips, 74–92. Stanford, Calif.: Stanford University Press.

Moi, Toril. 1994. *Simone de Beauvoir: The Making of an Intellectual Woman*. Oxford: Blackwell Publishers.

Moraga, Cherríe. 1983. "La Güerra." In *This Bridge Called My Back: Writings by Radical Women of Color*, ed. Cherríe Moraga and Gloria Anzaldúa, 27–34. New York: Kitchen Table: Women of Color Press.

Moraga, Cherríe, and Gloria Anzaldúa, eds. 1983. *This Bridge Called My Back: Writings by Radical Women of Color*. New York: Kitchen Table: Women of Color Press.

Morris, Phyllis Sutton. 1996. "Self-Creating Selves: Sartre and Foucault." *American Catholic Philosophical Quarterly* 70 (4): 537–49.

Moses, Claire Goldberg. 1998. "Made in America: 'French Feminism' in Academia." *Feminist Studies* 24 (2): 241–74.

Mouffe, Chantal. 1992. "Feminism, Citizenship, and Radical Democratic Politics." In *Feminists Theorize the Political*, ed. Judith Butler and Joan W. Scott, 369–84. New York: Routledge.

Murphy, Julien S., ed. 1999. *Feminist Interpretations of Jean-Paul Sartre*. University Park: Pennsylvania State University Press.

Nicholson, Linda J., ed. 1990. *Feminism/Postmodernism*. New York: Routledge.

O'Brien, Mary. 1981. *The Politics of Reproduction.* London: Routledge and Kegan Paul.

Okely, Judith. 1986. *Simone de Beauvoir: A Re-Reading.* London: Virago Press.

Okin, Susan Moller. 1989. *Justice, Gender, and the Family.* New York: Basic Books.

Phelan, Shane. 1989. *Identity Politics: Lesbian Feminism and the Limits of Community.* Philadelphia, Pa.: Temple University Press.

——. 1994. *Getting Specific: Postmodern Lesbian Politics.* Minneapolis: University of Minnesota Press.

Phillips, Anne. 1995. *The Politics of Presence.* Oxford: Clarendon Press.

Rabinow, Paul, ed. 1984. *The Foucault Reader.* New York: Pantheon Books.

Reagon, Bernice Johnson. 1983. "Coalition Politics: Turning the Century." In *Home Girls: A Black Feminist Anthology,* ed. Barbara Smith, 356–68. New York: Kitchen Table: Women of Color Press.

Redstockings. 1970. "The Manifesto of the Redstockings." In *Notes from the Second Year,* ed. Shulamith Firestone and Anne Koedt, 112–13. New York: Radical Feminism.

Rich, Adrienne. [1976] 1986. *Of Woman Born: Motherhood as Experience and Institution.* New York: Norton.

Riley, Denise. 1988. *"Am I That Name?" Feminism and the Category of "Women" in History.* Minneapolis: University of Minnesota Press.

Roberson, Noma L. 1996. "Exploring Health Issues and Health Status of African-American Women with Emphasis on Cancer." In *African-American Women's Health and Social Issues,* ed. Catherine F. Collins, 37–58. Westport, Conn.: Auburn House.

Rorty, Richard. 1989. *Contingency, Irony, and Solidarity.* New York: Cambridge University Press.

——. 1991. "Feminism and Pragmatism." *Michigan Quarterly Review* 30 (2): 231–58.

——. 1993. "Feminism, Ideology, and Deconstruction: A Pragmatist View." *Hypatia: A Journal of Feminist Philosophy* 8 (2): 96–103.

Ross, Loretta. 1998. "African-American Women and Abortion." In *Abortion Wars: Half a Century of Struggle,* ed. Rickie Solinger, 161–207. Berkeley: University of California Press.

Roth, Rachel. 1993. "At Women's Expense: The Costs of Fetal Rights." *Women and Politics* 13 (3/4): 117–36.

Ruddick, Sara. 1989. *Maternal Thinking.* Boston: Beacon Press.

Said, Edward. 1978. *Orientalism.* New York: Pantheon.

Sandoval, Chela. 1991. "U.S. Third World Feminism: The Theory and Method of Oppositional Consciousness in the Postmodern World." *Genders* 10 (spring): 1–24.

Sartre, Jean-Paul. [1948] 1955. *Dirty Hands,* in *"No Exit" and Three Other Plays.* Trans. Lionel Abel. New York: Random House.

——. [1943] 1956. *Being and Nothingness.* Trans. Hazel E. Barnes. New York: New Philosophical Library. Originally published as *L'Etre et le néant.* Paris: Gallimard.

——. [1952] 1965. "Reply to Albert Camus." In *Situations.* Trans. Benita Eisler, 54–78. Greenwich, Conn.: Fawcett Publications.

———. [1961] 1965. "Merleau-Ponty." In *Situations*. Trans. Benita Eisler, 156–226. Greenwich, Conn.: Fawcett Publications.

———. [1960] 1968. *Search for a Method*. Trans. Hazel E. Barnes. New York: Vintage Books.

———. [1969] 1974. "Itinerary of a Thought." In *Between Existentialism and Marxism*. Trans. John Matthews, 31–64. London: New Left Books.

———. [1946] 1976. *Anti-Semite and Jew*. Trans. George J. Becker. New York: Schocken Books.

———. [1948] 1976. *Black Orpheus*. Trans. S. W. Allen. Paris: Présence Africaine.

———. [1960] 1976. *Critique of Dialectical Reason*. Vol. 1. Trans. Alan Sheridan-Smith. London: New Left Books.

———. [1985] 1991. *Critique of Dialectical Reason*. Vol. 2 (posthumous, incomplete). Ed. Arlette Elkaïm-Sartre. Trans. Quintin Hoare. London: Verso.

———. 1992. *Notebooks for an Ethics*. Trans. David Pellauer. Chicago: University of Chicago Press.

———. [1971–72] 1981–93. *The Family Idiot*. Vols. 1–5. Trans. Carol Cosman. Chicago: University of Chicago Press.

Scarry, Elaine. 1985. *The Body in Pain*. New York: Oxford University Press.

Scheler, Max. [1913] 1954. *The Nature of Sympathy*. Trans. Peter Heath. London: Routledge and Kegan Paul.

Schor, Naomi, and Elizabeth Weed, eds. 1994. *The Essential Difference*. Bloomington: Indiana University Press.

Schutte, Ofelia. 1997. "A Critique of Normative Heterosexuality: Identity, Embodiment, and Sexual Difference in Beauvoir and Irigaray." *Hypatia: A Journal of Feminist Philosophy* 12 (1): 40–62.

Schwarzer, Alice. 1984. *After "The Second Sex": Conversations with Simone de Beauvoir*. Trans. Marianne Howarth. New York: Pantheon Books.

Scott, Joan W. 1992. "Experience." In *Feminists Theorize the Political*, ed. Judith Butler and Joan W. Scott, 22–40. New York: Routledge.

———. 1993. "The Tip of the Volcano." *Comparative Studies in Society and History* 35 (2): 438–43.

Sheets-Johnstone, Maxine. 1990. *The Roots of Thinking*. Philadelphia, Pa.: Temple University Press.

———. 1994. *The Roots of Power: Animate Form and Gendered Bodies*. Chicago: Open Court.

Sicard, Michel. 1979. "Interférences." *Obliques* nos. 18/19: 325–29.

Siegfried, Charlene. 1985. "*Second Sex*: Second Thoughts." *Women's Studies International Forum* 8 (3): 219–29.

Simons, Margaret A. 1981. "Beauvoir and Sartre: The Question of Influence." *Eros* 8 (1): 25–42.

———. 1983. "The Silencing of Simone de Beauvoir: Guess What's Missing from *The Second Sex*." *Women's Studies International Forum* 6 (5): 559–64.

———. 1986. "Beauvoir and Sartre: The Philosophical Relationship." *Yale French Studies* 72: 165–79.

———. 1999. *Beauvoir and "The Second Sex": Feminism, Race, and the Origins of Existentialism*. Lanham, Md.: Rowman and Littlefield.

———, ed. 1995. *Feminist Interpretations of Simone de Beauvoir*. University Park: Pennsylvania State University Press.

Singer, Linda. 1990. "Interpretation and Retrieval: Rereading Beauvoir." In *Hypatia Reborn: Essays in Feminist Philosophy*, ed. Azizah Y. al-Hibri and Margaret A. Simons, 323–35. Indianapolis: Indiana University Press.

Sivanandan, A. 1989. "All That Melts into Air Is Solid: The Hokum of New Times." *Race and Class* 31 (3): 1–30.

Smith, Adam. [1759] 1976. *The Theory of Moral Sentiments*. Ed. D. D. Raphael and A. L. Macfie. Oxford: Clarendon Press.

Smith, Barbara, ed. 1983. *Home Girls: A Black Feminist Anthology*. New York: Kitchen Table: Women of Color Press.

Smith, Barbara, and Beverly Smith. 1983. "Across the Kitchen Table: A Sister-to-Sister Dialogue." In *This Bridge Called My Back: Writings by Radical Women of Color*, ed. Cherríe Moraga and Gloria Anzaldúa, 113–27. New York: Kitchen Table: Women of Color Press.

Spelman, Elizabeth V. 1988. *Inessential Woman: Problems of Exclusion in Feminist Thought*. Boston: Beacon Press.

——. 1989. "Anger and Insubordination." In *Women, Knowledge and Reality*, ed. Ann Garry and Marilyn Pearsall, 263-73. Boston: Unwin Hyman.

——. 1995. "Changing the Subject: Studies in the Appropriation of Pain." In *Overcoming Racism and Sexism*, ed. Linda A. Bell and David Blumenfeld, 181–96. Lanham, Md.: Rowman and Littlefield.

Spivak. Gayatri Chakravorty. 1988. *In Other Worlds: Essays in Cultural Politics*. New York: Routledge.

Steele, Meili. 1996. "Language and African-American Culture: The Need for Meta-Philosophical Reflection." *Philosophy Today* 40 (1): 179–87.

Sullivan, Shannon. 1997. "Domination and Dialogue in Merleau-Ponty's *Phenomenology of Perception*." *Hypatia: A Journal of Feminist Philosophy* 12 (1): 1–19.

Sylvester, Christine. 1995. "African and Western Feminisms: World Traveling the Tendencies and Possibilities." *Signs: Journal of Women in Culture and Society* 20 (4): 941–69.

Taylor, Charles. 1991. *The Ethics of Authenticity*. Cambridge, Mass.: Harvard University Press.

Tronto, Joan C. 1993. *Moral Boundaries: A Political Argument for an Ethic of Care*. New York: Routledge.

Vaillant, Janet G. 1990. *Black, French, and African: A Life of Léopold Senghor*. Cambridge, Mass.: Harvard University Press.

Vaz, Angelina. 1995. "Who's Got the Look? Sartre's Gaze and Foucault's Panopticism." *Dalhousie French Studies* 32 (fall): 33–45.

Walker, Alice, and Pratiba Parmar. 1993. *Warrior Marks: Female Genital Mutilation and the Sexual Binding of Women*. New York: Harcourt Brace.

Walkowitz, Judith R. 1980. *Prostitution and Victorian Society: Women, Class, and the State*. Cambridge: Cambridge University Press.

Ware, Vron. 1992. *Beyond the Pale: White Women, Racism, and History*. London: Verso.

Warnock, Mary. 1970. *Existentialism*. Oxford: Oxford University Press.

Weiss, Gail. 1999. *Body Images: Embodiment as Intercorporeality*. New York: Routledge.

West, Cornel. 1990. "The New Cultural Politics of Difference." In *Out There: Marginalization and Contemporary Cultures*, ed. Russell Ferguson, Martha

Gever, Trinh T. Minh-ha, and Cornel West, 19–36. New York and Cambridge, Mass.: New Museum of Contemporary Art and MIT Press.

Whitmarsh, Anne. 1981. *Simone de Beauvoir and the Limits of Commitment.* Cambridge: Cambridge University Press.

Wilkinson, James John Garth. 1870. *The Forcible Introspection of Women for the Army and the Navy by the Oligarchy, Considered Physically.* London: F. Pittman.

Winter, Bronwyn. 1995. "Women, the Law, and Cultural Relativism in France: The Case of Excision." In *Rethinking the Political: Gender, Resistance, and the State,* ed. Barbara Laslett, Johanna Brenner, and Yesim Arat, 315–50. Chicago: University of Chicago Press.

Wispé, Lauren. 1991. *The Psychology of Sympathy.* New York: Plenum Press.

Young, Iris M. 1990a. *Justice and the Politics of Difference.* Princeton, N.J.: Princeton University Press.

——. 1990b. *Throwing like a Girl and Other Essays in Feminist Philosophy and Social Theory.* Bloomington: Indiana University Press.

——. 1994. "Gender as Seriality: Thinking about Women as a Social Collective." *Signs: Journal of Women in Culture and Society* 19 (3): 713–38.

——. 1997. "Unruly Categories: A Critique of Nancy Fraser's Dual Systems Theory." *New Left Review* 222 (March/April): 147–60.

Zahar, Renate. 1974. *Frantz Fanon: Colonialism and Alienation: Concerning Frantz Fanon's Political Theory.* Trans. Willfried F. Feuser. New York: Monthly Review Press.

Zerilli, Linda M. G. 1992. "A Process without a Subject: Simone de Beauvoir and Julia Kristeva on Maternity." *Signs: Journal of Women in Culture and Society* 18 (1): 111–35.

Index

Beauvoir, Simone de (*continued*)
  and social class, 45n.21, 66n.19
  and subjectivity, 33, 35–36, 37, 59, 64
—Works:
  The Ethics of Ambiguity, 35–36, 69n.22
  Letters to Sartre, 29
  The Prime of Life, 34
  Pyrrhus et Cinéas, 35
  The Second Sex, 27, 29–31, 33, 36–49,
    57, 68, 176
Beckett, Samuel, 16
Becoming a woman, 48, 51, 58, 69, 72, 81
Being and Nothingness (Sartre):
  and the autonomy of the subject,
    19–20, 31
  Beauvoir's relationship to, 29–30
  on consciousness, 124
  and the *Critique of Dialectical Reason*,
    32
  and Fanon, 90, 103
  and freedom, 8–9, 34–35, 49–50, 103
  on shame, 62–63
  and the struggle for recognition, 91
Being and Time (Heidegger), 7
Being-for-itself, 31
Being-for-others, 37, 43, 48, 66, 90, 94
Being-in-itself, 43–44
Being-in-situation, 37
Being-other, 47
Bell, Linda, 92n.21
Benhabib, Seyla, 15, 155n.3
Bentham, Jeremy, 57, 62
Bergoffen, Debra, 28, 30
Bergson, Henri-Louis, 10
Bhabha, Homi, 90
Bigwood, Carol, 164n.15
Binswanger, Ludwig, 10
Black Consciousness movement, 89
Black experience, 13, 97–103, 167n.18
Black identity, 89
Black Orpheus (Sartre), 102–3
Black Panthers, 87, 89
Black Power movement, 79, 87, 89
Black Skin, White Masks (Fanon), 21, 79,
    89–90, 97–103
Body, the:
  for Arendt, 164–65
  for Beauvoir, 29, 32–33, 40, 46–47, 49,
    71, 136–37, 164
  for Fanon, 98–99n.30
  for Foucault, 59
  generality of, 40

and global-difference feminism, 107
for Merleau-Ponty, 40, 46–47, 49, 164,
  167
for Rorty, 135–36
See also Feminine embodiment; Lived
  body
Body in Pain, The (Scarry), 165
Borderlands/La Frontera (Anzaldúa), 86
Bordo, Susan, 4, 157
Bracketing, 7, 8, 133
Breasted experience, 164
Brunschvicg, Léon, 10
Butler, Josephine, 169–71, 173
Butler, Judith, 17, 19, 28, 59, 70–75,
  87n.10

Camus, Albert, 118
Caring occupations, 121
Cartesian subject:
  and Judith Butler, 71
  and existentialism, 8–9, 10–11, 17–18
  and feminist theory in America, 3
  and phenomenology, 17–18
  and Joan Scott, 143
  See also Constituting subject
Césaire, Aimé, 88, 97
"Changing the Subject: Studies in the
  Appropriation of Pain" (Spelman),
  174
Chanter, Tina, 17–18
Chodorow, Nancy, 131–32, 158–59
Choice, 22, 45, 68, 81, 142–43, 144–45,
  175
Civil rights movement, black, 12, 84. *See
  also* Black Power movement
Class, 41n.16, 66n.19, 69, 102, 111, 122
Cleaver, Eldridge, 89
Clitoridectomy, 111, 160, 165, 172–73
Coalition politics, 83, 85, 106, 109–10,
  153–54, 159
"Coalition Politics: Turning the Century"
  (Reagon), 153
Code, Lorraine, 172
Collective change, 45–46. *See also* Praxis
Collectives, 41–42, 122–23
Collins, Patricia Hill, 14n.11, 132
Colonialism, French, 30, 89, 97, 104
Combahee River Collective, 82
Commonalities of embodiment, 33–34,
  151–52, 175
Communist Party, French, 7–8, 117
Complicity, 57, 60–61, 67–68